GARDEN PAINTERS

Contemporary Artists

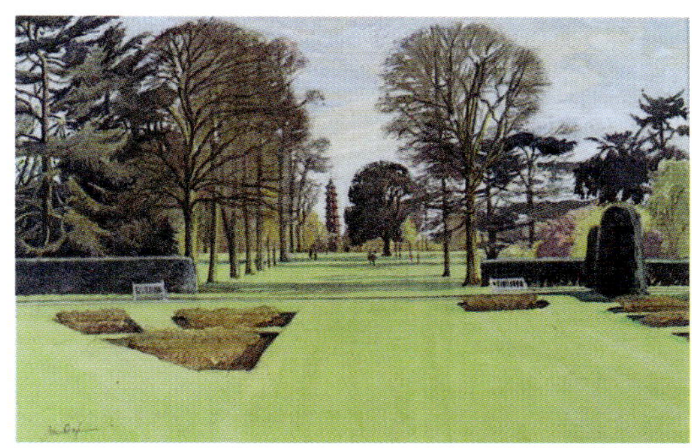

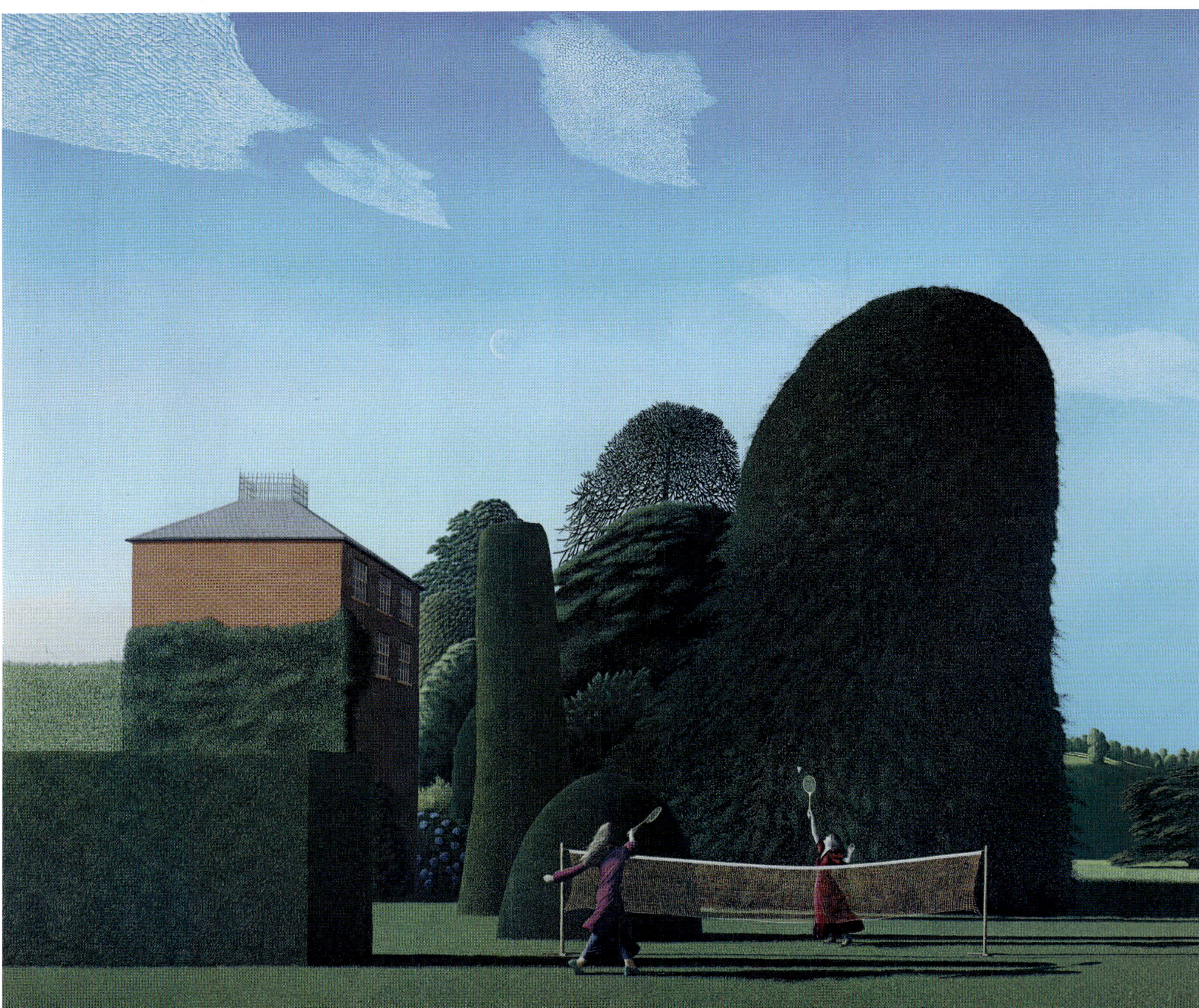

GARDEN PAINTERS

Contemporary Artists

Ariel Luke

FOREWORD BY SIR ROY STRONG

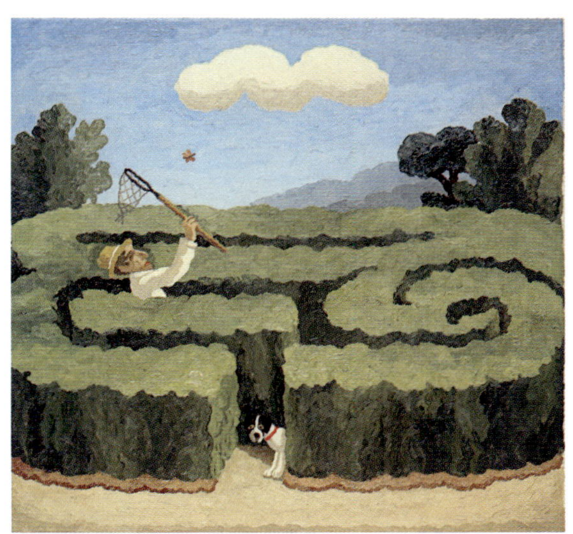

A & C BLACK · LONDON

Acknowledgements

First of all, I must thank the artists for their time and often hospitality, for supplying photographs of their work and for being so wonderfully talented.

I should also like to thank Linda Lambert and Anne Watts for encouraging me at the right moments and for being such a joy to work with. Friends have helped with tips and advice, principally Kate Baden Fuller, but also Caroline Annesley, Alastair Best, Anne Binney, Melissa Bonn, Sam Clarke, Moya Denman, Julia Dixon, Katherine Hodgkinson, Tom Juneau, Sheela Lampietti, Caroline Lightburn, Marie-Christine Paris, Richard Stokes, Fiona Warrender and Angela Williams. Maria Texeira has been invaluable in countless ways. Among galleries that have been supportive are the Francis Kyle Gallery, the Redfern Gallery, Long & Ryle, and Joshua Briggs in New York.

Finally, I thank Richard Whatmore.

PAGE 1 ILLUSTRATION: SEE PAGE 44.
FRONTISPIECE (PAGE 2): SEE PAGE 69.
PAGE 3 ILLUSTRATION: SEE PAGE 95.
PAGE 5 ILLUSTRATION: SEE PAGE 51.
PAGE 6 ILLUSTRATION: SEE PAGE 71.

First published 2009
A & C Black Publishers Limited
36 Soho Square, London W1D 3QY
www.acblack.com

ISBN: 978 0 7136 8206 9

Jacket designed by Sutchinda Thompson
Book designed by Susan McIntyre
Typeset in 10.5 on 13pt Celeste

Printed and bound by Tien Wah Press, Singapore

A & C Black uses paper produced with elemental chlorine-free pulp, harvested from managed sustainable sources.

Contents

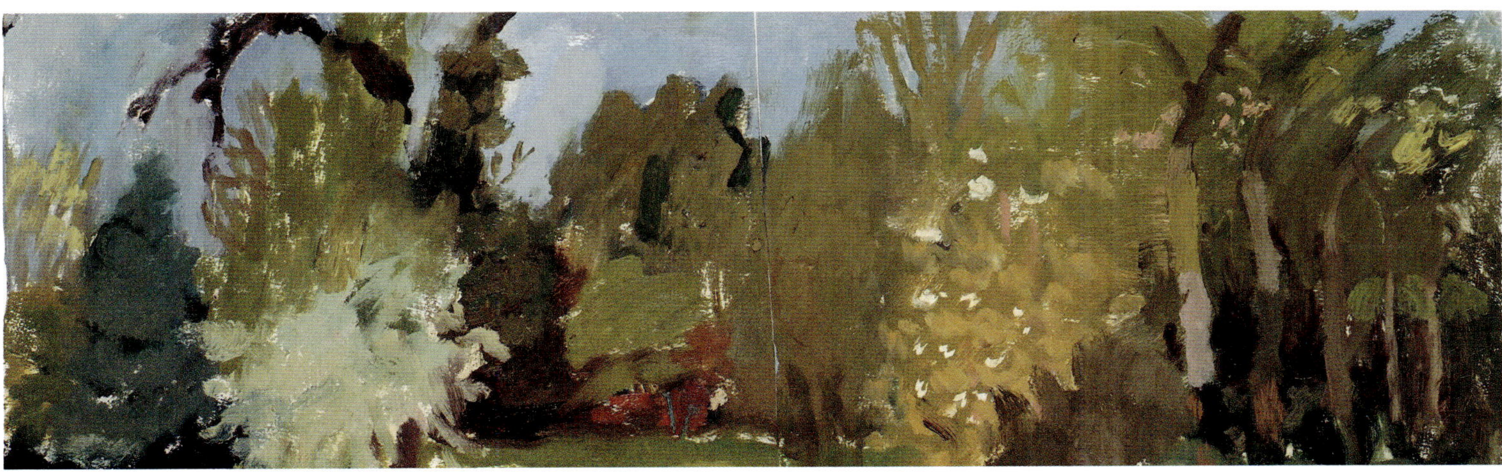

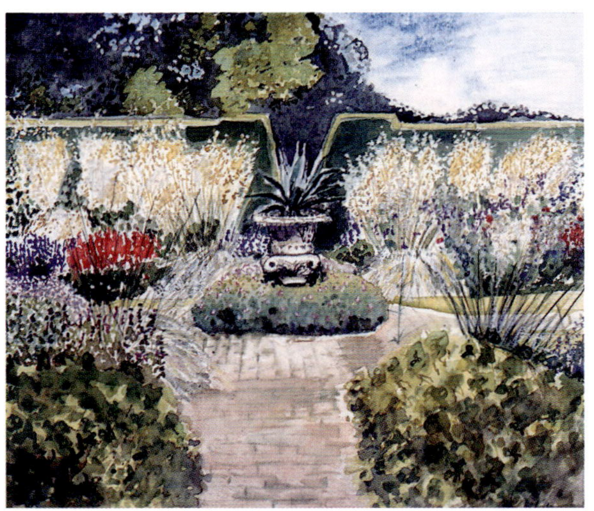

Foreword

This is a much needed book, a guide to many of those who are painting gardens today. The artists here all have quite different responses to their challenge, so inevitably we see a wide variety of approaches. These vary from the grand aerial views of Dick Smyly and Jonathan Myles-Lea to the close-up details of John Pearce or Angela Gladwell. There is the unashamed romanticism of Robert Bates and the surreal fantasy of François Houtin. There is not an artist here who doesn't have in some way a particular 'take' on the garden.

Gardens are themselves an artificial re-ordering of nature and the very act of painting them re-configures that artificiality through the eyes of the painter. So what we see here is one art overlaid on another, which, after all, is part of the fascination of garden painting.

Such pictures call upon the onlooker to share in the painter's visual experience. It will not be his own but it will be equally intriguing. In the case of the owner such a picture can come as a revelation making him look at his own garden with fresh eyes. That is what is so exciting and stimulating about garden pictures.

Roy Strong

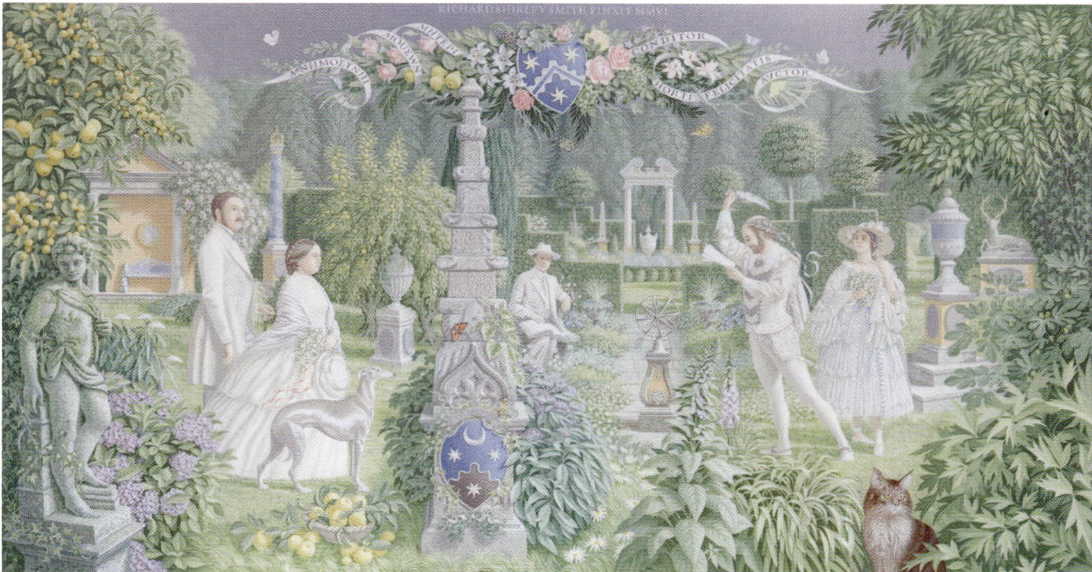

Richard Shirley Smith, *Lasket Shades*, 2006, acrylic mural on canvas, 8 × 4ft. PHOTO: CLIVE BOURSNELL

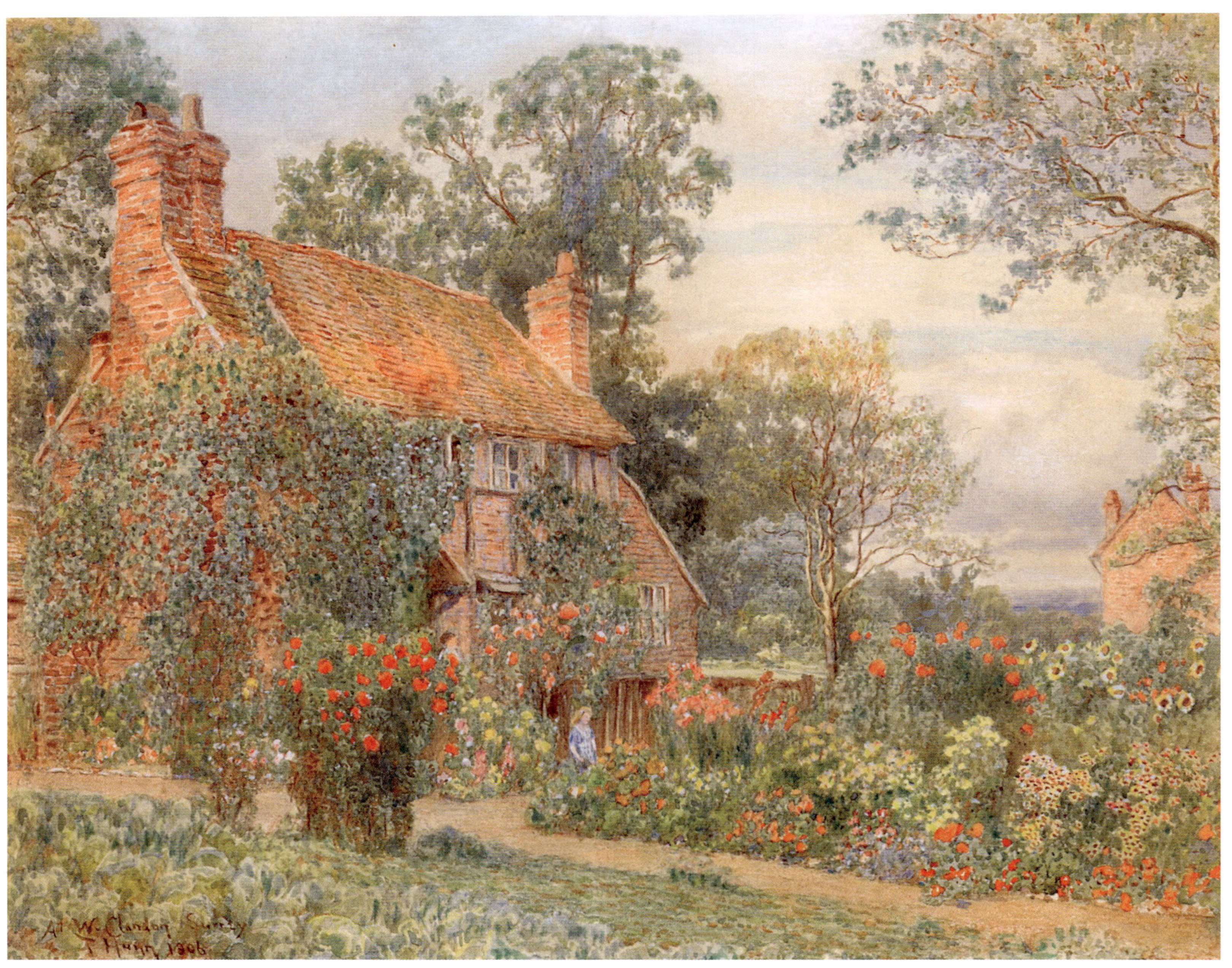

Thomas Hunn, *Cottage Garden, Surrey*, 1906, watercolour, 31 × 43cm. PHOTO: PROFESSIONAL COLOUR SERVICES

Introduction

Organising a celebration of work by garden artists has proved a most fascinating journey of discovery: visiting galleries, exhibitions and fairs, and talking. It has been an enormous privilege to visit the studios of the painters included in this book, to uncover the network of influences on them (those of painters past and present, of places, books, music ...) and to discover the mediums they use and, in some cases, their terror of exhibiting. This is a random and uncalculated selection of the kind of work that is being done in this field today.

The period of the 1960s and 1970s, with the colossal effect on art of influences from America – conceptual, abstract and minimalist – made landscape painting difficult to practise.

There is a tendency to see landscape painting as an activity for amateurs or for Academicians, but not for mainstream 'avant-garde' artists. It is hardly surprising that in so many conversations with artists the talk centres around the topic of going Pop or not, and of how to perceive landscape in today's terms.

The romantic legacy of landscape/garden painting, as Peter Fuller, the critic, wrote, 'may be tried and forced into hiding by Modernists but there are artists ready to reinvigorate a long-standing indigenous tradition.' Adrian Berg, for one, regards the English tradition as one of travelling, drawing, sketching and painting.

In 1975 David Inshaw and like-minded painters formed the Brotherhood of Ruralists to defend traditional practices and to move them on. The group was to become big and popular and to exert influence on other painters.

Some artists have so identified with landscape and garden painting that it has always been their principal activity and purpose. Some are known for other types of work – sculpture, portrait painting, fantasy decoration, even landscape architecture.

Commissioned work still has an important role, as it has had throughout the history of painting. It makes its own particular challenges as does work done exclusively from the imagination. The two genres of art in some ways feed off one another. It does seem evident, however, that an intellectual soul-searching is more prevalent today which, I believe, has created the most exciting work ever to have appeared around the subject of gardens.

The illuminators of medieval manuscripts depicted gardens as backgrounds, to show social settings and different seasons, just as decoration – not at all for any personal expression.

In the fifteenth century, Ghirlandaio painted his *Portrait of an Old Man and his Grandchild* with a view of the garden through a window. Sixteenth- and seventeenth-century portrait painters often incorporated such a view to give an extra dimension to the picture, probably to record the property and status of noble families. The 'lunettes' of Giusto Utens were documents principally depicting property belonging to the Medici family. Few of these rather stylised pictures have an especially painterly quality, but scrupulous precision was employed in order to include every detail. The unifying factor was the need to list and to define.

As a contrast to such work came the paintings of Fragonard (1732–1806) and of Gainsborough (1727–88) who clearly had a fundamental understanding of the quiet countryside and who depicted scenes with extraordinary charm and sensitivity.

Then came the nineteenth century with the Victorian era, when paintings of gardens were probably at their most popular. There were many members of the gentry and landowners of big estates who wished to have their gardens recorded. These

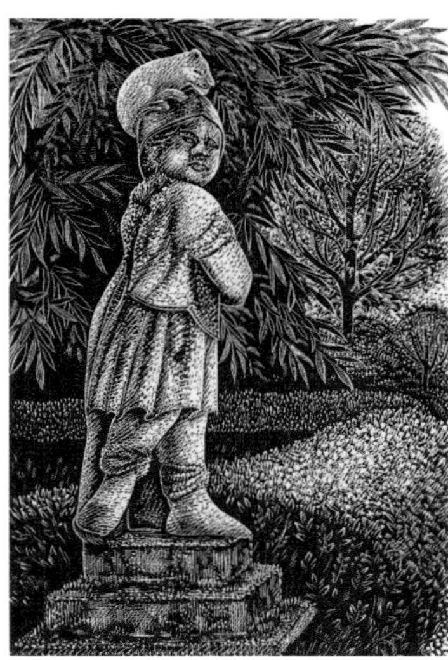

Yvonne Skargon, *Buscot Boy*, 2000, wood engraving, 9 × 6cm.

gardens had an emphasis on topiary, knot gardens, arbours and richly planted, labour-intensive, herbaceous borders. Painters such as George Samuel Elgood, Arthur Rowe and E. Alveno Brooke depicted these more formally designed gardens.

In contrast there were Helen Allingham, Beatrice Parsons and Arthur Claude Strachen who took delight in depicting the more casual gardens and lifestyle of the urban middle classes. These city dwellers were beginning to acquire cottages in the country and only had the time and budget for a simpler style of garden.

In effect the styles of painting were reflecting the battle of conflicting styles in the field of garden design. On the one hand, there were the traditional gardeners with their 'bedding out' and very labour-intensive schemes; on the other, Gertrude Jekyll and William Robinson with their strong views on a more naturalistic manner of gardening.

Most paintings of this period were carried out in watercolour. They give the impression that the sun is always shining even if in a hazy and rather delicate manner.

There developed a form of partnership between artists and gardeners. Several artists (such as Elgood, Rowe and Parsons) became specialist garden painters to the exclusion of almost all else. Others were called upon to illustrate garden periodicals at the same time as they were showing work at the Royal Academy of Art and being heralded as leading painters of the period. Since the time of Thomas Bewick in the eighteenth century, and particularly since the 1920s, the printing technique of wood engraving has become an art in itself. It lends itself readily to the depiction of gardens. An engraver of today, Yvonne Skargon, has produced many delightful illustrations for the well-respected gardening journal, *Hortus*, as well as for her own books.

In the twentieth century, Stanley Spencer was known to describe some of his garden paintings as 'pot-boilers', which funded his more figurative work. Between the 1920s and 1950s, he produced a social map of Cookham which has been so evocative that the village has become a kind of shrine for many art lovers. Yet he was not afraid to show concrete posts, barbed wire and tarred roofs. Similarly, Lucian Freud said of his painting *Garden from the Window*, 'I realised that I could sustain the drama that I wanted in the picture ... by giving all the information I can.' Patrick Heron's *Autumn Garden* is completely different. It is made up of abstract patterns of colours that depict dripping paint.

Artists all approach their work differently. Some spend a long time just looking for the right place. They then keep travelling there and stand in the rain under umbrellas and awnings – as is particularly the case with John Pearce, Jonathan Warrender, Annabel Gault and myself. (In this respect things haven't changed. Henry Terry wrote in 1892, 'Worked in the garden under an umbrella in the morning and for an hour in the afternoon, then gave it up as a bad job. Rained all day.') Others take many sketches, notes and photographs which can contribute later to a composite picture carried out in the studio.

Works shown in this book demonstrate a wide range of materials and techniques, from oil and watercolour to pastel, tempera on gesso, graphite on tracing paper, screenprints, copperplate etchings and murals.

Members of the public today still seek to commission paintings of their own gardens, to buy pictures of gardens, to visit art exhibitions that display them. Good artists are sought after, they have international reputations of a high order.

This book is to celebrate them and at the same time to introduce their work and the whole subject of garden art to an even wider audience.

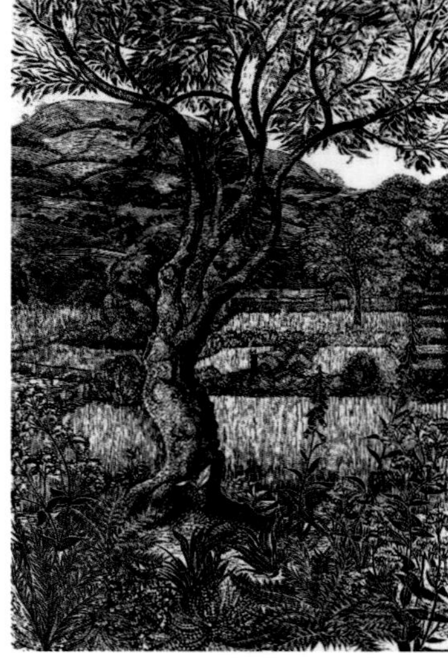

Yvonne Skargon, *Ryder*, 1998, wood engraving, 15 × 10cm.
PHOTO: PROFESSIONAL COLOUR SERVICES

Ivor Abrahams

I had known of Ivor Abrahams' sculpture for many years but it was while researching the work of another artist in Bath that I was reminded of Ivor Abrahams' 'Garden Suites' of the 1970s which employed innovative techniques and featured the garden.

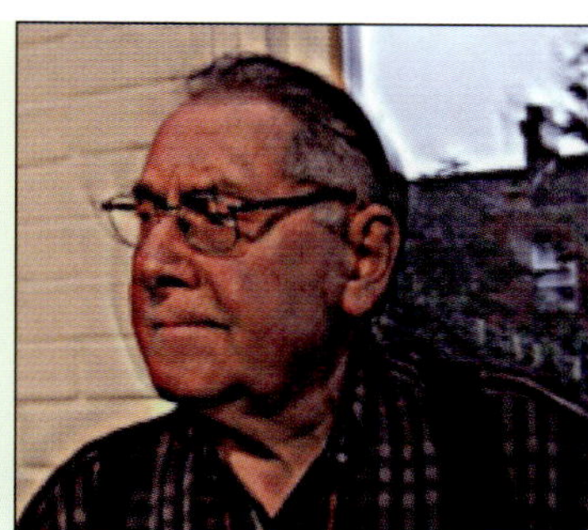

The Artist.
PHOTO: EVELYN ABRAHAMS

Ivor is known primarily as a sculptor, but in the early 1970s he also made his name with prints: several 'suites' of lithographs and screenprints. (Screenprinting was a relatively new medium for artists at that time and its strong colours and clean outlines were suited to the dazzle of Abstract Expressionism and the fun of Pop that was current in those years.) Ivor also developed images that were a combination of photographic cuttings (from popular magazines such as *Amateur Gardening* and *Popular Gardening*) with hand-drawn material.

After first studying at St Martin's School of Art, Ivor continued at Camberwell School of Art where there was a more rigorous ethic. He became a sculptor because it was found that he was partially colour blind and had difficulty distinguishing greens, yellows and red. This may have been an advantage to him in some ways, as colours in his prints are especially distinctive and vivid.

He showed promise as a student and was later taken on by Camberwell to teach there two or three times a week. He had some success in a gallery in the 1960s, but it was in the 1970s – with the 'Garden Suites' – that he was able to give up teaching altogether. These prints sold out instantly, distinguished not only by their large scale but also by their use of innovative techniques such as flocking. They catapulted him into a very successful career. There then followed a show in New York of big sculptures and another in Cologne where he achieved international prominence. He has since shown worldwide, principally with the Bernard Jacobson Gallery and, for the

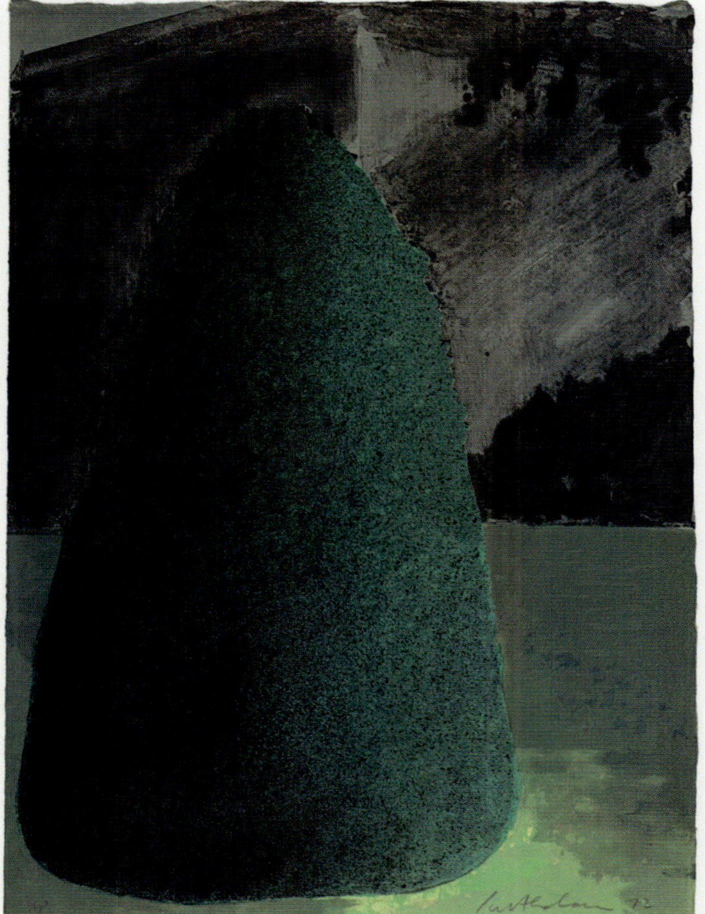

Ivor Abrahams, *Suburban Shrub II: Dusk*, 1972, lithograph on paper, 83.1 × 63cm.
COURTESY: TATE, LONDON, 2008

last twenty years, with the Mayor Gallery. He became a Royal Academician in 1991.

It is not hard to detect the links between images and sculpture: clipped topiary, hedges, dials and urns provide shapes and forms that are bold and distinctive. Ivor says that his prints and sculpture go along together '… the prints often inform the sculpture. Obviously the more sculptural things were, the more attractive they were to me. In the beginning, when I started out, topiary gave me a repertory of shapes. I wasn't interested in the way a garden was laid out. The garden wasn't my image, it was everybody's image – a desire, an English preoccupation. I honestly feel that my work should be accessible to a large number of people.' Ivor is not so much interested in the aesthetics of individual gardens but of a larger picture, a passion open to all. In *Privacy Plots V*, outlined hedges are set in front of a street; in *Privacy Plots II*, there is mass planting, probably begonias (like those in a park). In another picture, a funeral urn stands by itself, perhaps to symbolise death.

Ivor works on his sculpture maquettes at home in London and in several studios. He also works with fabricators from the film industry who bring a different form of talent and versatility to the way of making things and can grasp ideas quickly. He still uses a venue in Perivale to draw from the figure. 'I have always worked between the figure and landscape. Using the figure was all part of the academic tradition and it has always stood me in good stead. Although I have at times been criticised for getting into a more traditional role, it has never bothered me too much.' He gave up the figure when he began the 'Garden Suites' but later reintroduced it, and continues to make reference to it today. Acrobats and dancers have been a recurrent inspiration. Animals and architectural themes have more recently played their part.

He moves on to keep his interest going. 'You can get known for something and that can just get boring. You can have a style

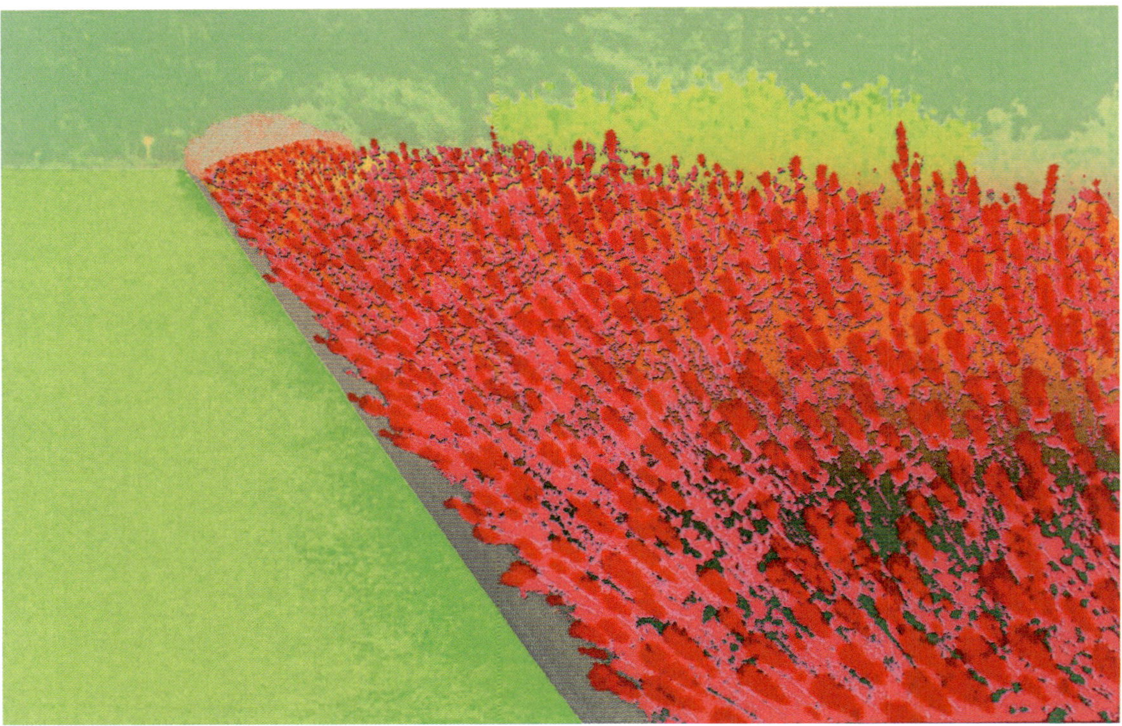

Ivor Abrahams, *Privacy Plots II: Flower Garden*, 1970, screenprint and flock fibre on paper, 38 × 61.1cm. COURTESY: TATE, LONDON, 2008

and it can become a sort of signature and the temptation could be to carry on doing it, but I just throw it away and do something else. I am interested in the difference between the artificial and the real – those are my preoccupations, but I change the subject.' At present he is heavily engaged in yet another challenge – he is teaching at the Royal Academy Schools and preparing for his next exhibition at the Mayor Gallery.

FACING PAGE Ivor Abrahams, *Privacy Plots V: Hedge and Street*, 1970, screenprint and flock fibre on paper, 40 × 59.5cm. COURTESY: TATE, LONDON, 2008

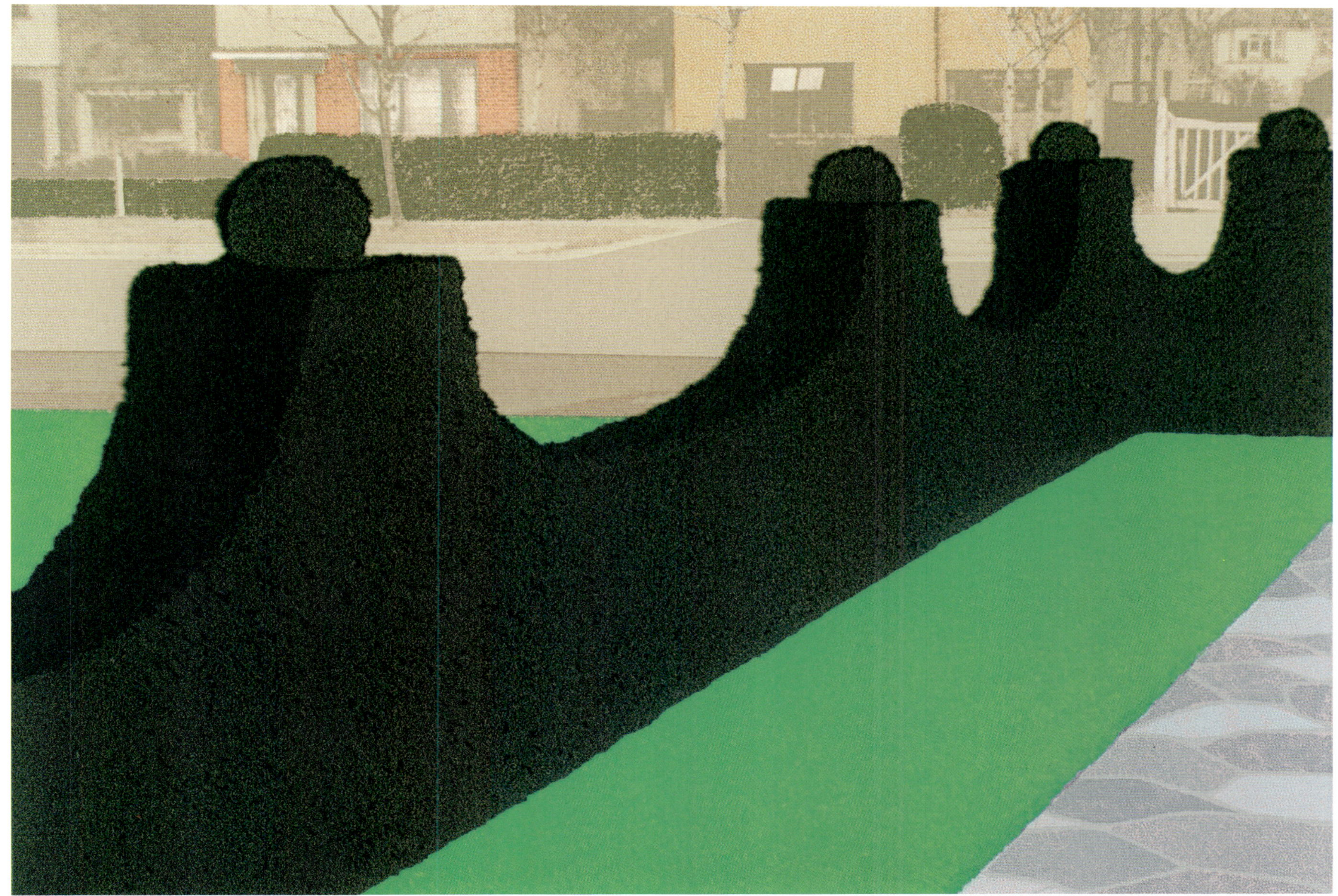

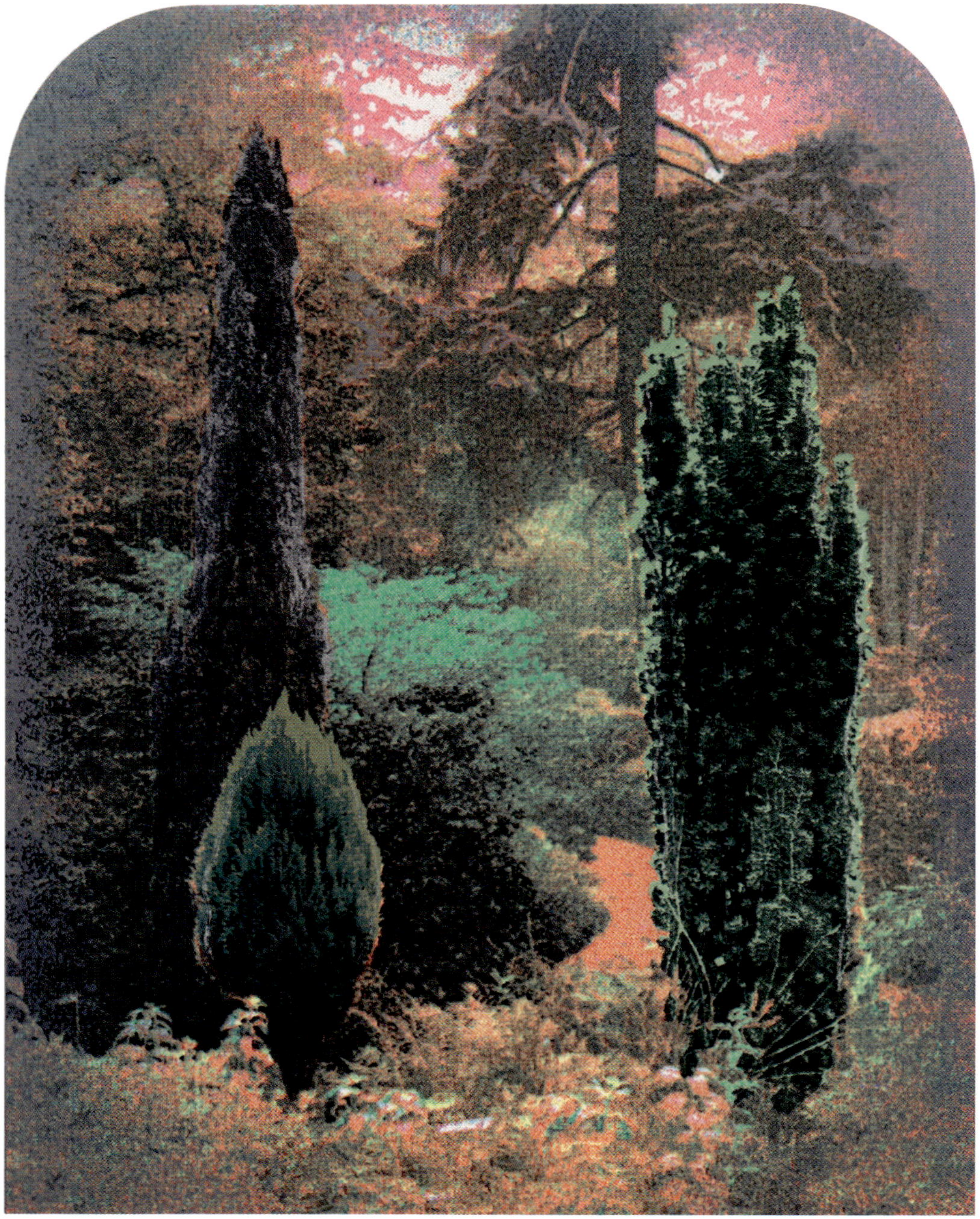

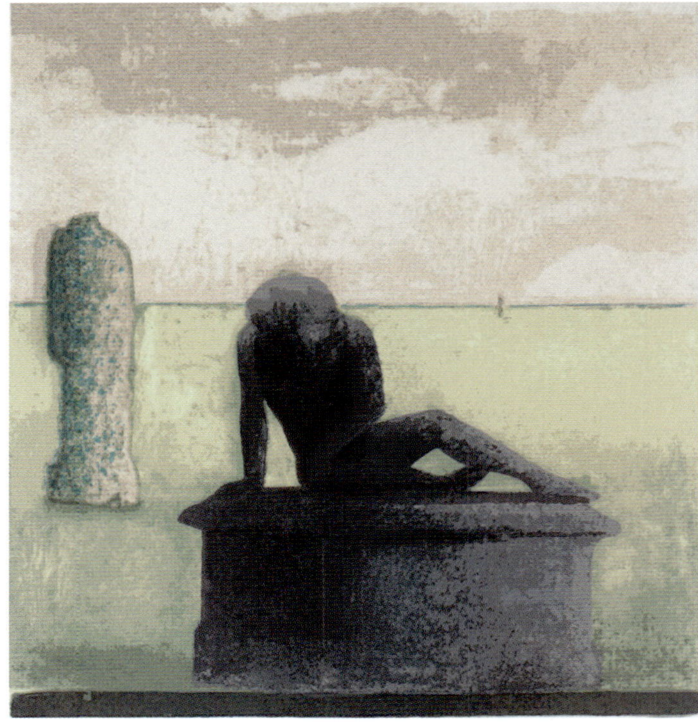

Ivor Abrahams, *Alone*, from E. A. Poe, *Tales and Poems*, 1976, screenprint on paper, 18.9 × 18.2cm. COURTESY: TATE, LONDON, 2008

LEFT Ivor Abrahams, *The Domain of Arnheim*, from E. A. Poe, *Tales and Poems*, 1976, screenprint on paper, 22.6 × 16.6cm. COURTESY: TATE, LONDON, 2008

Graham Bannister

Graham Bannister first came to my attention when we were both commissioned to paint two of the same gardens. Since then I have attended his exhibitions.

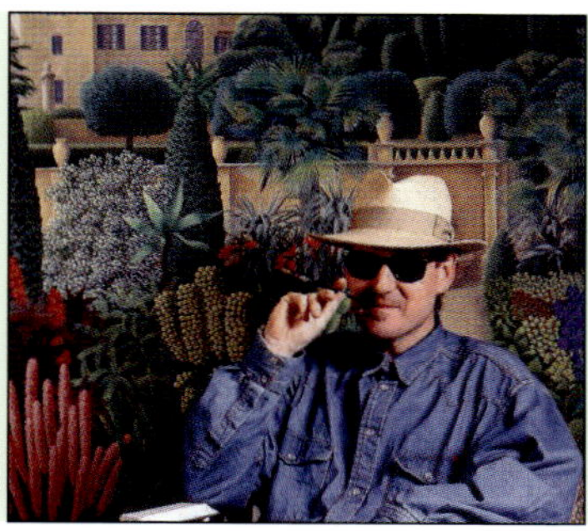

The Artist.
PHOTO: GRAHAM BANNISTER

Graham lives and works in the small village of Yvignac La Tour in northern Brittany, not far from the impressively fortified fishing port of St Malo. Here there is a rural enchantment overlying the countryside. Tender greens of feathery grasses contrast with the bold outlines of Charolais cows. Graham himself lives in a charming and, no doubt, very old cottage, with bright ultramarine painted shutters acting as the background to magenta hollyhocks and various hostas in pots. His studio is nearby and there is an impression that these surroundings have benefited his latest style of work.

It was at the very early age of eight that Graham was first attracted to painting. He was sent to art therapy to help him overcome his extreme shyness. 'I painted my dreams,' and even now when you study the work done at Stourhead, Wiltshire, for instance, it's possible to detect a dream-like quality. This therapy clearly intrigued him enough to persevere with painting.

After leaving school he didn't attend an art college but worked as an Artist-in-Residence at the Brillig Art Centre in Bath where he was influenced by the group called the Brotherhood of Ruralists. These artists saw themselves as carrying forward the principles of the Pre-Raphaelites with rural life as their predominant theme. It was they who experimented with the exacting requirements of painting in oil in the open air – addressing 'healthy nature'. Peter Blake, David Inshaw and Graham Arnold were amongst this group. Graham readily admits that the way he depicts foliage and some of his heavily darkened foregrounds have been influenced by David Inshaw's work.

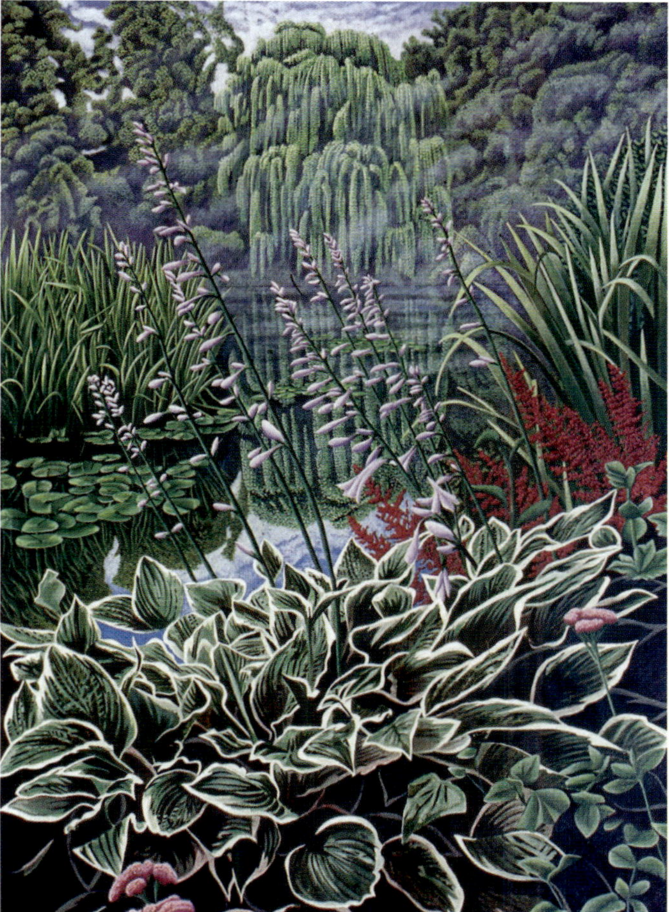

Graham Bannister, *Hosta aureomarginata, Giverny*, 1999, 600g Arches paper on board, with acrylic underpainting and wax, resin & pigment overpainting, 150 × 100cm.
PHOTO: GRAHAM BANNISTER

However, the manner in which leaves and flowers are drawn by Graham Bannister is very reminiscent of Henri Rousseau, with the often gaudy greens seeming to dance across the canvas in bold and almost hard-edged outlines. Another influence has been Monet whose work energised him to play with the effect of light. (Graham has since been to paint Monet's own garden at Giverny.)

When Graham left the Brillig Art Centre he went to live in a remote cottage in Cornwall and it was here, living a rather reclusive life, that he was able to consolidate his style. This period culminated in an exhibition at Camelford, and trips to Greece and Venice. Ironically, it was later – while living in Tuscany – that he began to work on commissioned paintings of houses and gardens in England: the first of about forty commissions which have been interspersed with his own creative work. Other notable garden commissions have been Wateringbury in Kent, Trebah in Cornwall and Stourhead.

It is well understood that the lifestyle of artists is precarious. It is often necessary to be versatile and ready to go with the flow. Graham's career has been a good example. Other than living in Bath and Cornwall, he has lived in Wales, in Winkfield, Berkshire, and overseas in Tuscany, Italy, the South West of France and, since 1993, in Brittany. All these venues have affected his particular style to some degree or other.

His exhibitions have been spread even more widely. He has shown in the Grand Palais (Paris), Madrid, the Museum of Modern Art in Peking, Delhi, USA, Japan and, of course, London and other venues in the UK.

In 1985 he enterprisingly created the idea of Visual Aid for Band Aid which included the work of a hundred and four artists in one print. The list of artists involved reads like a *Who's Who* of art in our present time: Howard Hodgkin, Peter Kinley, Elizabeth Frink, David Hockney and Peter Blake, to name but a few. Another more recent project in 2002 was the IBA Human Rights Institute.

Since settling in Brittany he has established a good relationship with the French Société Nationale des Beaux-Arts and

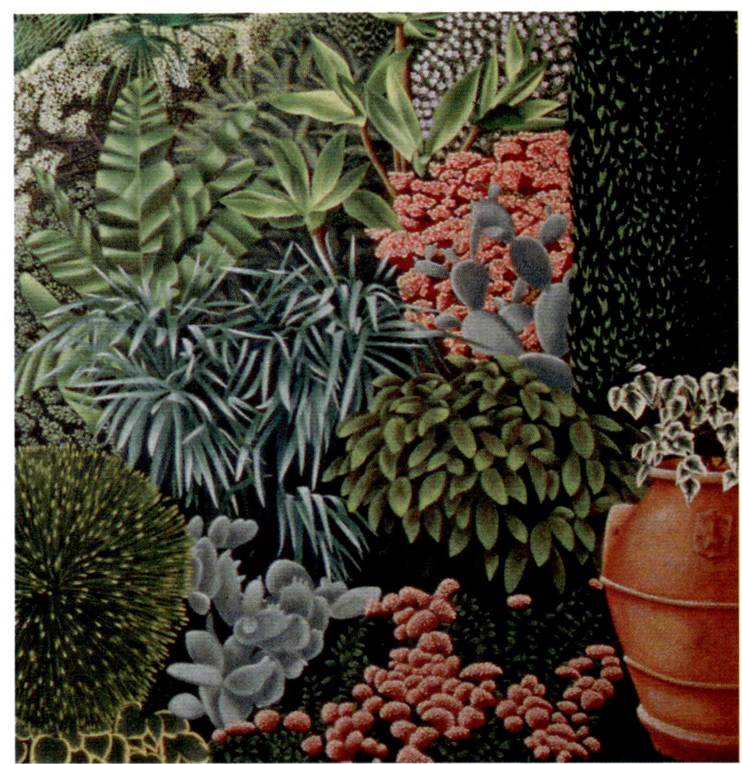

Graham Bannister, detail from *Villa Balbianelo, Lake Como, Italy*, 1998, acrylic on canvas, 250 × 350cm. PHOTO: GRAHAM BANNISTER

they have awarded him the Médaille d'Honneur d'Argent. He exhibited at the Grand Louvre in 2001 and 2003.

Graham started out painting in the traditional mediums of watercolour and oil paint but now mostly paints with a mixture of dammar resin and wax, plus pigments, from an old recipe. This gives greater depth to the image, making serrated foliage appear almost three-dimensional. The larger works are on canvas, but other works are painted on $600gm^2$ watercolour paper to give texture. He also works in a freer style using Caran d'Ache water-soluble crayons and acrylic. The paintings are first drawn and

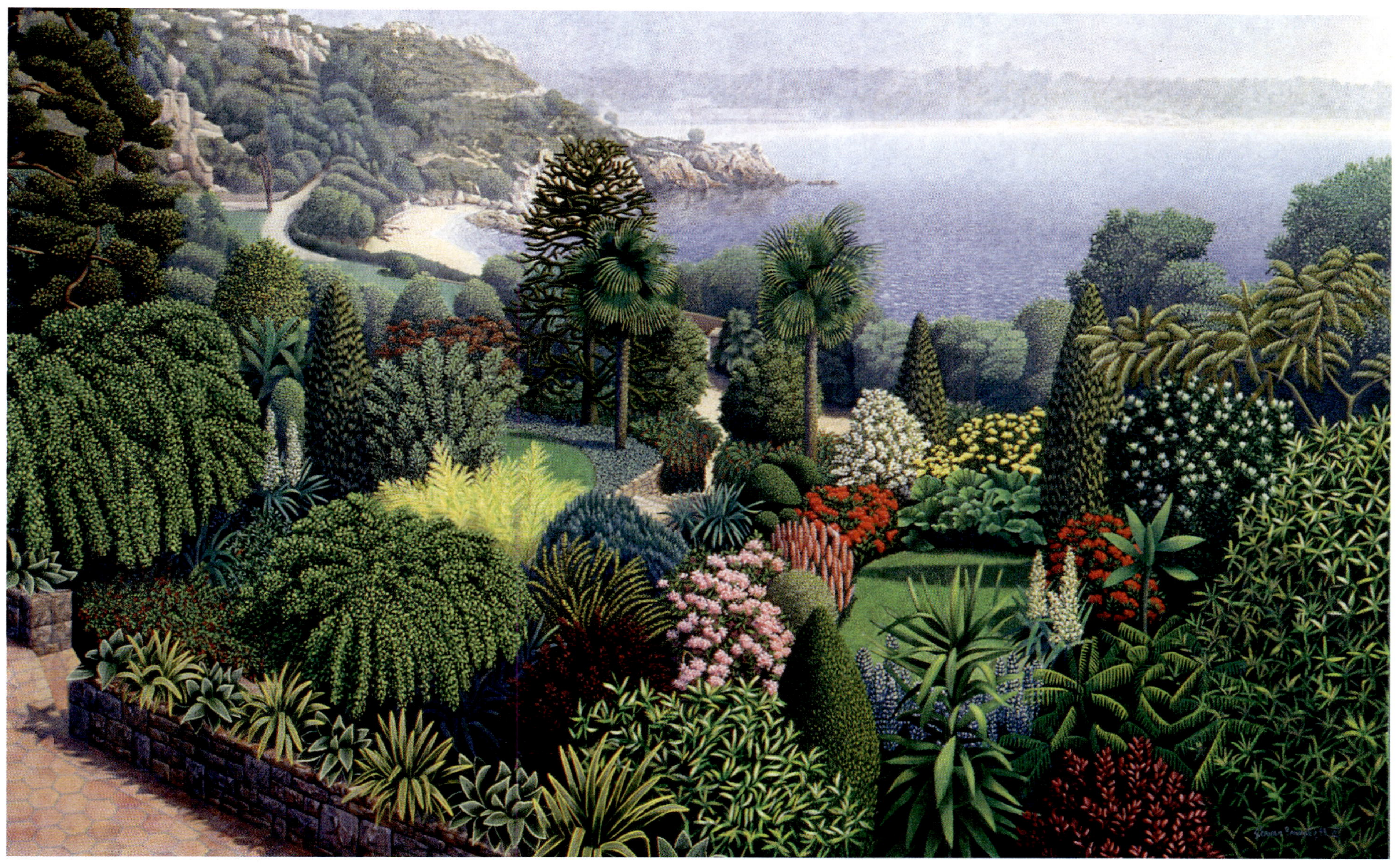

Graham Bannister, *Morning Side, Jersey*, 1994, acrylic on canvas, 96 × 162cm. PHOTO: GRAHAM BANNISTER

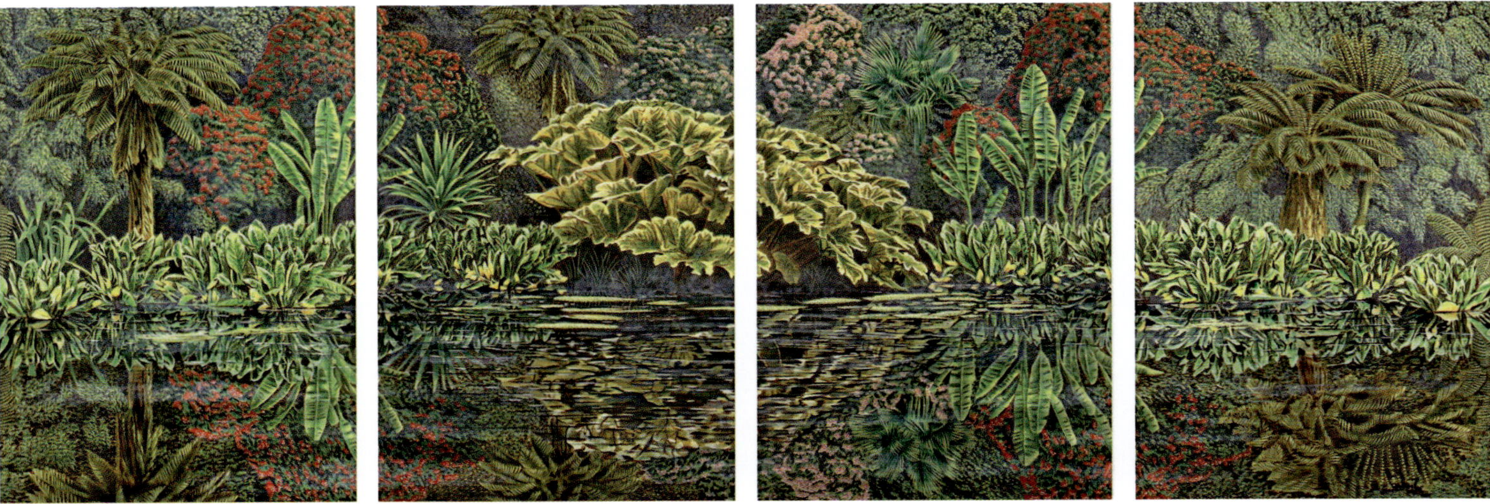

Graham Bannister, *Cornish Jungle, Cornwall*, 2002, 600g Arches paper on board, with acrylic underpainting and wax, resin & pigment overpainting, 80 × 240cm. PHOTO: GRAHAM BANNISTER

then painted in three tones to create the whole image, so that corrections can be resolved before colour is added. A rather unique aspect of these works is a method of interchanging one part of a picture with another. For instance, the painting of a Cornish jungle is executed on four panels which can be swapped around as the design follows from one panel to another.

Graham suggests that one of the reasons for living in Brittany is so that he can concentrate on his work and get away 'from the sometimes incestuous and overly exciting atmosphere of London where it is difficult to concentrate in an uninterrupted way'. However, he continues to show regularly and to take on garden/house commissions. Even so, there is a feeling that this period may be one of transition. His latest images depict bold, massive trees and trunks with entwined branches, painted with the considerable detail that is an essential part of his work. These large-scale pictures are mostly executed in monochrome, sometimes with muted shades of colour showing damp-looking shade, contrasted by small spots of bright sunlight. The art critic Terence Mullaly once wrote of Graham 'that there is an almost alarmingly assured air about his pictures'. These comments appear very apt with regard to these exhilarating new images.

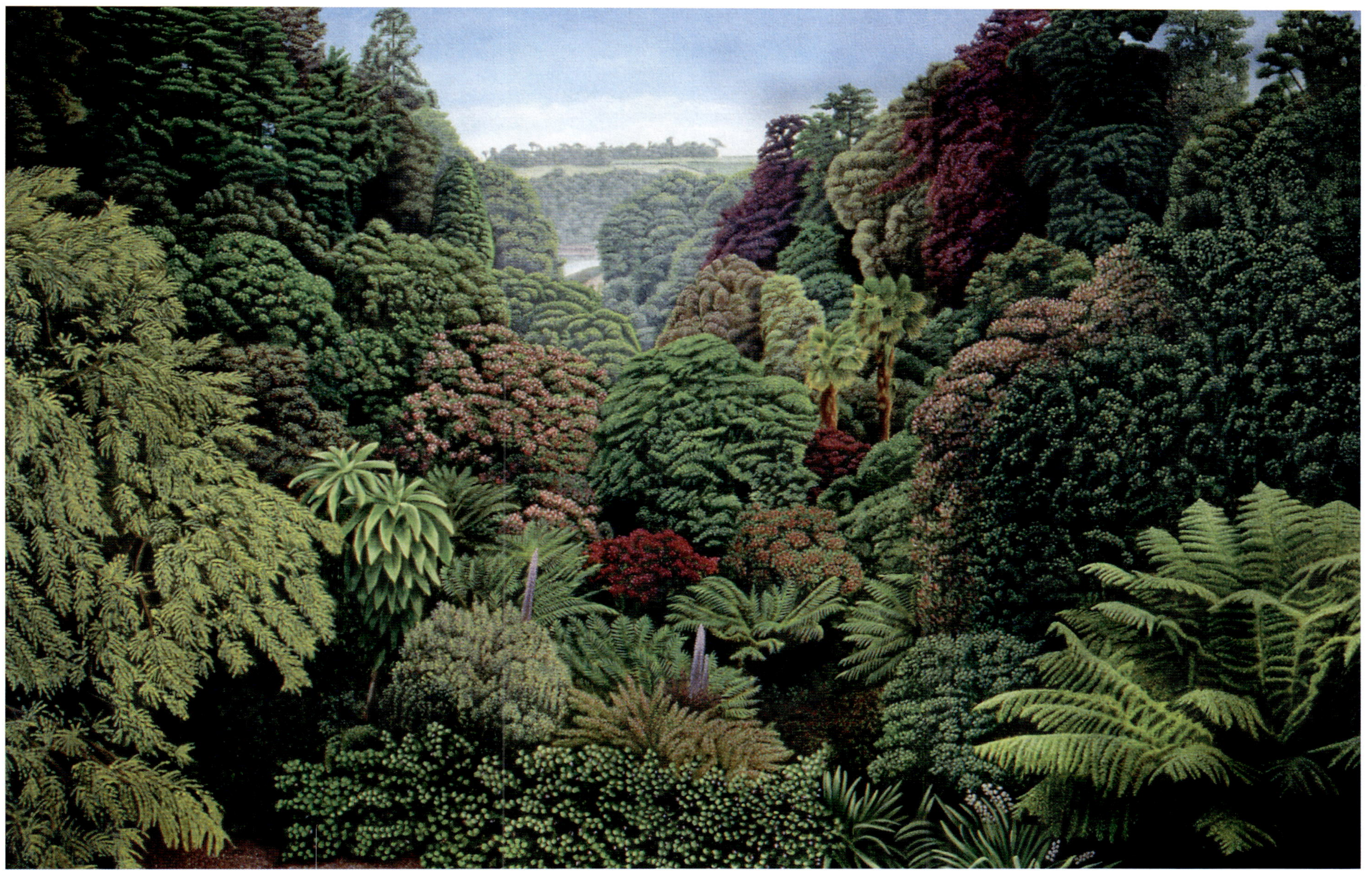

Graham Bannister, *Trebah, Cornwall*, 2005, 600g Arches paper on board, with acrylic underpainting and wax, resin & pigment overpainting, 100 × 150cm. PHOTO: GRAHAM BANNISTER

Jennifer Bartlett

A childhood friend, Moya Denman, lived in Washington in the 1990s. It was through her and her friend Sheela Lampietti that I was introduced to Jennifer Bartlett's work. An e-mail read 'the famous contemporary artist who does gardens'.

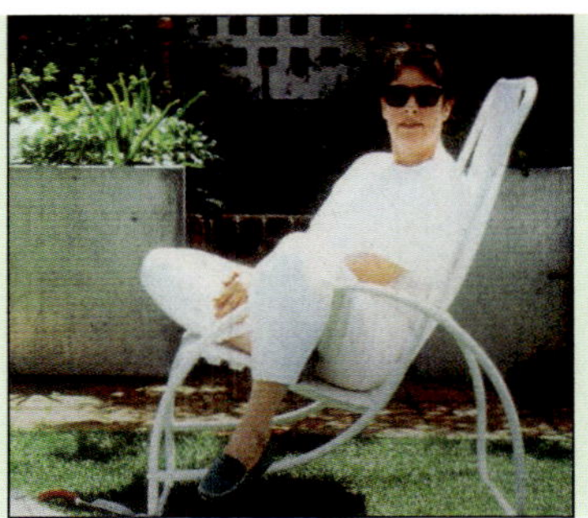

The Artist. PHOTO: ERIC BOMAN

When the renowned New York garden designer, Madison Cox, wrote his book *The Artists' Garden*, he subtitled the volume 'Claude Monet to Jennifer Bartlett'. This is some indication of the importance of this painter's work and of her long association with gardens.

Jennifer grew up in Long Beach, California, from where she probably gained her fascination with water and light. After studying art on the West Coast, she moved to the Yale School of Art and Architecture to complete her studies. Her influences were much as to be expected during this period: Jasper Johns, Andy Warhol, Jackson Pollock, the minimalists and conceptualists. Across the Atlantic you can see the influences of Seurat with his pointillism technique, a version of which she has often used, and Matisse whose chapel at Vence she readily acknowledges as being influential when she lived in Nice. After graduation she became part of the New Image group, showing widely and consistently and at the same time winning prestigious prizes.

A highly disciplined and, by her own admission, ambitious worker, she has not only been recognised in the USA, but elsewhere. She took part in the Venice and Paris Biennales and has exhibited some of her larger landscapes at Tate Britain, London.

She came to prominence in the 1970s with the showing of her major work *Rhapsody*, which was described by one critic as 'the most ambitious single work of new art that has come my way since I have started living in New York'. This elaborate work focused on many stylistic tendencies and was 7ft 6in high

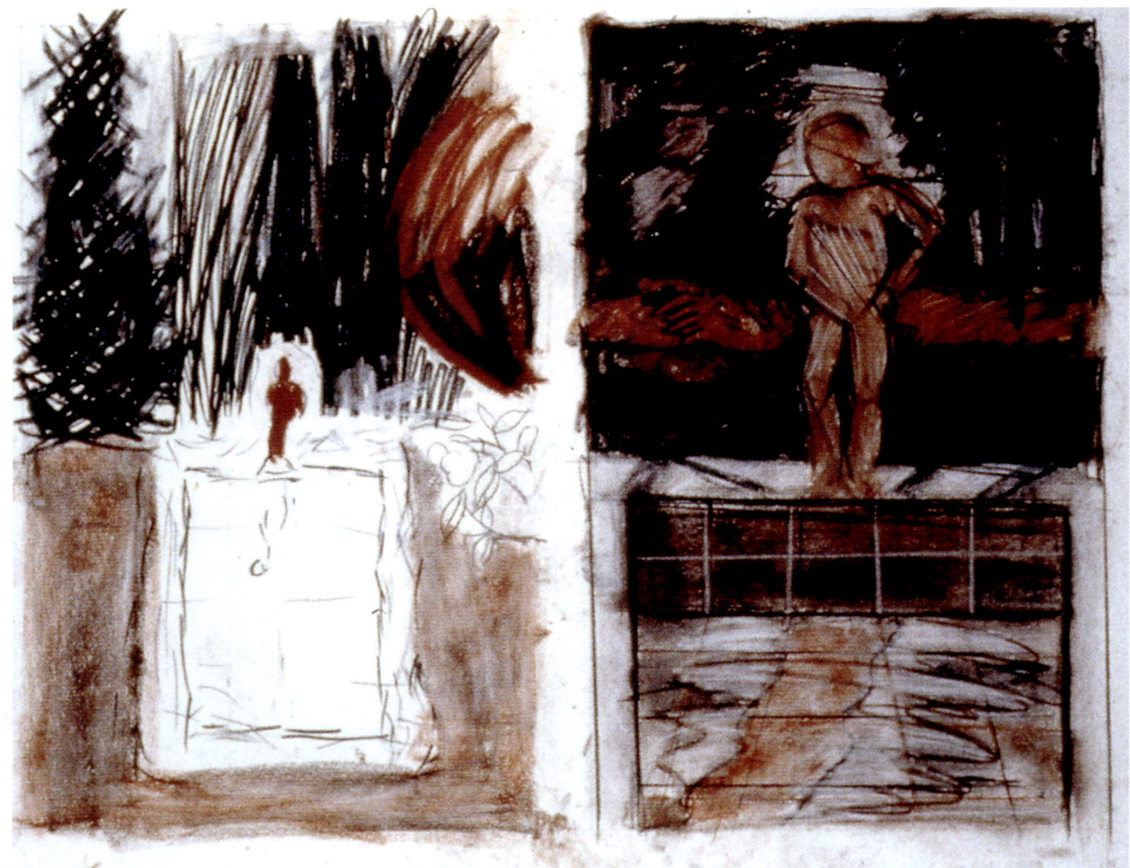

Jennifer Bartlett, *In the Garden*, drawing no. 40, 1980, Conté crayon on paper, 19.5 × 26cm.
PHOTO: GEOFFREY CLEMENTS

and 153ft long. There were figurative images of mountains, trees and a house – landscape – vividly composed in twenty-five separate colours. A kind of tidal tug or cumulative movement of spontaneous sketches, often abstract in form, which went from left to right with a vital energy.

Jennifer's involvement with the painting of gardens came about in the early 1980s when she and her sister did a house swap with a well-known writer, who took her house and studio in New York, while they moved to his house in Nice, France, for a period of fifteen months. Initially she was disappointed with this undistinguished villa and its garden in a dull quarter of town. Having at the time started work on a series of paintings which didn't really succeed, she decided to use the garden as subject matter for a collection of drawings in about ten different mediums: watercolour, charcoal, coloured pencils, pastels, etc. The garden was not elaborate: there was a pool, a statue of a boy, an olive tree, an orange tree and a stretch of cypresses, a few roses and peonies. Jennifer approached the theme in a very meticulous way, starting with drawings done from life and directly in front of her, then moving on to abstract drawings until there was a cumulative momentum of compositions concentrating on specific features. In some drawings there is a dynamic vigour for a brisk and blowy climate, in others there is extraordinary sensitivity and delicacy of line and colour. All in all, when the entire collection was shown in New York there was a sense of 'defiant fun', a speed and lightness of touch; and the critic John Russell wrote that it represented 'one of the most endearing achievements of our present decade – and one of the most substantial'. This surely is an extraordinary demonstration of the breath of feeling that drawing can evoke.

When she travels now she is mainly using pastels on paper, generally 31in square. 'I just draw what is in front of me as a kind of gravitation, a discipline.' Such explorations give her images that are then amalgamated and developed into paintings,

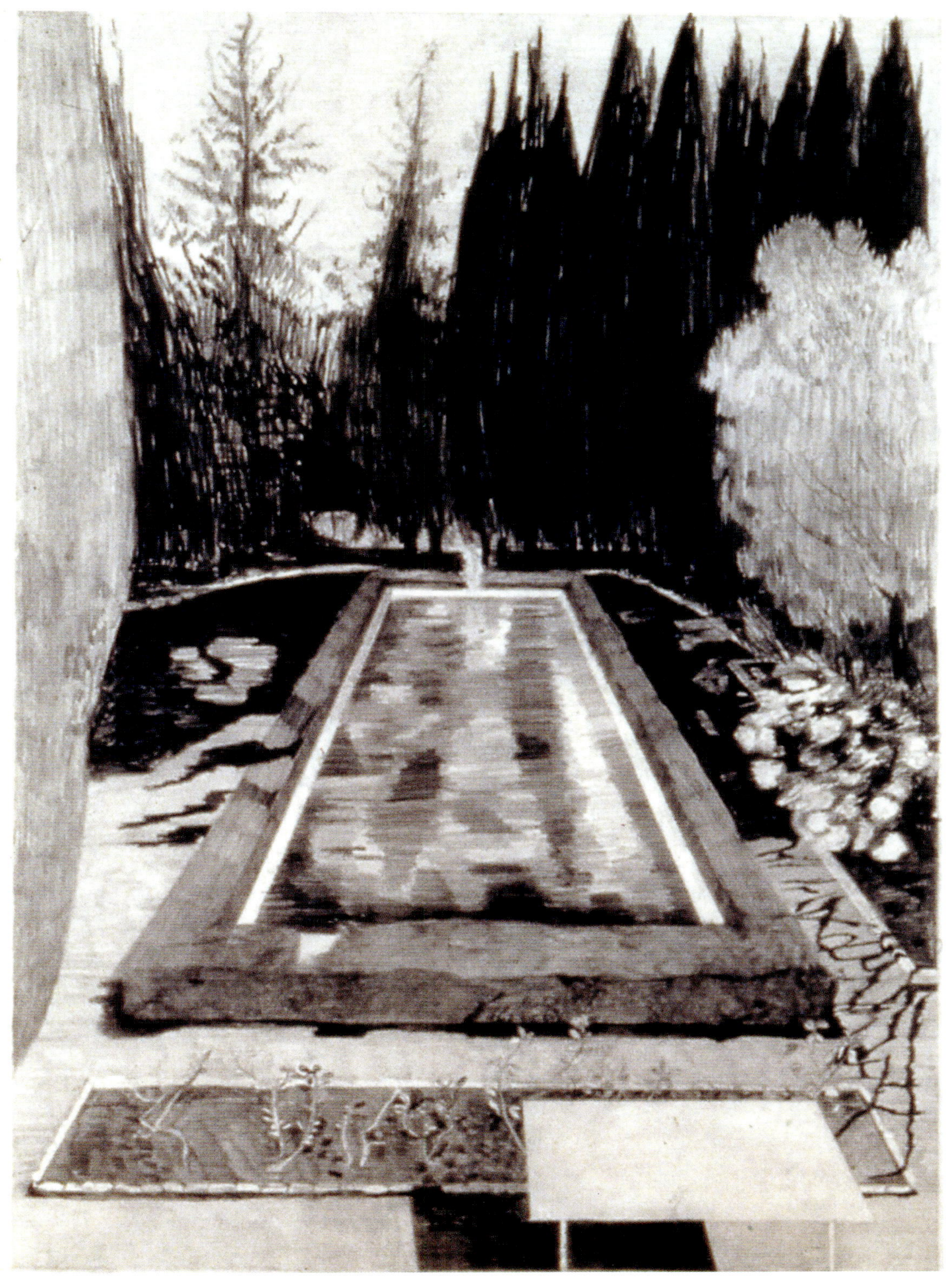

Jennifer Bartlett, *In the Garden*, drawing no. 65, 1980, pastel on paper, 26 × 19.5in. PHOTO: GEOFFREY CLEMENTS

'but I do a lot of preparation and there will always be something happening in the process.'

Her work over the years has been an exploration of many different mediums, including Japanese inks and other materials. Careful, meticulous handling is a byword of Jennifer's technique. This facet is demonstrated in a monumental work for Washington Airport where she reworked paintings, using glass collages in gold, silver and platinum leaf. The final work measured 24ft by 440yd. On other occasions she has used layers of steel plates baked onto enamel surfaces – a technique unique to her. Then there has been her interesting use of silkscreen inks, sometimes as many as seventy-nine colours, both transparent and opaque.

Landscape and, almost inevitably, gardens have 'popped in and out of her work' and she has since travelled with her friend, the garden designer Madison Cox, to see many of the renowned gardens in England (Hidcote for instance) and others in France and Italy. Bartlett herself became involved with the design and development of Manhattan's Battery Park City South Garden that 'unfortunately became an enormous political football.' However, with the help of Madison Cox, she has imaginatively designed her own garden at a Greenwich Village warehouse where she lives and has her studio. 'I am continuously interested in gardens, they have a lot of symmetry and shape; there are muscular gardens and pretty gardens and there are so many different goals set out by the gardeners – it is really like architecture and I have always been interested in architecture.' It is hardly surprising that the designer who helped her with the garden in Manhattan found the experience 'most liberating'.

One feature that is so admirable about this artist's work is an almost fearless approach at times, an audacity. As she says, 'I think people find it disturbing that there isn't a kind of signature painting – that I shift gears and that there are so many layers, so to speak.' There is ruthless abstraction and, as one critic put it, 'the 'romantic' and the 'classical' side by side. She manages to pull witty irregularity out of diligent regularity.'

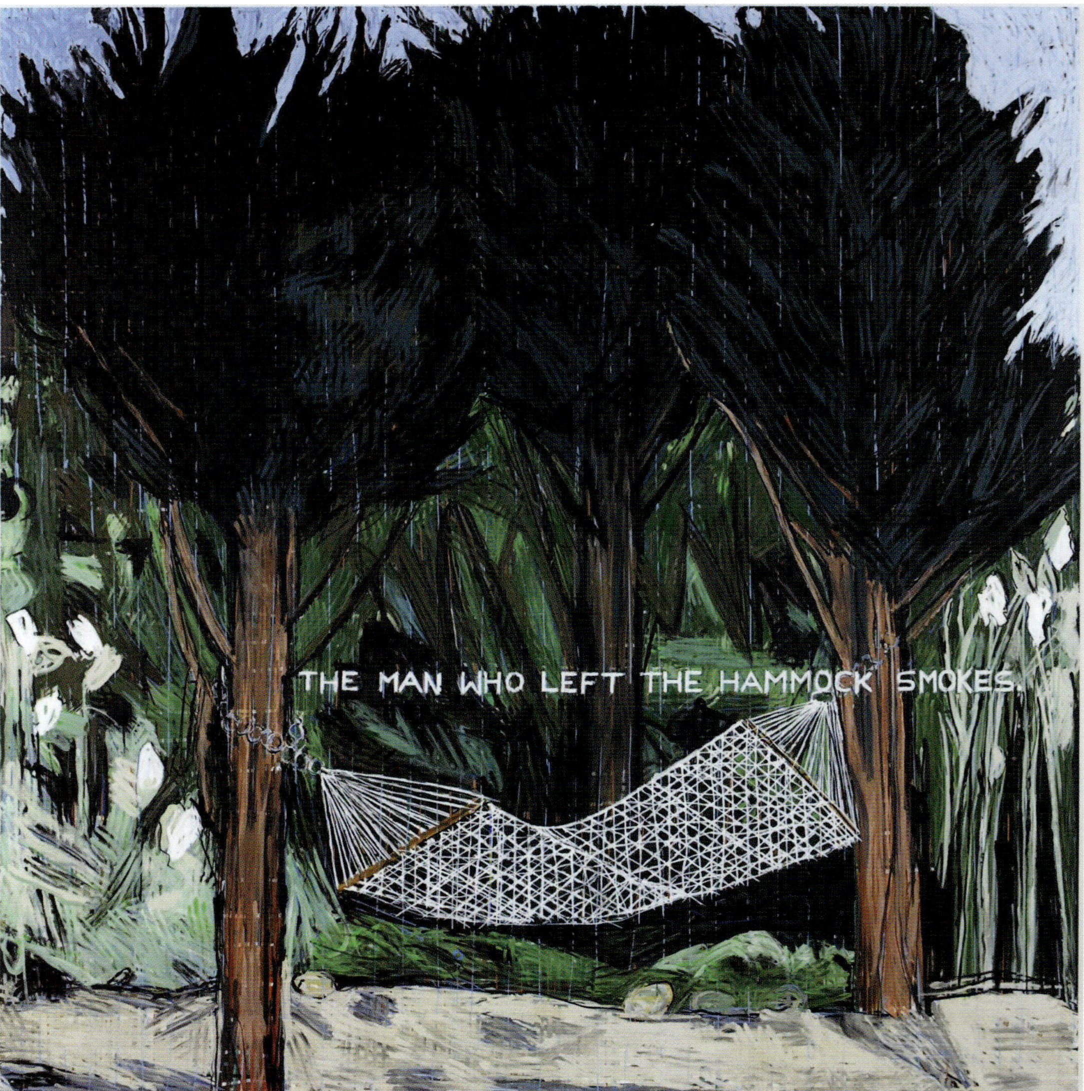

Jennifer Bartlett, *Smokes*, 2006, oil on canvas, 108 × 108in. PHOTO: TOM POWELL

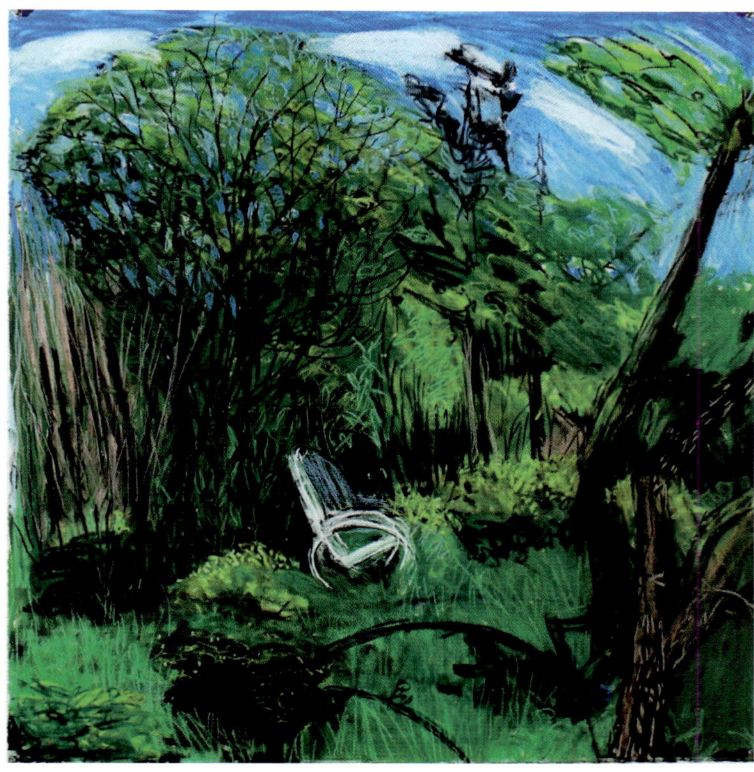

Jennifer Bartlett, *Amagansett*, June 2007, pastel on paper, 30 × 30in.
PHOTO: TOM POWELL

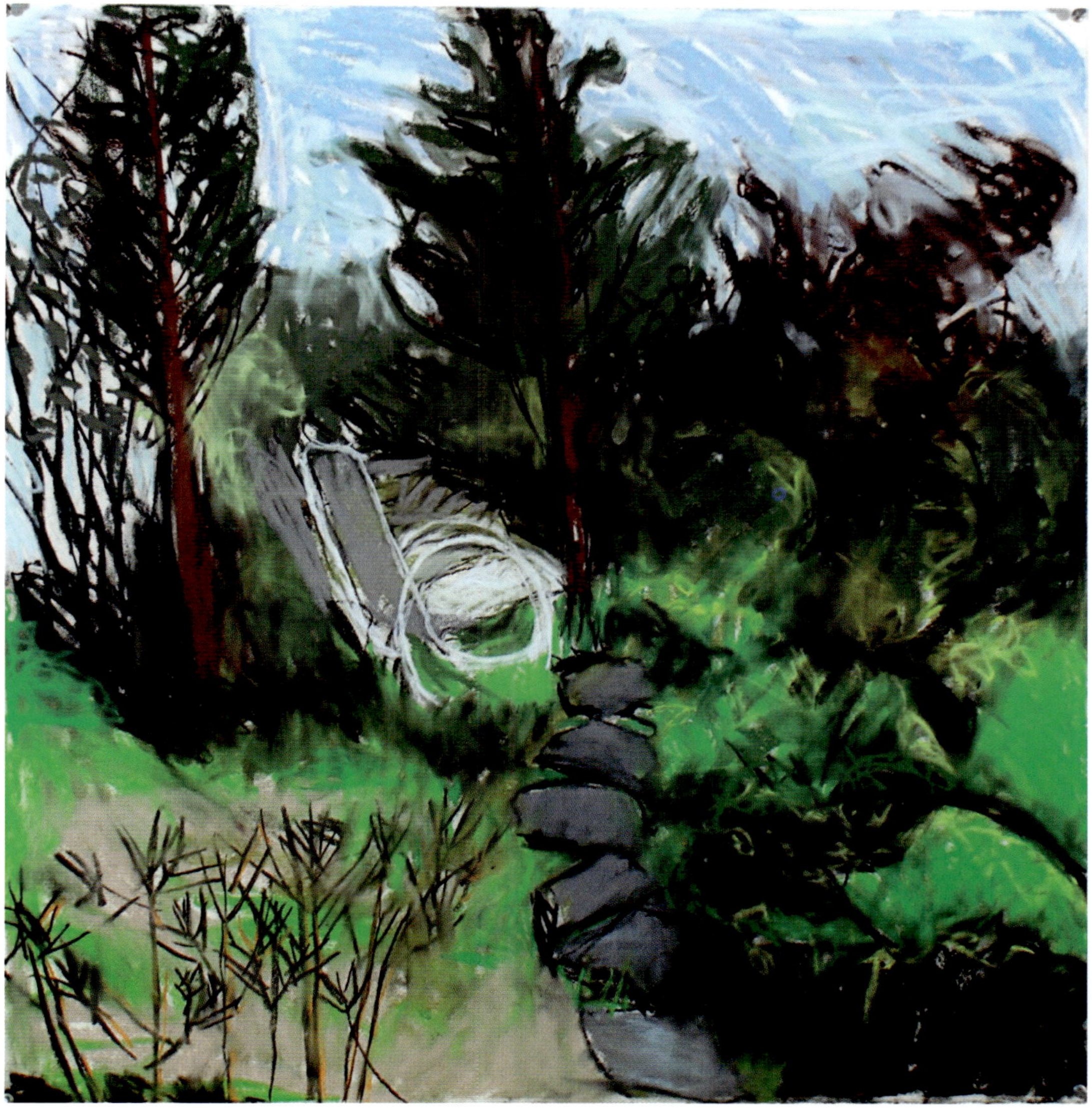

Jennifer Bartlett, *Amagansett*, May 2007, pastel on paper, 30 × 30in. PHOTO: TOM POWELL

Robert Bates

I have known Robert Bates' work since the 1970s when he first showed at the Lumley Cazalet Gallery. During the thirty-four years of the gallery's existence, he and I both had work there. My husband and I bought two of his jewel-like images at one of the earlier exhibitions.

The great traditions of the English landscape artist live on with the romantic and atmospheric images of this painter. There is a subtle poetry in the exquisite way that Bob, as he is known, handles watercolour, but he avoids sentimentality by combining the uglier aspects of the world we live in with nature itself. As Fenella Crichton wrote in *Art International*, 'He produces most unattractive products with the same exquisite care that is expended on the brilliant butterfly ... Telegraph poles stud the purple-tinged hills ... A railway siding, grey and water-sodden ... These become transformed into amulets of peace.'

This unusual talent was encouraged at an early age as he attended the Moseley School of Art in Birmingham in the days when there were schools that specialised in art as distinct from grammar schools and secondary modern schools. By his third year, he had three days studying art and only two days' general studies. At this stage he intended being a commercial artist. He moved to Birmingham College of Art at sixteen; he entered the Fine Art department where the work of such artists as Stanley Spencer and Samuel Palmer was introduced to him. He also started printmaking – etching and lithography.

This stage was followed by a move to the Royal College of Art which had just been through a Golden Period. He did not feel at home in the hot-house atmosphere and indeed felt repressed by a 'sense of guilt' about the work he was producing. He looked around at the work everyone else was doing and tried doing something similar but never felt comfortable about it. He missed the enthusiasm he had encountered in Birmingham.

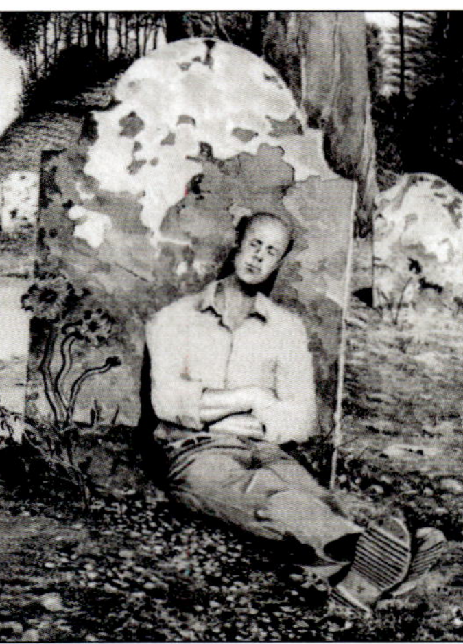

Detail from *The Watercolourist Dreaming in his Watercolour*, 1993, watercolour on paper.
PHOTO: ROBERT BATES

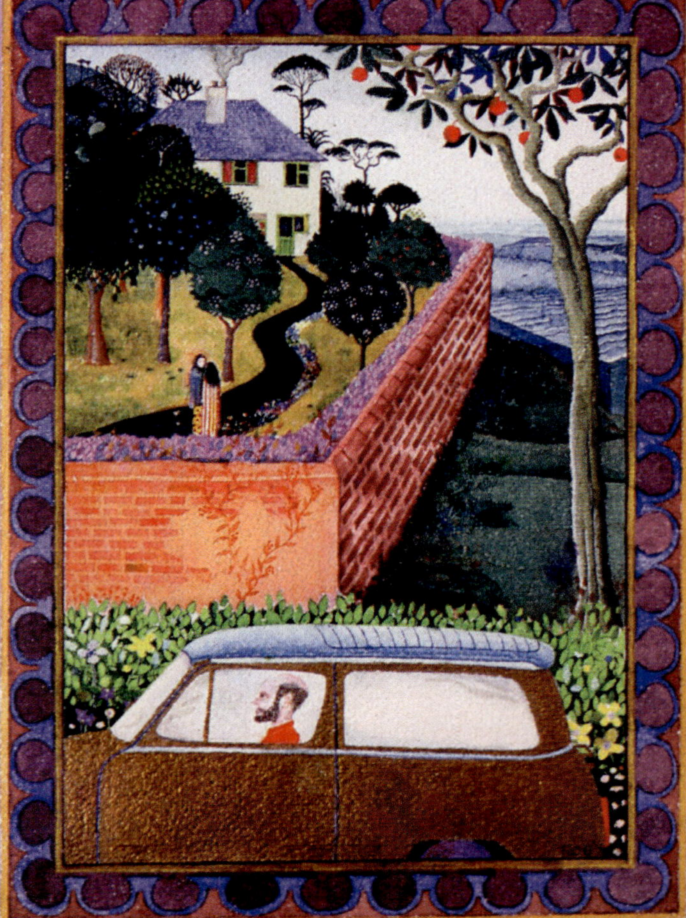

Robert Bates, *Riding in Barbara's Car*, 1970, watercolour on paper, 15.3 × 11.4cm.
PHOTO: ROBERT BATES

Fortunately, in his last year at college a few of the students went to show on the railings in Bayswater Road on Sundays, and this led to a significant encounter. A young man, just down from Cambridge, bought a few pictures and offered to take a portfolio of Bob's work round the galleries. It wasn't long before the Lumley Cazalet Gallery on Davies Street agreed to take his work. Initially, it took his prints, but later the gallery broke its rule of 'only graphics' (which included prints from limited editions by Bonnard, Matisse, Frink and Giacometti) and included his watercolours as well.

For Bob, now teaching near Canterbury, had recently bought his first box of watercolours. He then became inspired by the illustrations of a book containing the letters from Miguel Cyrano to Herman Hesse. After years of printing in black and white he found it very exciting to work in colour – Indian, Persian and French miniatures were a source of inspiration – and, as a result, started incorporating elaborate borders in his own work. His first one-man show of watercolours in 1970 was successful, and he has worked only in this medium ever since. A relief really as he describes the printing methods of that period as far too cavalier and risky. There were no extractor fans and Bob sometimes tested the strength of nitric acid on the tongue!

In the early 1970s, at around the time he started showing at the Lumley Cazalet Gallery, Bob and his wife Barbara moved to Shropshire, a county he has had a particular affinity with ever since, despite a twenty-one-year stint in Ireland. In Shropshire, he is able to define with rare tenderness the poignant scenes that surround him. In hindsight, he describes with affection his first cottage with no running water and no mains electricity.

Bob still paints in miniature dimensions, only in watercolour. His brushes start from size 000 and go no larger than size 6. The images are carried out with exceptional skill, often incorporating a figure, 'say, a watcher by the pool under a lemon sky' and you feel that the figure, too, is 'experiencing the wonder and we can sense it'. The moon appears to hold a certain magic for him, too. In 1997 he had an exhibition around the theme 'Moonlit

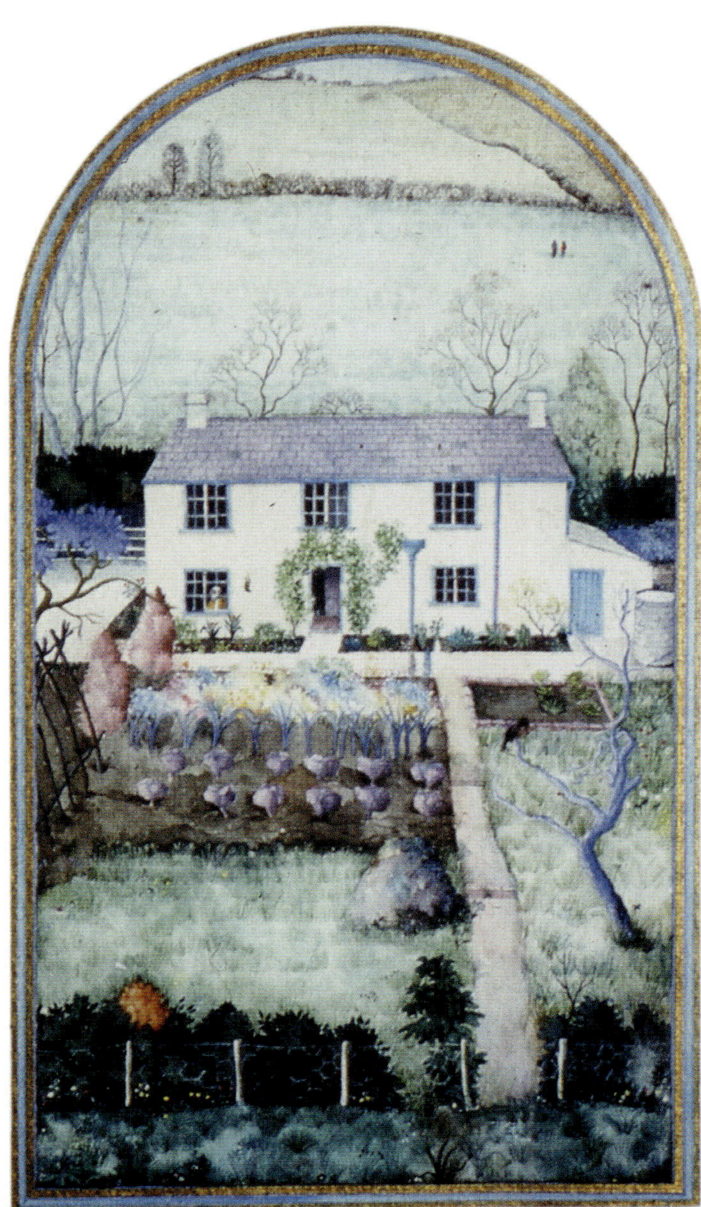

Robert Bates, *The House Gradually Filling with Happiness*, 1972, watercolour on paper, 18.6 × 10.9cm.
PHOTO: ROBERT BATES

Landscapes' and his painting of Will Fielden's house with the vegetable garden in the foreground has an ethereal quality to it.

Pictures take two to three weeks on average, sometimes being put away for weeks or even years and taken out again, when 'I realise that they are not finished and I'll add to them.' Watercolours have a reputation for demanding immediate accuracy, but with the use of various techniques Bob is able to rebuild some of his images with layers of colour.

Bob now shows at the Molesworth Gallery in Dublin and his last show went well. He finds that as he gets older he is slower but, 'You have more skills so the images are achieved more readily – there is work that I did in my twenties that I couldn't do now. The gifts of painting are given to you not once but over and over again and it's something you can't count on. I find that at the start of every painting there is that fear and trembling that it isn't going to work – I've still got my fingers crossed. You should be able to get two inches square to work. There is always a spark that either comes or it doesn't.' He finds that during the last few days of painting, something generally pops in that wasn't there before, which is in itself a kind of stepping stone, a knife edge, when it is either going to work or you've got to do something radical to make it work. 'There are times, a few months or even years later, when what I thought was a fairly mundane image turned out to be a good picture.'

Bob has two ways of working, there is one using more fantasy with distorted perspective and bright colours and another using straightforward landscapes. 'In some ways I think my imagination isn't as spontaneous as it was. Early on, there was the youthful innocence when childhood was still close and one still had that capacity to dream. Nowadays the creativity is more sculpted with a more probing observation of natural detail showing the tones and seasonal colour.'

Bob doesn't get much involved with gardening, but he does grow vegetables, hence the fact that he's always loved painting vegetable gardens, 'The big bean poles and rows of cabbages have an intimate feel and cosiness about them.' He may be very far from being a botanical painter but there is always a hint as

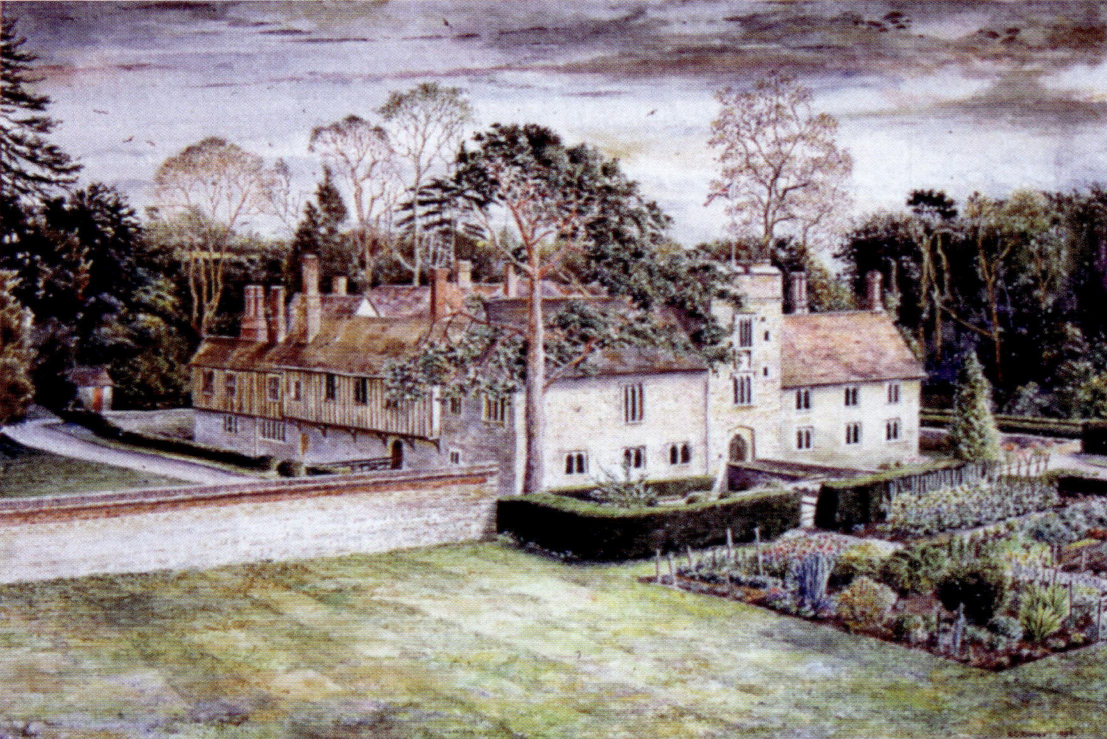

Robert Bates, *Ightham Mote*, 1990, watercolour on paper, 4.75 × 7in.
PHOTO: ROBERT BATES

to what the plants may be as a result of his own close involvement. He has painted Lambeth Palace Garden, Alan Whicker (the broadcaster)'s, garden in Jersey, Jacob Rothschild standing in a garden in Corfu and other renowned gardens, but you feel his thoughts are mainly focused on the overgrown walled garden or fairly simple gardens to which he can add his own mythical interpretation. Titles give a clue to this thought process: *A Poem on the Other Side of the Wall, Unexpected Ascension of an Ordinary Man in his Garden*, or *The Magic Back Garden* – and many others.

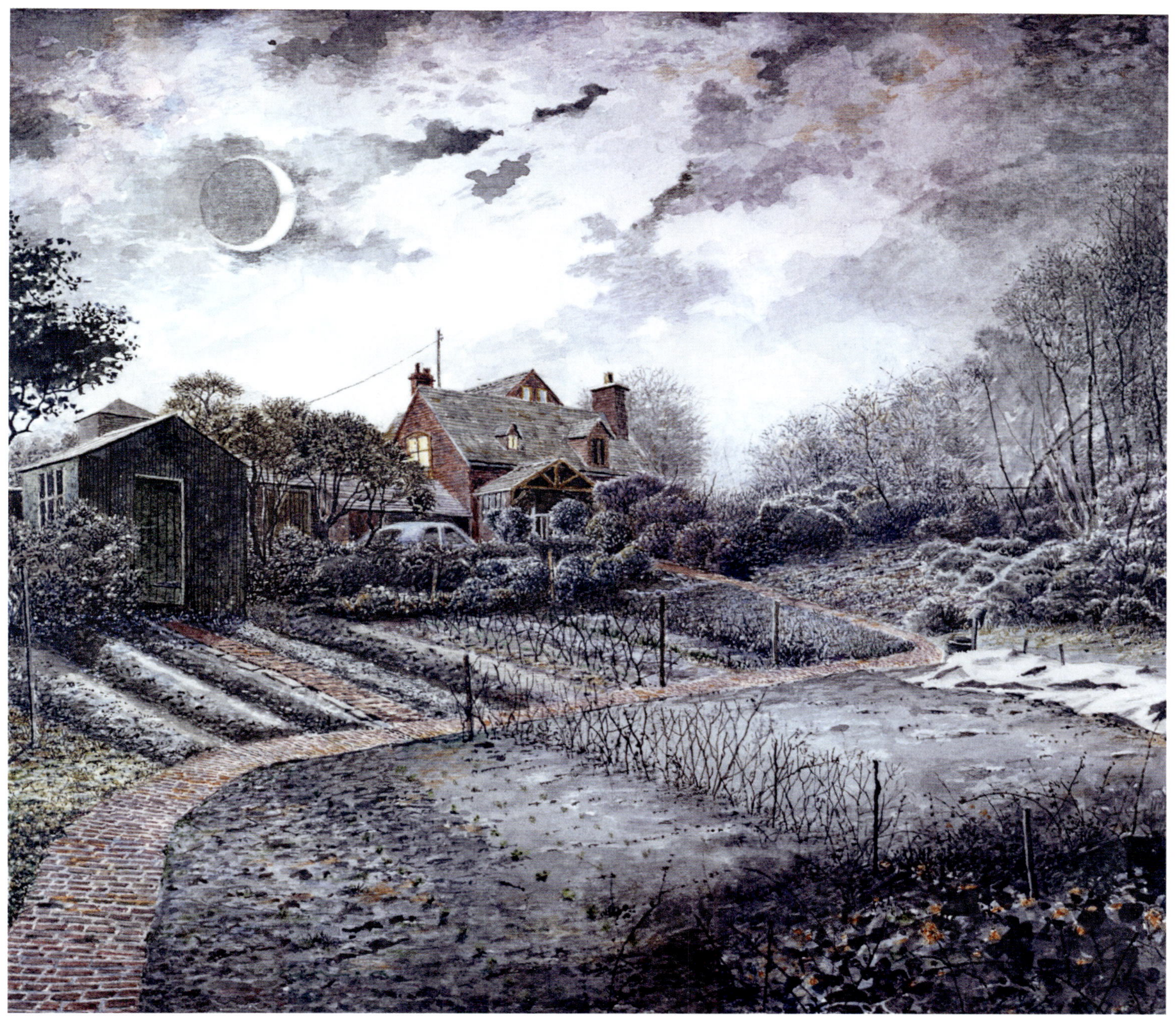

Robert Bates, *Will Fielden's House in Shropshire*, 1996, watercolour on paper, 12.8 × 14.8cm.
COURTESY: LUMLEY CAZALET LTD

Bob's work shows us an interesting blend of 'urban sprawl' meeting 'haunted nature'. Here there is, as Oswell Blakeston of *Arts Review* puts it, 'some truth about poetic pleasure in the world'. Combining memory and imagination, the artist painstakingly paints to a remarkable level of finish with formidable ability.

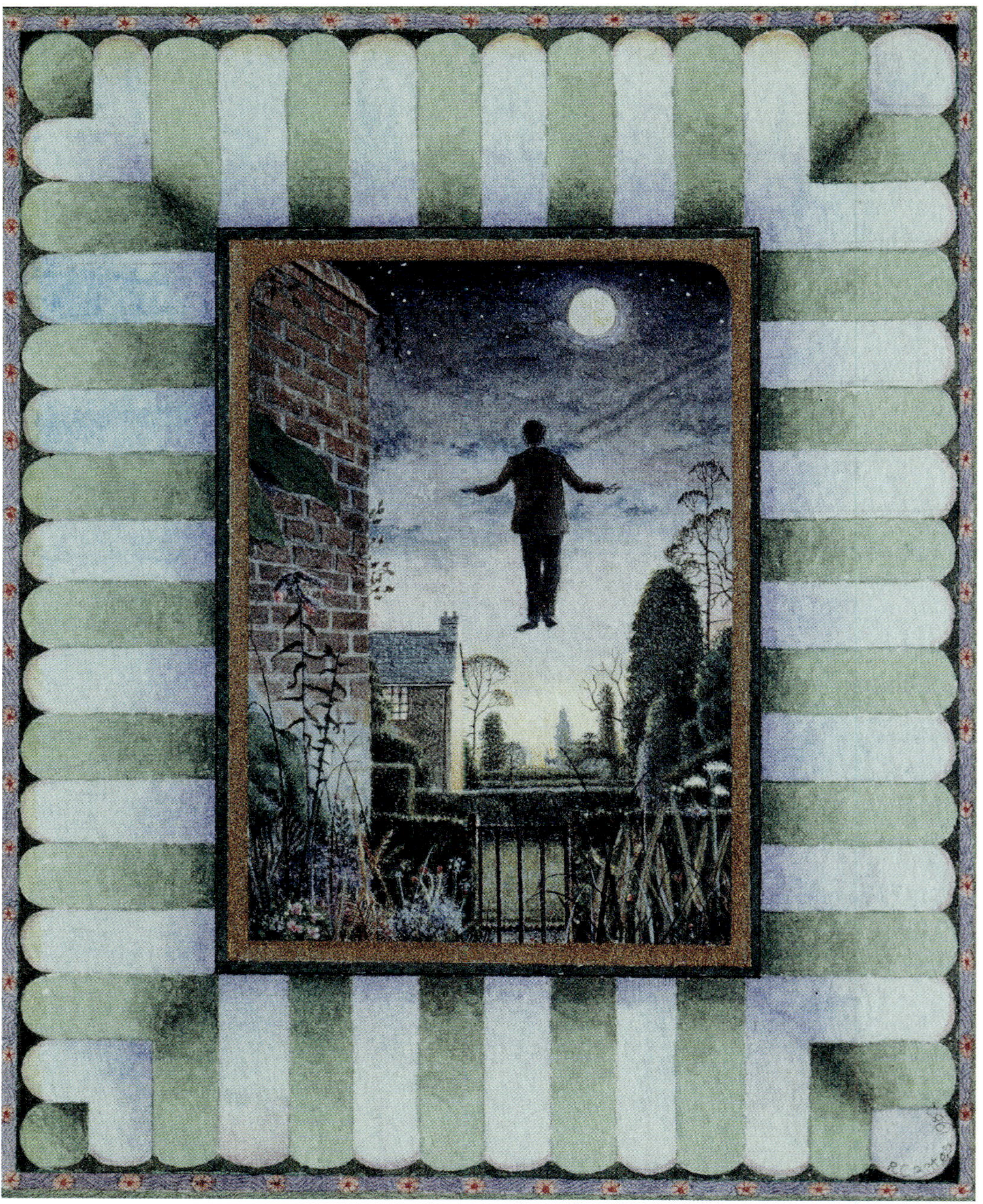

Robert Bates, *Unexpected Ascension of an Ordinary Man in his Garden*, 1982, watercolour on paper, 13 × 11 cm. PHOTO: ROBERT BATES

Adrian Berg

For several years now I have been an admirer of Adrian Berg's joyous and unique series of paintings of Regent's Park from Gloucester Gate, one of which is at Tate Britain. While I was at art school a visiting lecturer, Peter Kinley, introduced me to the wonders of Indian and Persian miniatures that he and his friend Howard Hodgkin had started to buy. It is possible to detect the same kind of influence in Adrian Berg's work.

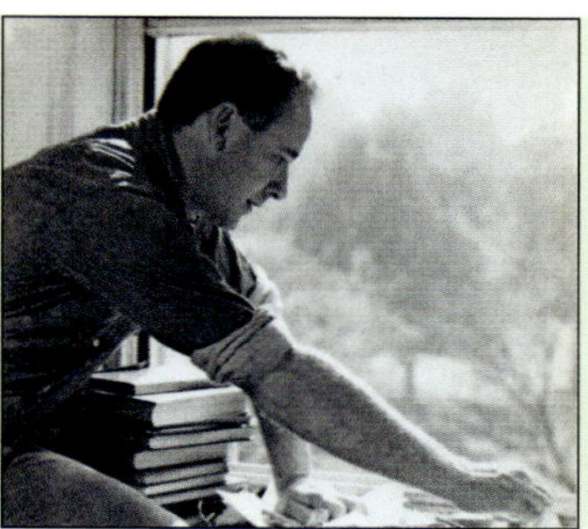

Artist at Gloucester Gate, Regent's Park, 1963.
PHOTO: RICHARD ADENEY

Maybe on account of his father being a psychoanalyst, Adrian was encouraged to study medicine. However, he took a degree in English at Cambridge and went on to study education at Trinity College, Dublin, despite the fact that everyone knew that from the age of three all he ever did was draw. Both at Prep School and at Public School he won drawing prizes based on imaginary landscapes of Regent's Park.

It was while at Cambridge, because the academic year ended so early and he had about six weeks to kill, that he spent time at Chelsea School of Art. Ceri Richards was in charge: 'He was marvellous, absolutely marvellous and I so enjoyed my six weeks that although, when I was finally able to study art, I went to St Martin's School of Art for Intermediate, I knew I had to go on to Chelsea.'

At St Martin's, Adrian was taught watercolour painting by Douglas Holden. Every Wednesday he would be taken out to some place in London to practise this medium. He had done the same thing even when at Cambridge. One summer he hitch-hiked all over France; the following year he drove a motorcycle to Venice, painting there for the entire summer; and the following year he motorcycled to Spain staying in a pensión by the Alhambra Palace. He painted the gardens there for the first time. Also staying in the pensión were some older French artists, who had known Pierre Bonnard. He recalls one of them telling him that Bonnard had the eyes of a child. He has many an anecdote of these trips. 'Once in Spain, when I was drawing away on a street corner, somebody let down a chair from a window for me

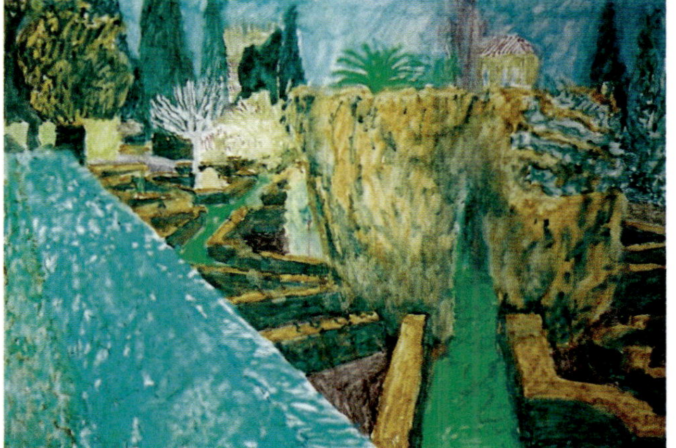

Adrian Berg, *The Alhambra, Granada*, 19 March and 3 April 2001, watercolour, pencil & crayon on paper, 35.5 × 50.8cm.
PHOTO: SAM CLARKE

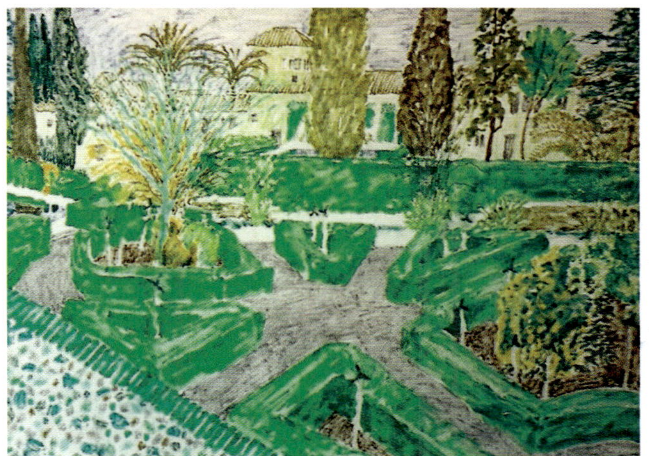

Adrian Berg, *The Alhambra, Granada*, 2003, watercolour, pencil & crayon on paper, 61 × 76.2cm. PHOTO: SAM CLARKE

to sit on.' A similar instance occurred in Amsterdam when he was drawing from the Mint Tower for a couple of hours and when he had finished a couple of policeman saluted him. He hadn't seen them, but they had been standing outside re-routing the traffic. 'They had their priorities right.'

While at St Martin's School of Art, Adrian used to walk down Bond Street from Harley Street, where he lived, taking in all the shows, including Lucian Freud's first show. He often stresses the importance of looking at and talking art. 'Students today do not need an art education so much as an education.'

Chelsea School of Art was run by Harold Williams, who employed fifty London-based artists as part-time staff. 'Wasn't he a clever man? I mean he ran the school superbly. The only artists we didn't have were Graham Sutherland, Henry Moore and John Piper because they were too rich and busy to come.'

From Chelsea, Adrian moved to the Royal College of Art and then began to teach.

He lived in Gloucester Gate from the 1960s to the 1980s and would often paint Regent's Park from the studio window or balcony. He developed over time a most intriguing format for what became for him a compulsive subject. His paintings incorporated the abundant growth of the changing seasons and the varying colours of foliage and flowers during the year. These images acted almost like a diary of the seasons. He then devised a unique way of using a square canvas on which multiple views fitted together to give an overall view. The picture can be hung from any of the four sides. There is no conventional perspective – the effect is more like carpet or tapestry. He painted such scenes 'because what I see outside sometimes looks unimaginably beautiful'. As Peter Fuller, the critic, wrote, 'He was working entirely within the traditions, disciplines, limits and skills of painting ... yet his work always seemed fresh, varied and full of discovery.'

During these years, Adrian taught at Kingston, Chelsea, the Slade and Camberwell. He became senior tutor at the Royal College of Art 1987–88. At this time there was an extraordinary camaraderie and interaction among artists. Ron Kitaj once said to Adrian while they were both at the Slade, 'Did you find that

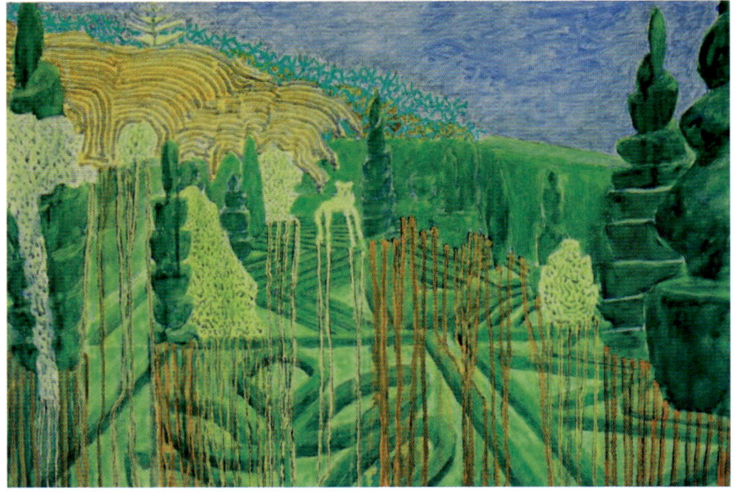

Adrian Berg, *The Botanic Garden, Madeira*, 25 October 2005, oil on canvas, 66 × 96.5cm. PHOTO: FXP PHOTOGRAPHY, COURTESY: JOHN RIDDY

you talked more than you ever talked in your life?' He has been at the epi-centre of the British Art scene for a long time and talking to him is like talking to an art historian of the period.

At the time there was the colossal influx of American Minimalism and Abstract Expressionism that one way or another affected so many artists: William de Kooning, Jackson Pollock, Ashile Gorky and others. 'Easels were going Pop everywhere.' Adrian remembers seeing a Jackson Pollock exhibition at the Whitechapel Gallery and telling his sister afterwards that 'He'd been up all night trying to catch the drip – I was trying to do a Pollock.'

Despite these influences Adrian felt that 'there was a sacrifice of emotional significance' and he has essentially kept to an English tradition of travelling, drawing, sketching and painting. He generally works outside from spring to autumn with 'days spent in the studio the exception'.

Since that time Adrian has made several ambitious series of paintings of parks and gardens of England: Wakehurst Place, Kew Gardens, Sheffield Park and Nymans, to name but a few. In these pictures he records changing seasons and changing times of day but interprets the scene in his uniquely colourful manner, giving a real sense of vibrating light and life.

FACING PAGE Adrian Berg, *Stourhead*, 26 June 1992, oil on canvas, 52 × 74in. PHOTO: SAM CLARKE

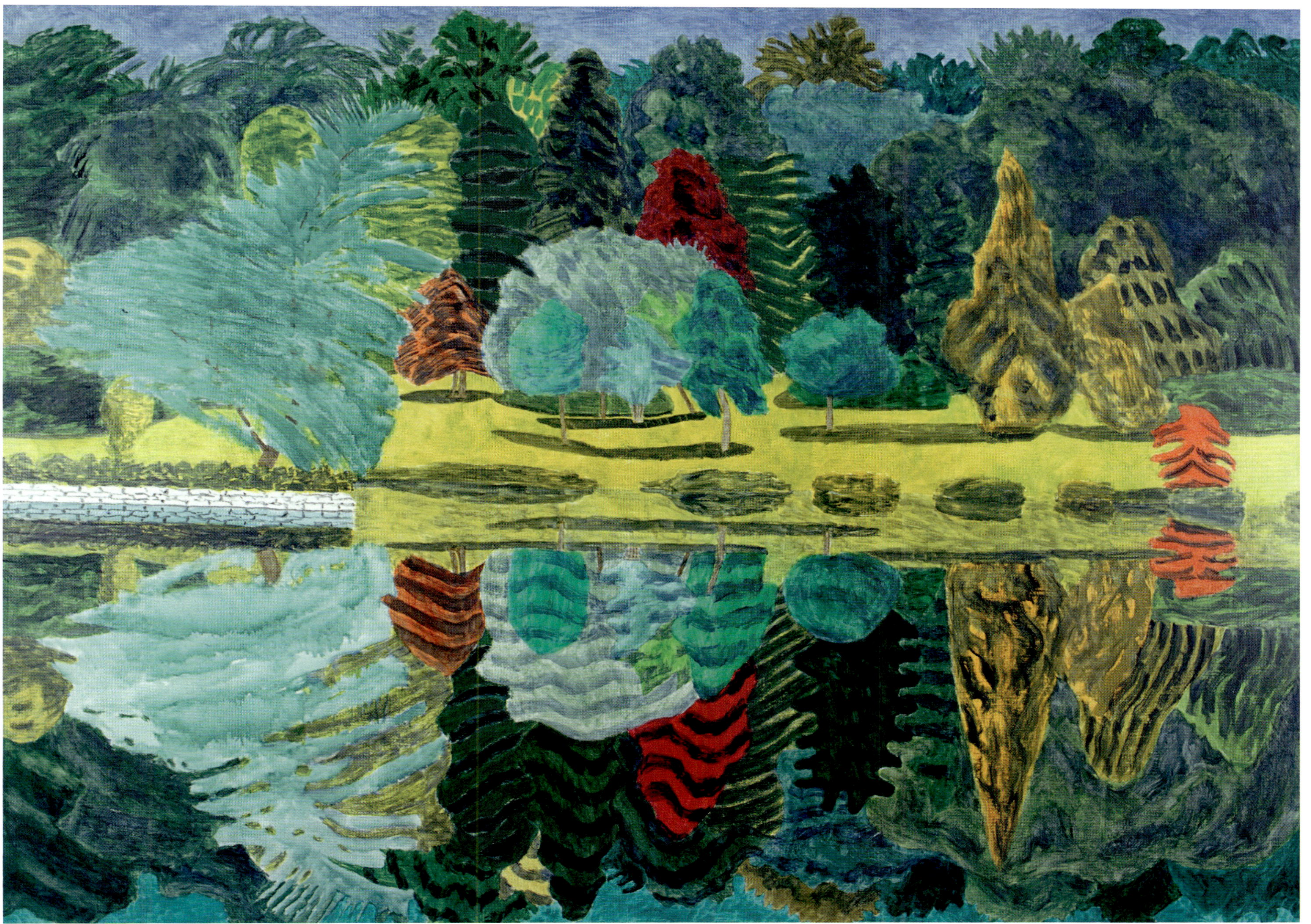

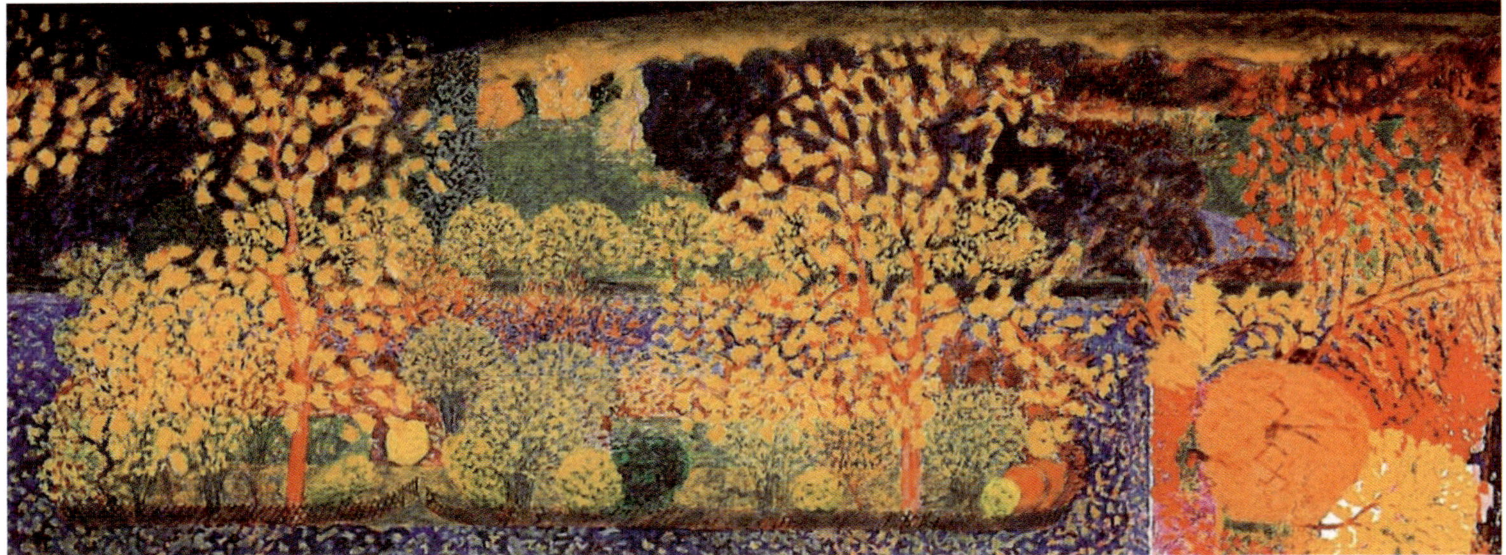

Adrian Berg, *Gloucester Gate, Regent's Park: Night, Autumn*, 1981, oil on canvas, 91.5 × 244cm.
PHOTO: MIGUEL HENRIQUE DE PINA OSMUND

On two occasions he has drawn for the National Trust at Stourhead, living there for a month in order to capture its essential magic. The British Council was responsible for sponsoring a month-long visit to Japan and the gardens there – a much-enjoyed trip. Other sources of inspiration have been the Botanic Gardens in Madeira and a further visit to the Alhambra Gardens in Spain.

Throughout his life he has shown his work at the most prestigious galleries – Arthur Tooth & Sons, Waddington Galleries and more recently at the Piccadilly Gallery from 1985–99. Adrian was made a Royal Academician in 1992 and has been involved in the organisation of Summer Shows.

At the Summer Show in 2007 his own work occupied the 'hot spot' to the left of David Hockney's pictures and his work was described 'as more than surviving, with a group of intensely colourful, joyous paintings partly inspired by Persian miniature painting'. There is a Persian-style carpet at the top of the stairs as you enter his studio.

After early use of watercolour, there was a short period after college when he painted in tempera. Now the shelves in his studio are stacked with neatly arranged oil paints in a vast range of hues, ranging from dark to light, particularly with the greens. Canvases are stacked, stretched and primed ready for use behind an easel and the walls are lined with black and white drawings done with reed pens. ('Rembrandt used them when they were three centuries out of date and I use them when they are six centuries out of date.')

An Australian artist once said to Adrian, 'How lucky you are to have that English tradition of painting behind you.' I thought, 'This is what you are up against, this isn't something you move in on, this is something you have to compete with – you have to compete with Constable and Turner, not to mention Girton and Samuel Palmer and so on.' Adrian feels that as a painter, 'You mustn't just paddle your feet, but swim.' This may account for the reason he will return again and again to the same subject, as for instance at Gloucester Gate, then again at Stourhead where he returned four years later and at Kew where he returned day after day. In this way he captures an intelligence of feeling, an intensity, a vivacity.

FACING PAGE Adrian Berg, *Gloucester Gate, Regent's Park*, 1982, oil on canvas, 178 × 178cm.
COURTESY: TATE, LONDON, 2008

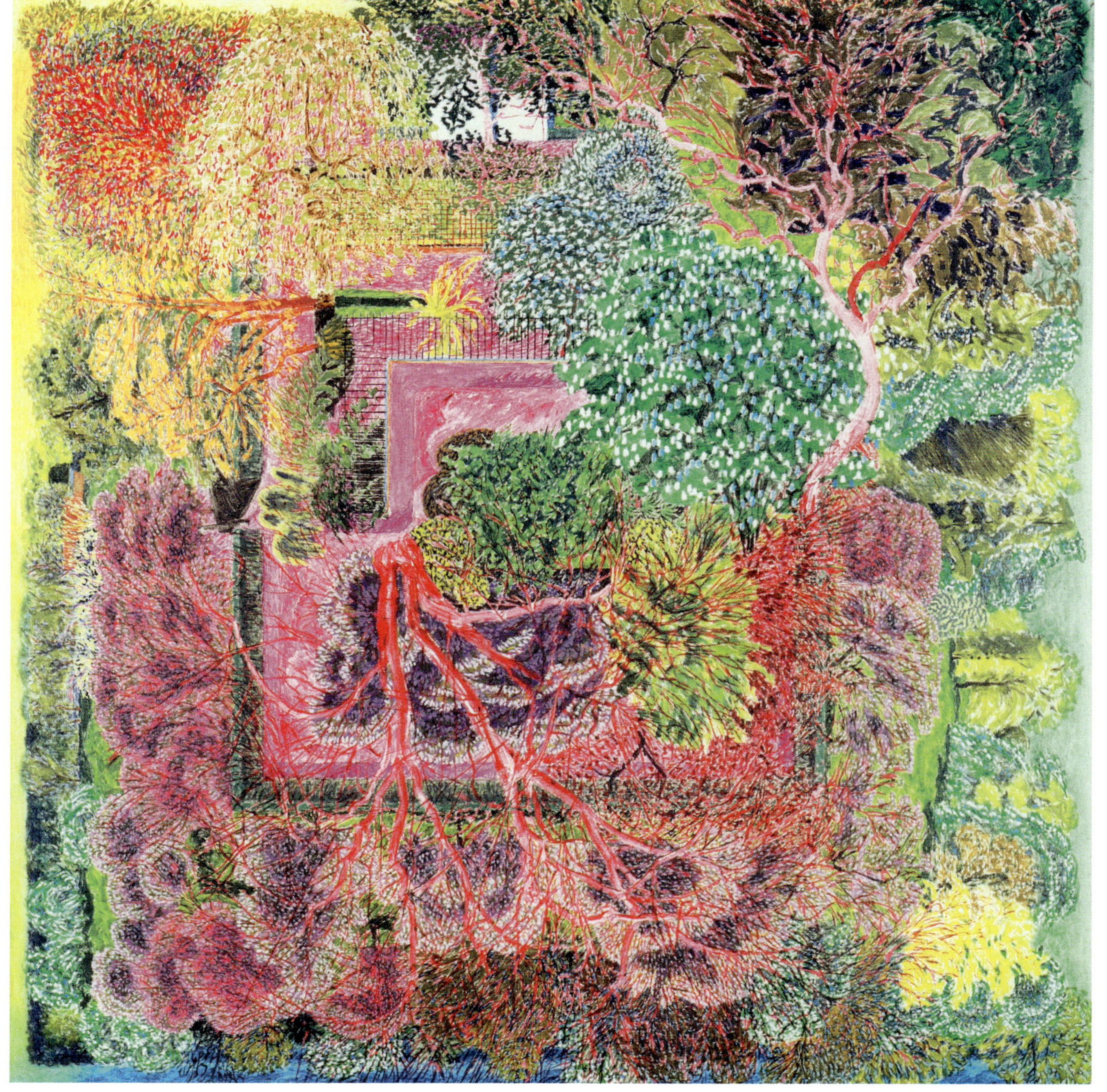

June Berry

While researching the artists to be included in this book, I heard the name June Berry mentioned on several occasions and when I saw the photograph of *The Bird Watcher* in the Royal Watercolour Society's recent book I knew I'd really admire her work.

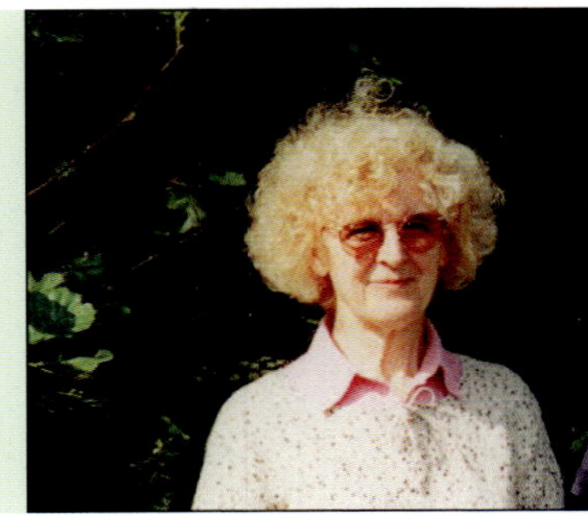

Portrait of the Artist.
PHOTO: JOHN BERRY

June's work is essentially the observation of the life taking place around her, either in the area of Deux-Sèvres, rural Poitou (France), or around Beckenham in South London. Her subjects are neighbours talking over a garden wall, taking tea in a garden, or perhaps working in a vegetable patch (in France). The vivid but warm colours have a similarity with the palette of Pierre Bonnard, her 'all-time hero', but the intimacy and sympathy with which all the scenes are depicted could recall the work of Edouard Vuillard (even though hers are principally exterior scenes, as opposed to Vuillard's interiors). Amongst the English artists who have worked around the same themes are Carel Weight and Ruskin Spear.

Despite having had no artistic background or encouragement at home, June gained a place at the Slade School of Art in 1942 and pursued her painting studies there after three years' war service in the WRNS. She was awarded a postgraduate year in 1949. The Slade has always been renowned for its teaching of draughtsmanship. The benefit of such training is easily observed by the accomplished manner in which she depicts the comforting shapes and feelings of a rustic village community. For the first term, the tuition centred on the drawing of plaster casts, followed by separate life classes for male and female students. Thereafter there was the usual instruction in painting. One of the visiting lecturers at that

June Berry, *Three Sisters in the Garden*, 1993, watercolour, 19 × 24in.
PHOTO: FXP PHOTOGRAPHY

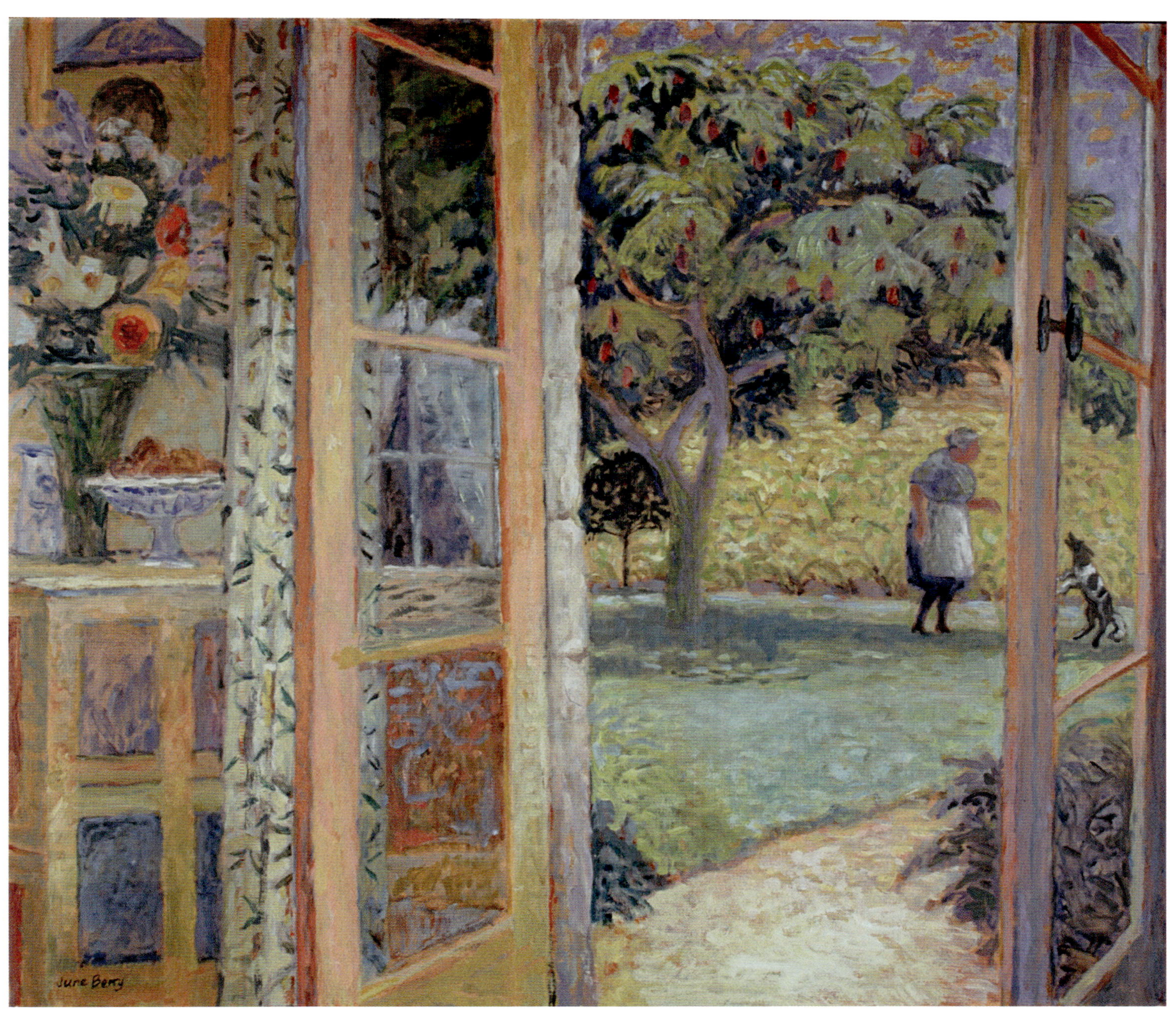

June Berry, *Through the Studio Window*, 1998, oil on board, 20 × 24in. PHOTO: FXP PHOTOGRAPHY

time was Stanley Spencer who would occasionally perch on her stool while giving a 'critique'.

Since then there has been a 'long, long learning experience', which she has described as 'slow-burning'. There were fifteen years devoted to part-time teaching, getting married and raising a family.

She used printmaking as a way back into painting and gaining confidence after all the intervening years, and considers that she has only really got into her stride over the last ten years. Nevertheless, during these years she has been able to assimilate experience and acquire a visual memory both of which have added to the character and poetic vision of her work. Her immense professional skill and consistent hard work have meant that she now has work in the collections of Her Majesty the Queen, the Ashmolean Museum, the Victoria & Albert Museum and the Graphotek, Berlin, among many others. She has had eighteen solo exhibitions and taken part in a long list of mixed exhibitions, being an award winner on five occasions, three of which were for watercolours. She has shown at the Royal Academy Summer Exhibition many times since the mid 1950s and is a member of no fewer than three Royal Societies – the Royal Watercolour Society, the Royal West of England Academy and the Royal Society of Painter Printmakers.

June is very orderly in the approach to her quietly anecdotal studies of everyday life. She has many small notebooks with copious closely observed figures and always prepares for a new picture with drawings and compositional studies of approximately half the size of the final painting. These are clearly an essential part of her creative process.

The drawings are a way of recording information, and 'reminding myself because I can't remember exactly how it was, and it is often quite a while before a painting follows on. When I'm awake at night I think, "Oh yes, I could do that, or alter that".' The drawings made on the spot are dotted with pencil notes about colour, such as 'cream/pink', 'yellow leaves and stalks', 'dark foliage', etc. The margins contain little studies of cats, birds, butterflies or people as these appeared on the scene.

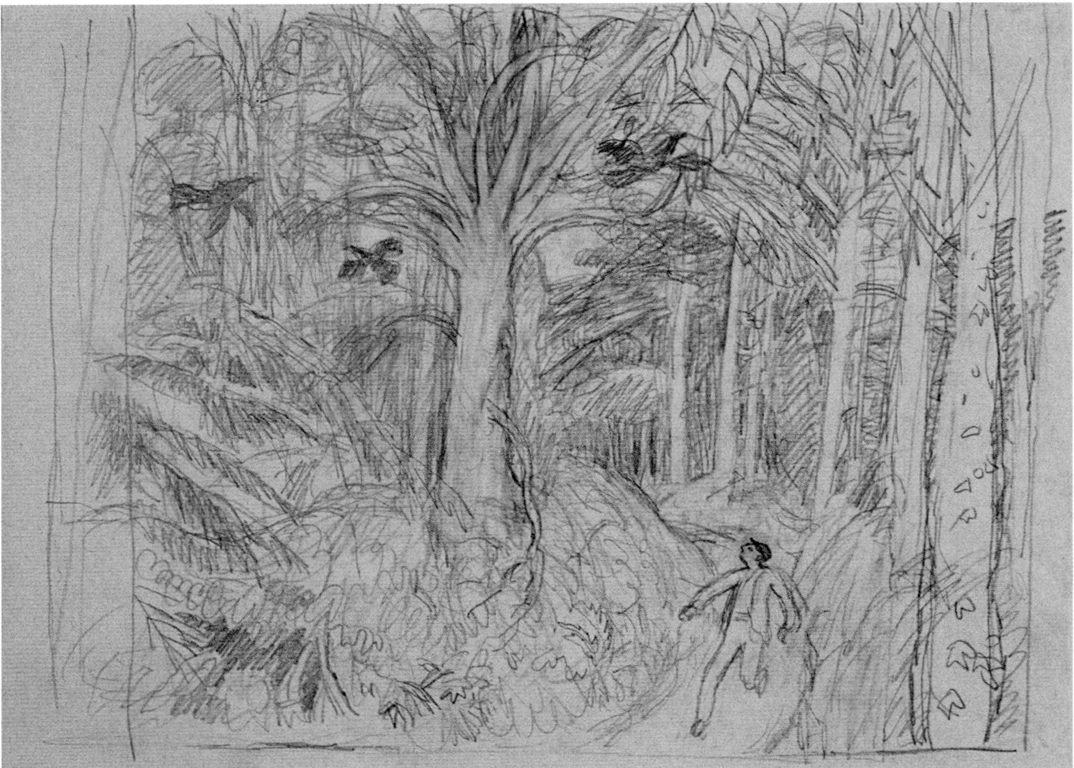

June Berry, *A Noise of Wings*, 2003, pencil drawing, 40 × 55in.
PHOTO: ALAN ROBERTSON

Her preparatory drawings and studies are private records that she doesn't exhibit but are essential to the development of the picture as it progresses, so that the paintings don't necessarily end up looking like the drawings. Approximately half her work is painted in oils and half in watercolour.

Although she has done commissioned work, it has been undertaken on the understanding that it has to be from her own perspective. If the commissioner doesn't like the result, that is 'OK'.

June spends about four months a year painting in her studio in France but finds the light and colour there difficult in summer. Over the years, her colour density and strength have become more saturated. It's interesting to observe the contrasting subjects

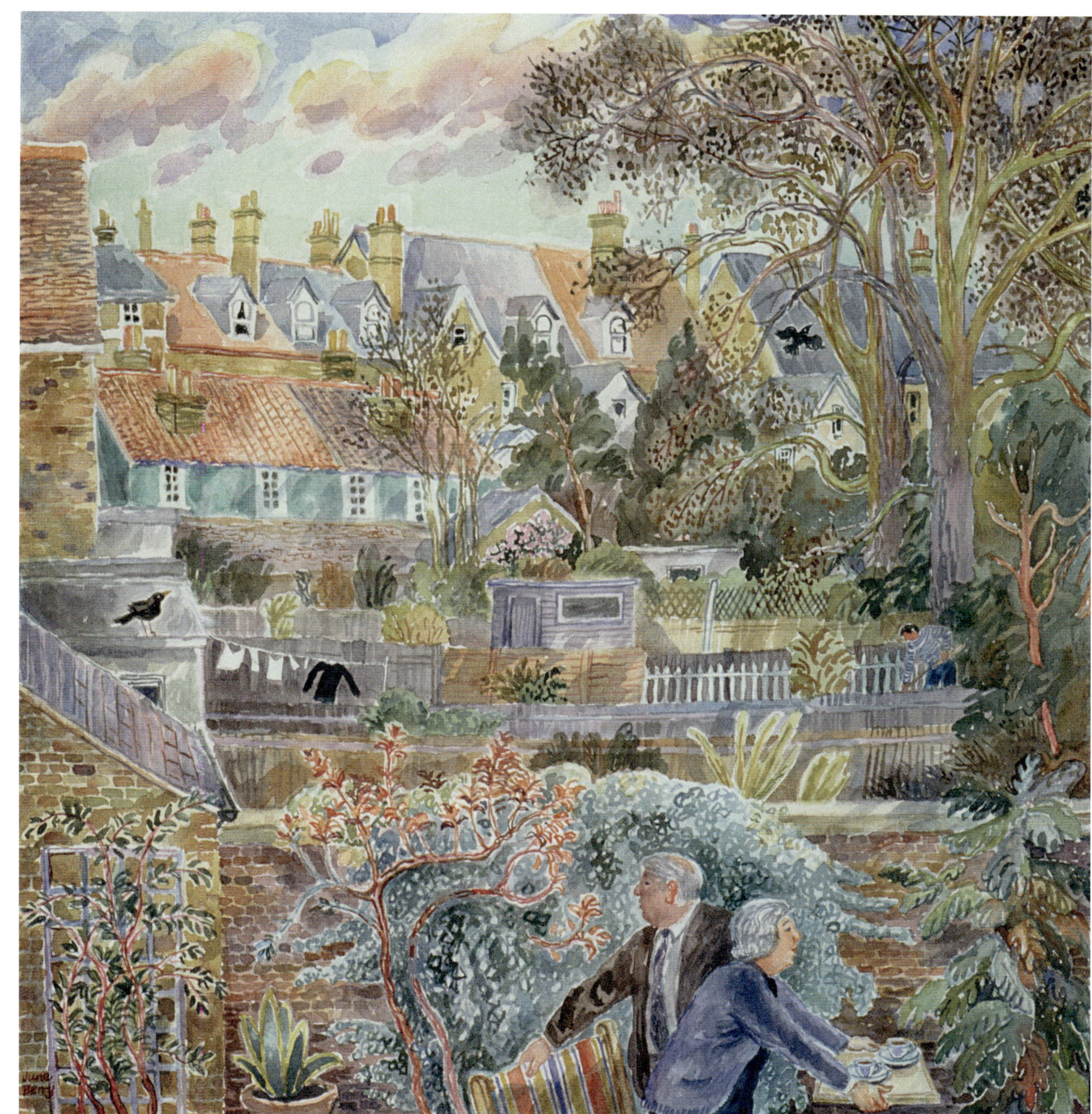

June Berry, *Tea in the Garden*, 1995,
watercolour, 22.5 × 23in.
PHOTO: FXP PHOTOGRAPHY

of her French and English pictures. In the French gardens there are chickens, dogs and donkeys, and an abundance of vegetables that signal the ethic: 'If you can't eat it, don't have it.' The English scenes tend to depict the more urban life of outer London.

Some time ago June was chosen to take part in a project involving the Royal Horticultural Society and the Royal Watercolour Society and this project produced some charming images from different parts of England. It is while studying these paintings that you detect her interesting and varied compositions of shapes and lines. In her painting of a grand vegetable garden at Calke Abbey in Derbyshire, there is emphasis on the zigzag line leading through the image whereas in *Belinda's Garden* in East London (where the owner jams all the plants together), the lines have more of a swirl and an intricate pattern. *Choosing Shrubs*, which is another French picture, focuses on an interesting big tree down the middle with the balancing figures and objects on either side unobtrusive, seemingly unconscious. Then there is *Tea in the Garden* where the shapes made by the figures' arms reflect the shapes of the roofs – all such details enhance the narrative interest that blends effortlessly with the effervescent use of colour and pigment. There is a kind of subliminal effect that results in a 'poetic fusion' because you keep thinking, 'Oh, that shape again.'

June has an impressive body of work and still produces about sixty paintings a year. She exhibits on a very regular and consistent basis, but you know that her present ambition is to succeed with her joyful but contemplative study of everyday life in her close environment. She enjoys conveying and reflecting the concerns and occupations of real people.

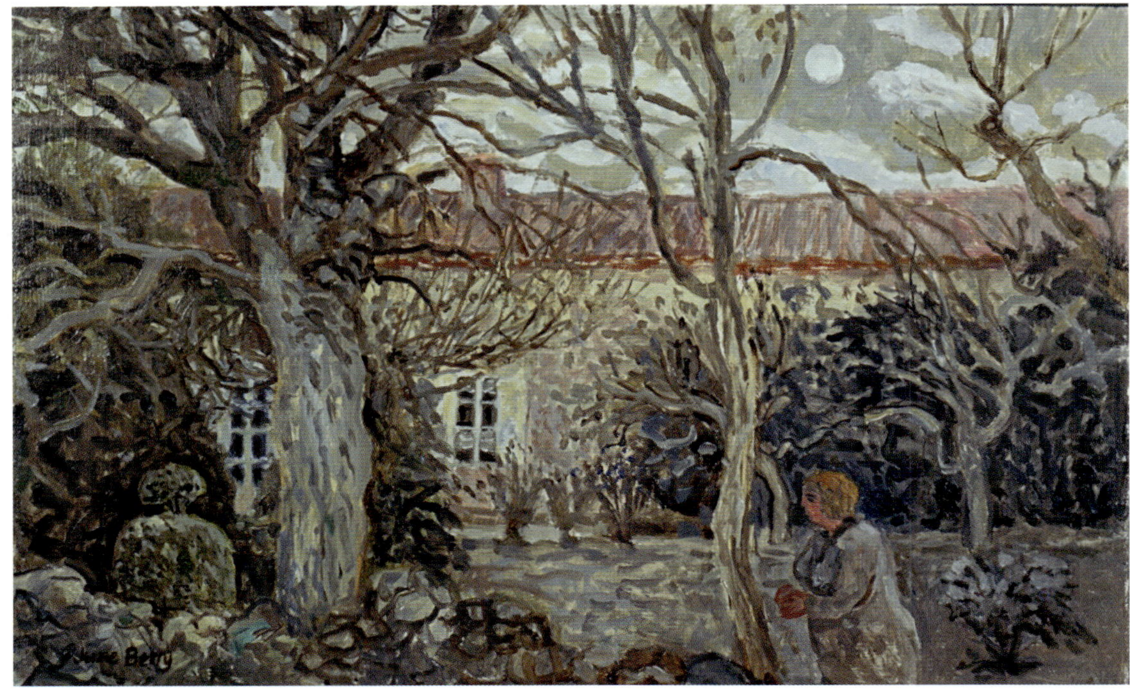

June Berry, *Winter in the Garden*, 2006, oil on board, 8 × 13in.

Michael Dillon

A while ago, after collecting some paintings from an exhibition in Dorset, I went to see John and Lizzie Wilsey, friends from childhood. On the walls of their conservatory was a delightful mural depicting scenes from their garden painted by Michael Dillon.

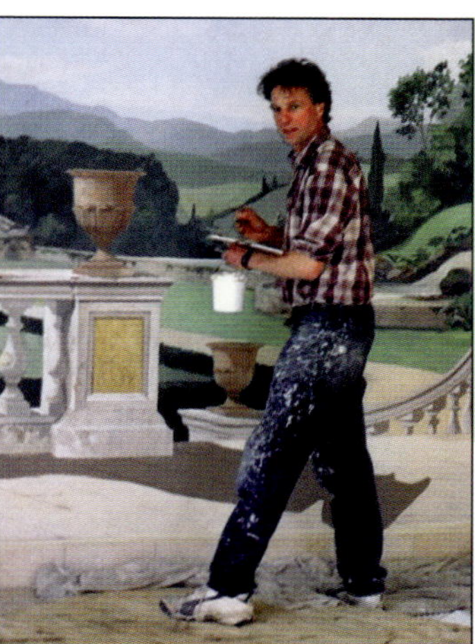

Artist painting a Tuscan Garden Swimming Pool.
PHOTO: ARTIST'S COLLECTION

Michael specialises in fantasy murals, historical decorations and *trompe l'œil* images. His interest in painting started when he drew and painted many of the different varieties of birds to be found in the countryside on the east coast of Ireland where he grew up. Even now there is a great profusion of birds of all varieties shown in his work, from the exotic to the more ordinary. At school, he wasn't particularly inclined to develop his art skills. He went on to study agriculture at college. After graduating he went to farm in New Zealand and in England, and finally worked near Lisieux in Normandy, France, where he looked after sheep and cattle.

He returned to painting in the late 1980s by joining Alec Cobbe, his brother-in-law, who had other skills – picture restoring, glass engraving and murals – as well as being an expert on many aspects of painting. During the two years that Michael worked with Alec, he visited many well-known houses and was introduced to historical decoration in all its various forms. One of the projects was at the Clyde Museum in Powys Castle, Wales.

A mural is art painted directly on a wall making it an integral part of the wall and ceiling. The late 1980s were a good period for such works when 'young yuppies were making a lot of money', but this form of expression is likely to continue as there will always be a desire to decorate surroundings and express ideas and beliefs. The subject matter is extremely varied, and it is to Michael's credit that his murals show such unfailing skill, gifted flare and imagination.

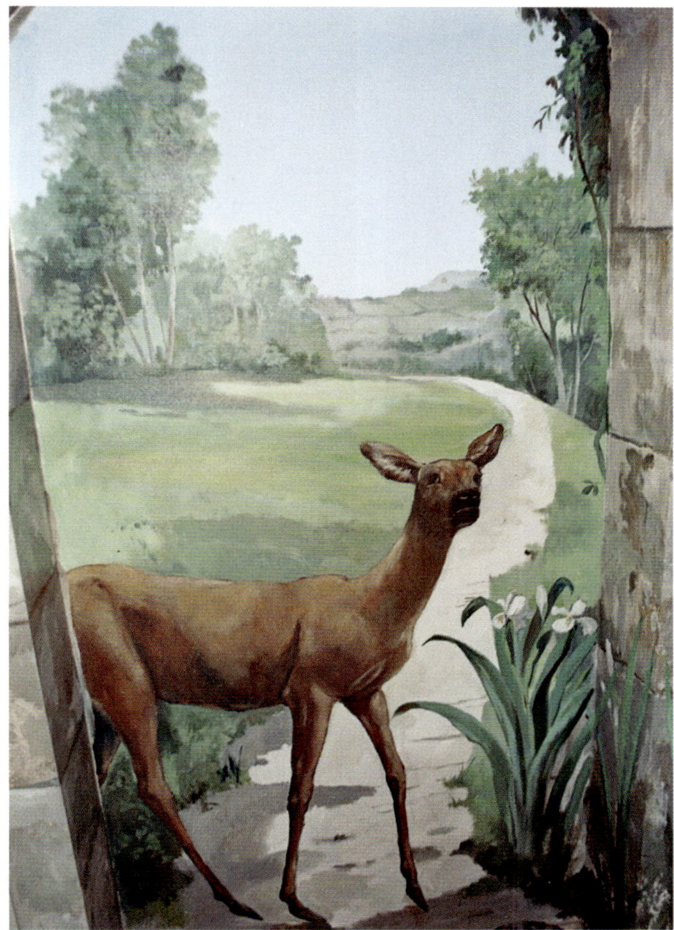

Michael Dillon, part of *Garden Mural, Dublin*, 2005, acrylic on wall, 400 × 200in.
PHOTO: MICHAEL DILLON

This period gave Michael the confidence to start his own business which he did by organising flyers and mail shots, and by contacting architects and interior designers. Amongst early assignments was work for the Hatfield House restaurant and Fortnum & Mason. For the latter, he did some designs for the Fountain Restaurant and also various lunettes for the Food Hall. Owing to recent refurbishment at Fortnum & Mason, Michael's paintings became part of an important and successful sale and have been dispersed around Europe. He has also worked for the National Trust and various hotels in Ireland, but otherwise most of his work is in private houses.

Michael travels a huge amount. He has worked not only in Great Britain, but also in France, Spain, Germany, Mustique and the USA, and even in the woodlands of Quebec and, in 1998, in Zimbabwe. During long journeys, when there is a lot of waiting around, he makes copious sketches of people and takes the opportunity to make notes and to develop designs.

When Michael takes on a new commission he is meticulous about his approach, making detailed small oil or acrylic paintings before the final images. If, for instance, he is asked to paint an Italianate garden (such as the example in Madrid, called the *Pompeian Ruin Room with Venetian Views*) he will try to visit some gardens in this genre, to do several sketches and to take photographs. After long experience, he has a good memory for detail and a good library for reference. He knows the gardens of Andalusia particularly well as he has done many drawings there, with notes on the plantings and, of course, there are cross-references from there to other styles. In future, he intends exhibiting some of the small preparatory oil designs as they have an appeal all their own. In any case, they help clients decide if they want to make last-minute changes, and for Michael it's important to have an accurate composition to work from.

On my visit to his vast and airy studio, there was on display a large canvas 6 × 6ft which was an oil sketch of a garden for a London house. He was changing the design around to decide where a summer house, a column and pots should be, so that major decisions for the mural were made in advance.

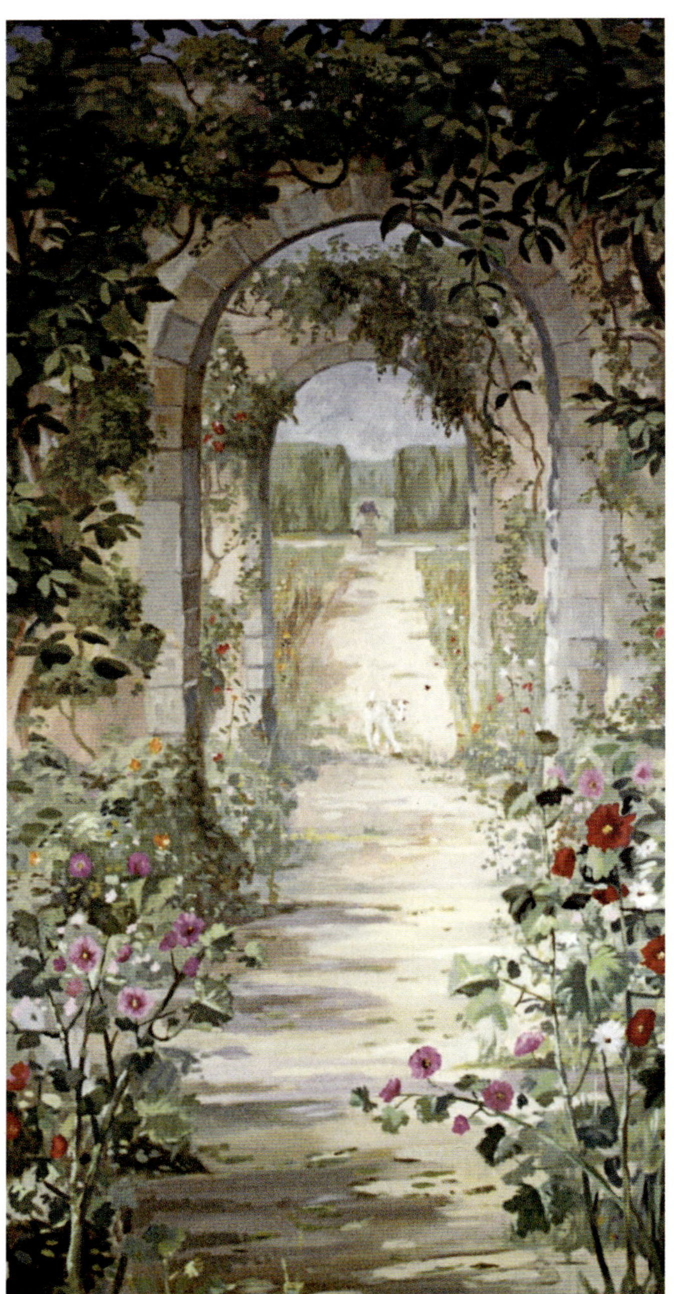

LEFT Michael Dillon, *Garden Mural*, inspired by gardens at the Château de Canon, Normandy, 1995, oil on board, 230 × 100cm. PHOTO: MICHAEL DILLON

FACING PAGE Michael Dillon, detail from *Garden Mural, Dorset*, 2006, acrylic on canvas, 170 × 350cm. PHOTO: MICHAEL DILLON

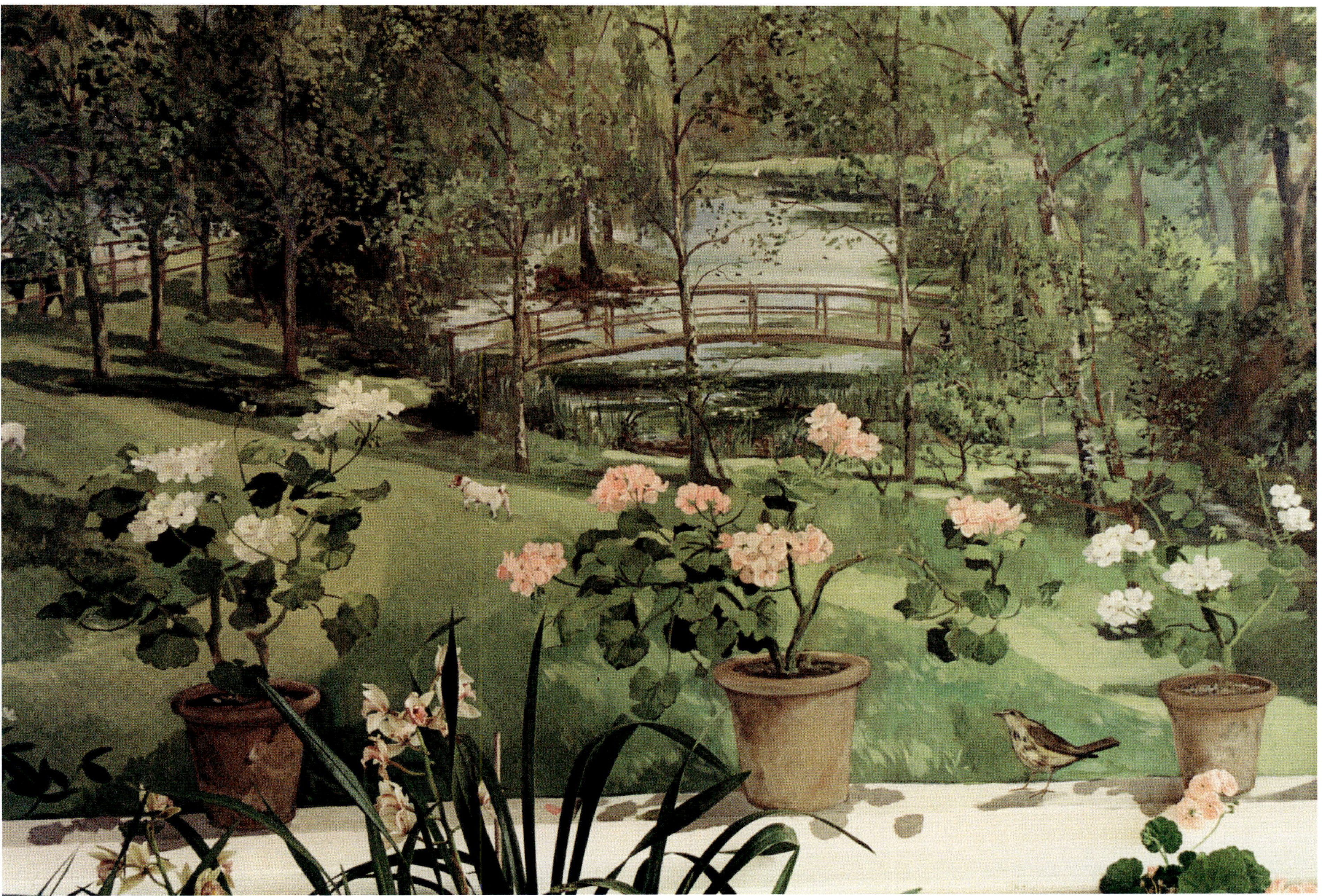

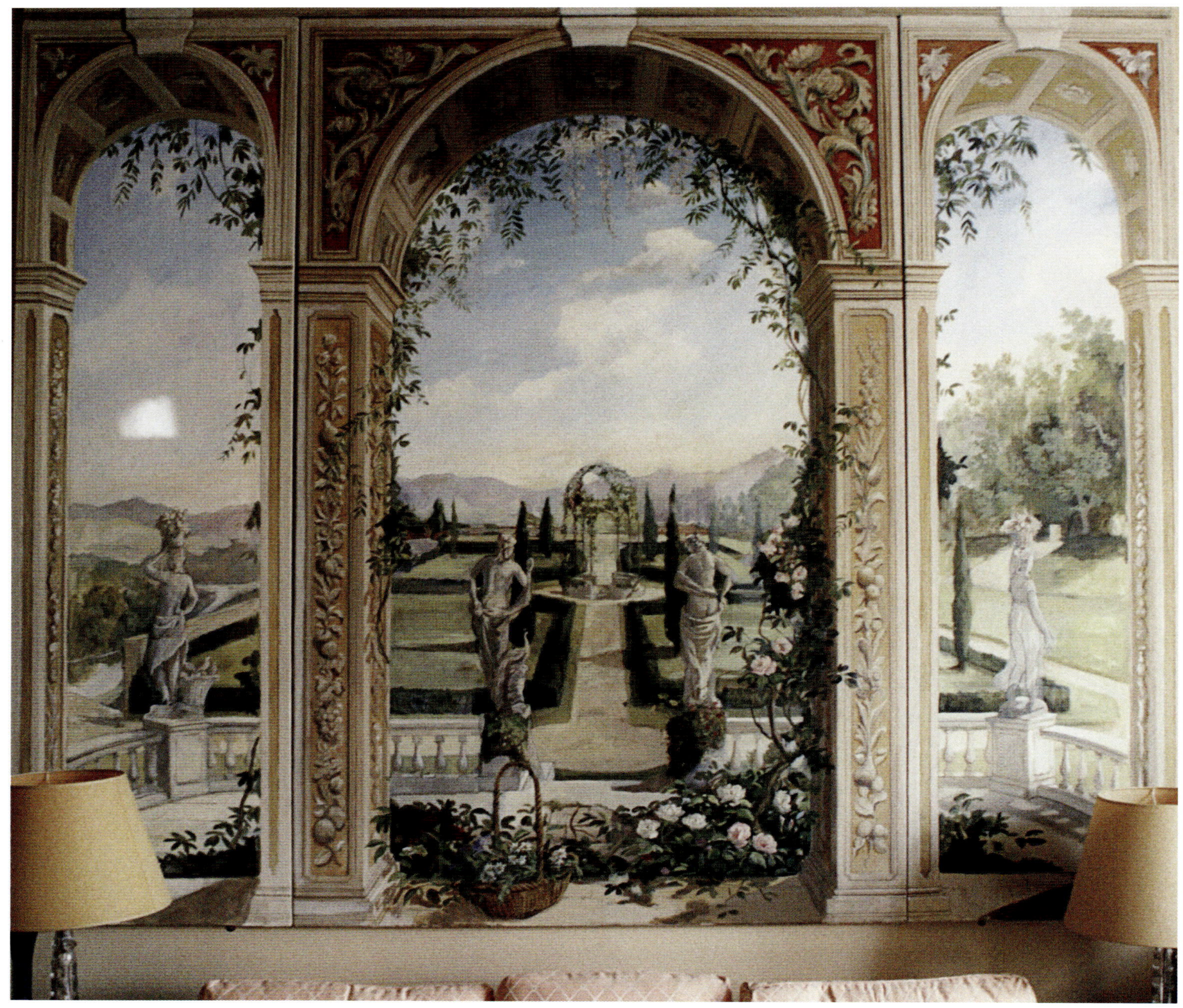

Michael Dillon, *Garden Fantasy*, triptych, 2002, oil on canvas, 230 x 370in.
PHOTO: MICHAEL DILLON

The flowing brush strokes and subtle variation of greens resulted in a piece of work that was probably looser and more painterly in style than the final mural.

The smaller murals are often painted on canvas. They can then be attached to the walls with batons and surrounded by a decorative moulding, or glued to the walls by a technique called *marouflage.* (In the Belle Époque period, murals of this kind, often produced in Paris, would almost always have been painted on canvas in a studio and then stuck onto walls in the same way as wallpaper.) The bigger murals are painted directly onto plastered walls. Some of these may take three weeks or more so Michael often employs assistants to do some of the more repetitive work. In a formal Pompeian scene they might draw out and paint the stone capitals. Assistants are occasionally 'borrowed' from friends working in the same field or sought locally in whichever part of the world he happens to be.

Michael has to be commercial in his approach to work and is encouraged by recent successful sales of his paintings at auction. 'I often suggest to my clients that I paint on canvas or panels rather than directly onto a wall, being aware that there may be a resale value. I strive to produce good and varied work – there is a lot more to learn.' An excellent critic for new designs is his wife who works part-time for the old master gallery Hazlitt, Goode & Fox.

Exhibiting hasn't been a necessity in the past as work is generally lined up for six months in advance, but Michael now plans to display in a forthcoming exhibition his collection of decorative tables and other furniture on which he has painted vignettes. These landscape and garden scenes are exquisitely painted with brushwork similar to that of English nineteenth-century artists and the foliage executed in the manner of Gainsborough.

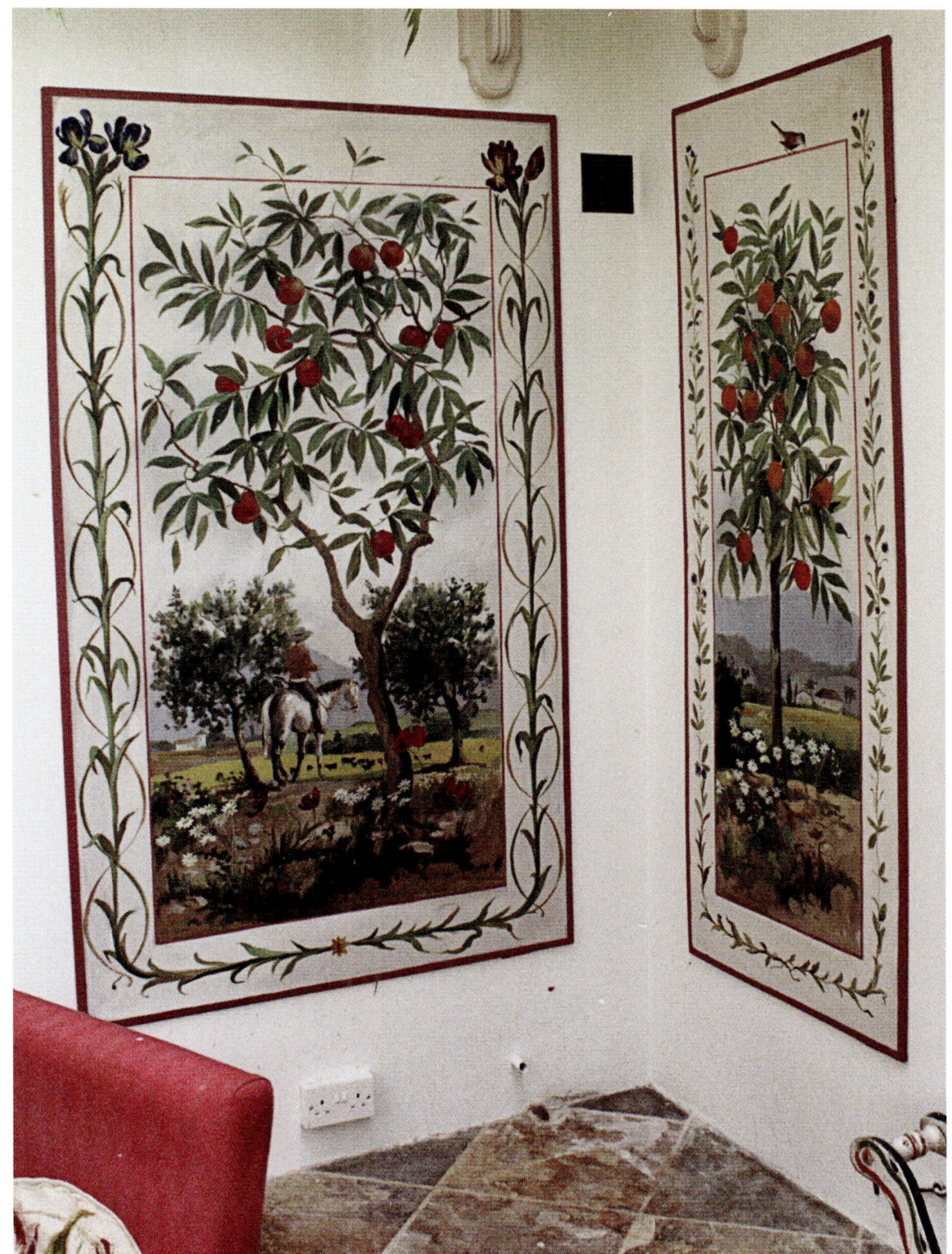

RIGHT Michael Dillon, Two sets of panels in a conservatory near Shaftesbury that illustrate fruit trees, with Spanish landscape in background, 2006, acrylic on canvas, each set 2 × 1m. PHOTO: MICHAEL DILLON

John Doyle

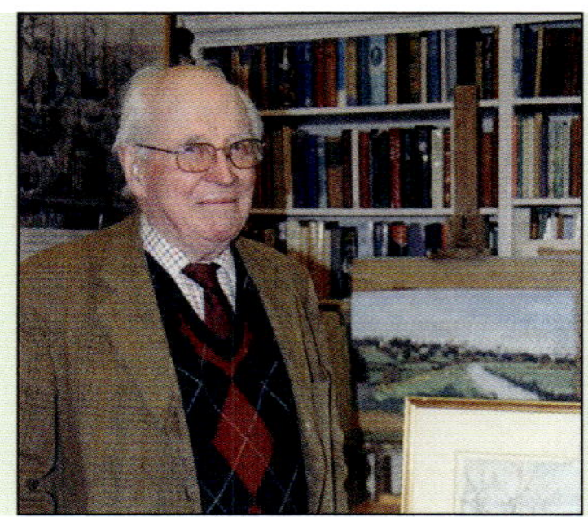

Artist in studio. PHOTO: ARIEL LUKE

In May 2006 there was an exhibition of contemporary work called *Artists' Kew* at Kew Gardens. It was here that I noticed two watercolours of *The Palm House* and *The Temperate House* by John Doyle. The intuitive drawing and instinctive painting combined to make these paintings particularly appealing.

When John Doyle was asked to paint for *Artists' Kew* he was returning to a familiar subject as he had painted there in the past. He chose to paint *The Palm House (1844–48)* and the *The Temperate House (1859–99)* essentially because of the architectural features which emphasised the effect of the light as it came through the glass and enhanced the contrast of the living leaves and the solid iron framework. He usually painted for two to three hours at a time which was when the light changed and then returned the next day, taking about three weeks in all.

John Doyle's studio is a converted barn in his garden, in the heart of the Kentish countryside, the Garden of England. It is a large room lined to the ceiling with books and with cabinets for his work. Despite this idyllic working area, John is an artist who consistently makes voyages and pilgrimages in search of his subject matter. 'I paint what I see and prefer painting outside with the wind on my face. If it's cold, I feel cold, if it's hot I feel that, too. I am committed to nature, I can never create from my imagination.'

John was conceived in Venice, 'a good start for an artist', a fact that even appears in his *Who's Who* entry. He was educated at Sherborne School in Somerset and because he was hopeless at sport was allowed off on his bicycle to venture forth into the very beautiful Dorset countryside to paint. These frequent expeditions nurtured his love of painting even though it was a while before he could devote his entire time to the subject.

After school he ran an iron foundry, only having time to study in the evenings, but when he discovered a manager to

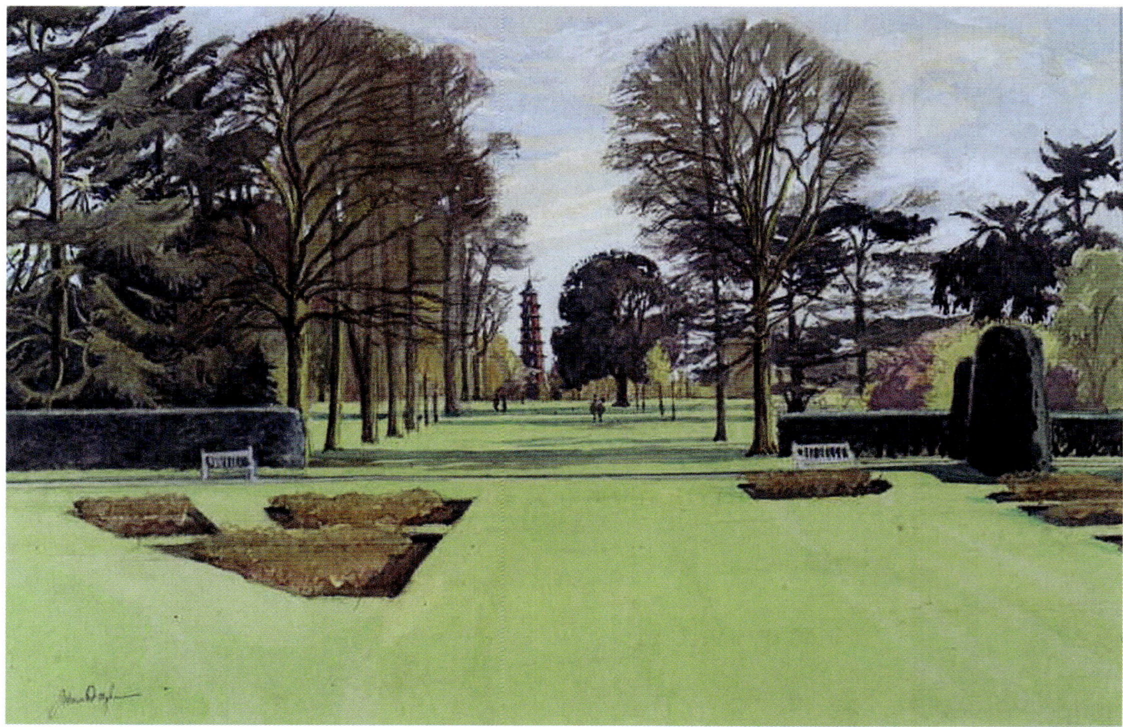

John Doyle, *The Pagoda from the Palm House, Kew*, 2006, watercolour on paper, 29 × 44cm. PHOTO: MICK DUFF

run his business he was freed from the rat race and able to paint full-time. This was followed by a fortuitous meeting on the steps of the Royal Academy with John Ward who had just become an associate member and who lived and painted nearby in Kent. Before long the two painters took off to Venice where they rigorously followed a strict routine: rising early, painting a picture before breakfast and then moving every two hours to follow the sun, generally working on five pictures at a time and returning at the same time each day until they were done. He was given little guidance except 'to start at the top and work downwards' and 'to buy some better pencils'. After two weeks there was quite a collection of work and it was suggested, much to his surprise, that he submit some work for the Royal Academy Summer Show. Two of the three paintings accepted were sold.

A solo expedition to Rome then followed and a small sell-out exhibition in Kent. From that time on, there grew a pattern of finding a 'theme' and going to live and work around the location. For three years he lived and worked in and around Oxford, and because the promised exhibitions didn't materialise on account of university politics, he secured a venue with Anthony Spink, London, in 1981. This was a happy association which continued until Spink's was taken over by Christie's.

The pilgrimages continued. As John once wrote, 'I find my compositions by exploring.' A journey of note resulted in the publication in 1996 of *An Artist's Journey down the Thames*, which took about a year. 'When looking for a suitable boat I was offered one for hire at £50 a day, with a small cabin, so I bought one for £750 with a pram dinghy towed behind. At the end of a year, I sold it for a profit.'

Living not far from Canterbury, John has had a long association with the Cathedral and has raised money for its various projects. There was an exhibition with John Ward and John Piper in 1973 and a solo exhibition in 1976, then came the altogether

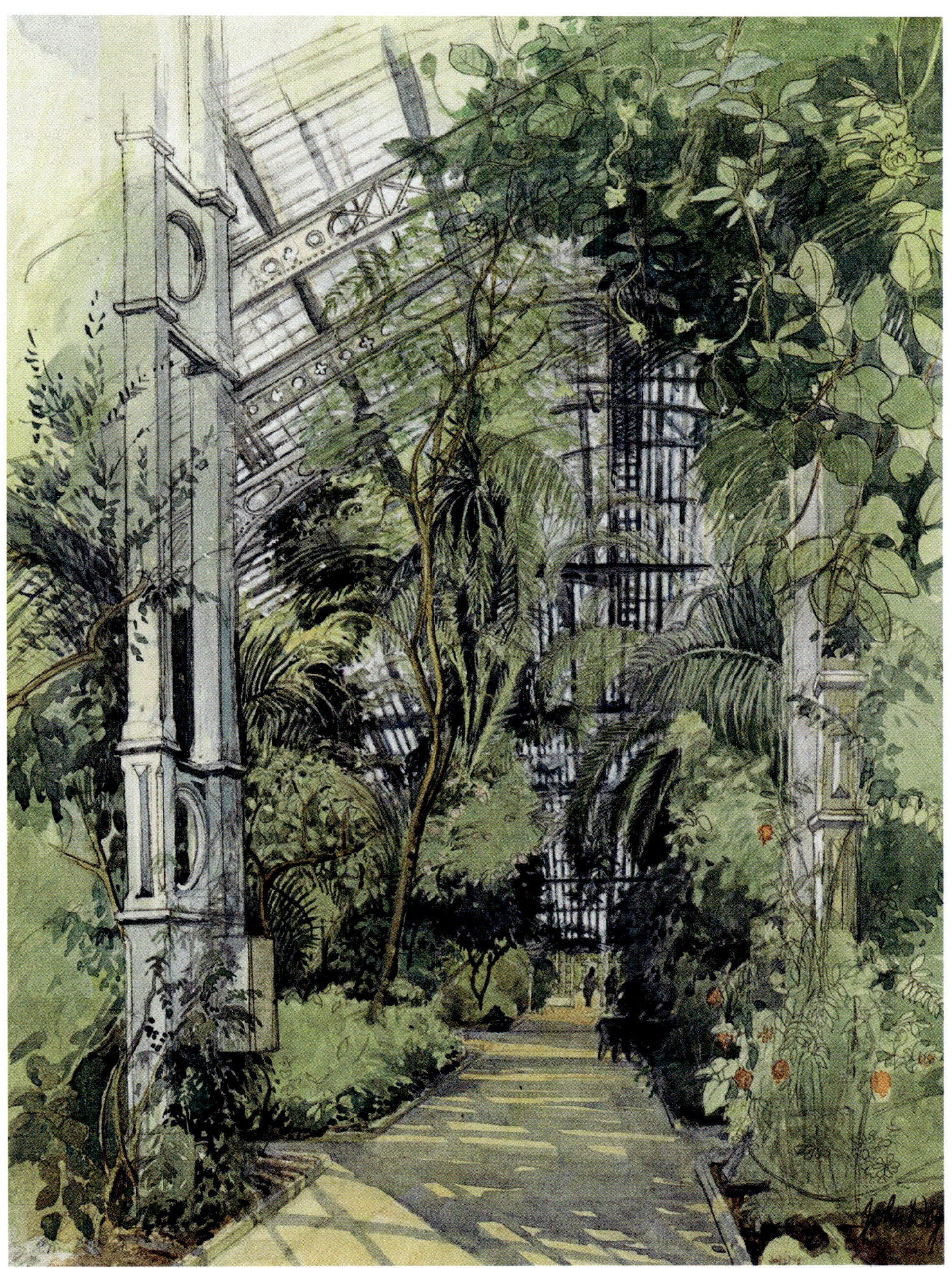

RIGHT John Doyle, *The Temperate House, Kew*, 2006, watercolour on paper, 44 × 29cm. PHOTO: MICK DUFF

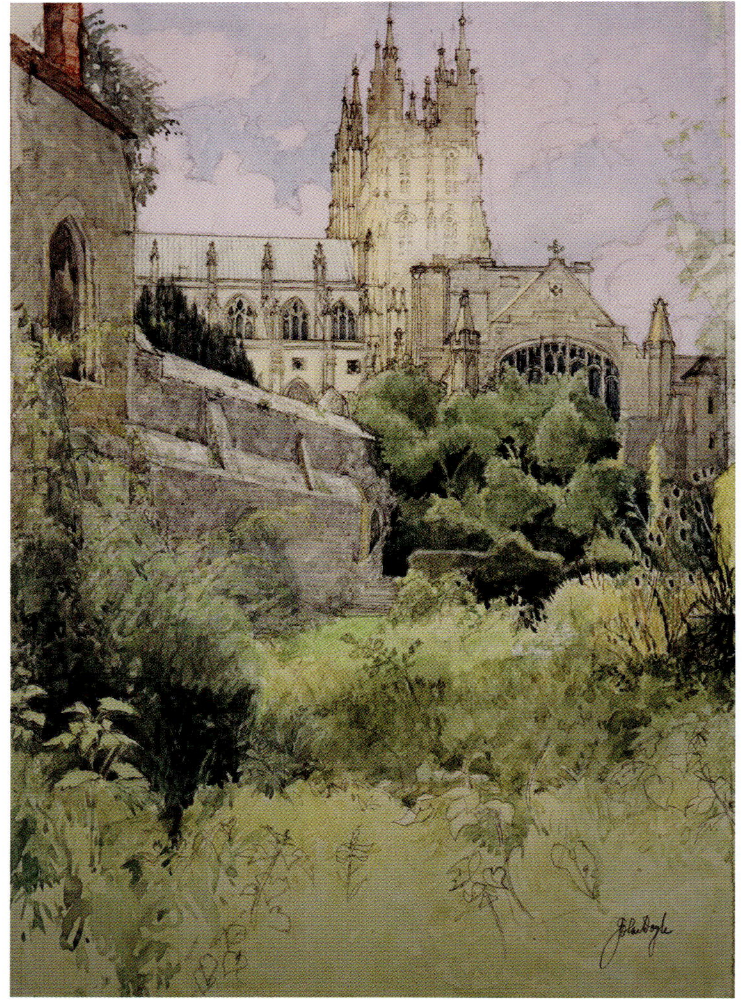

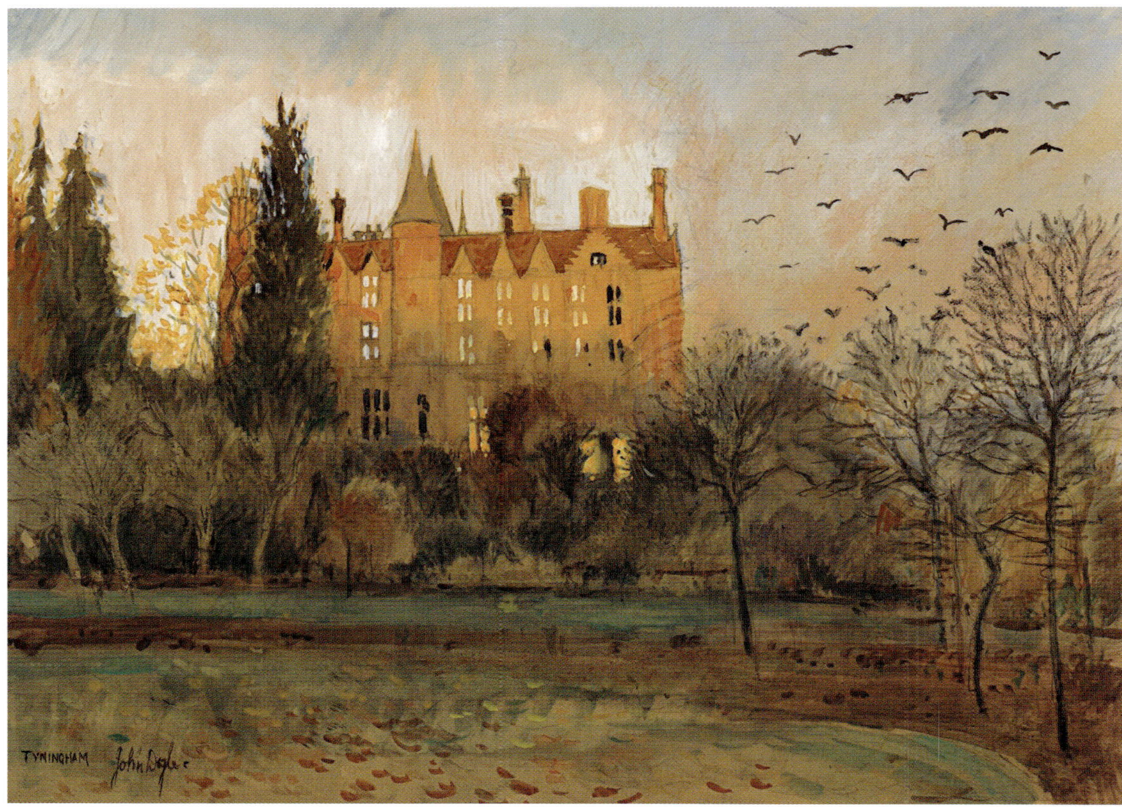

John Doyle, *Tyringham*, 2005, watercolour on paper, 43 × 58cm.
PHOTO: MICK DUFF

LEFT John Doyle, *The Archdeacon's Garden, Canterbury*, 2006,
watercolour on paper, 33.3 × 45.7cm. PHOTO: MICK DUFF

bigger task of celebrating the 1400th anniversary in 1997 with another exhibition. This resulted in the most extraordinary journey of all – walking from Canterbury to Rome (approximately 2000 miles) and painting on the way. Each day he would walk about ten miles in the morning, lunch and then walk a further ten miles in the afternoon (with stopovers for painting when a subject was particularly appealing), returning each evening by bus, train or taxi to collect his car which contained his materials. The journey was not done in consecutive order and John returned home at times. There were sections from Arles through Provence to Menton, Genoa, up the Arno to Florence, across Tuscany to Siena, and onto Rome, not forgetting the fun of walking across Paris. The walk ended in a meeting with the Pope who was presented with a painting of Canterbury Cathedral. 'When the Pope embraced, I really felt I was in the presence of a saint – his warmth and love absolutely engulfed me.' Nearly three hundred and fifty paintings resulted from this journey.

John locates his subjects by travelling about until he finds one that appeals to him. Inevitably the watercolour medium is very important to him. These paints 'can be slipped into a coat pocket and are not too bulky or messy with the added advantage that they dry quickly.'

John became a member of the Royal Watercolour Society in 1978 and its President in 1998. Still today he serves on the Committee.

John's approach is dictated by the subject he is painting: he uses body colour in a free style for atmospheric effects; he uses a tighter, more detailed method (based on careful drawing) for more clearcut forms such as trees and architecture. Sometimes the two styles are brought together – then the painting sings! Essentially John lets nature be his guide, 'If you look, the answer is nearly always in front of you but oh, how often we don't look.'

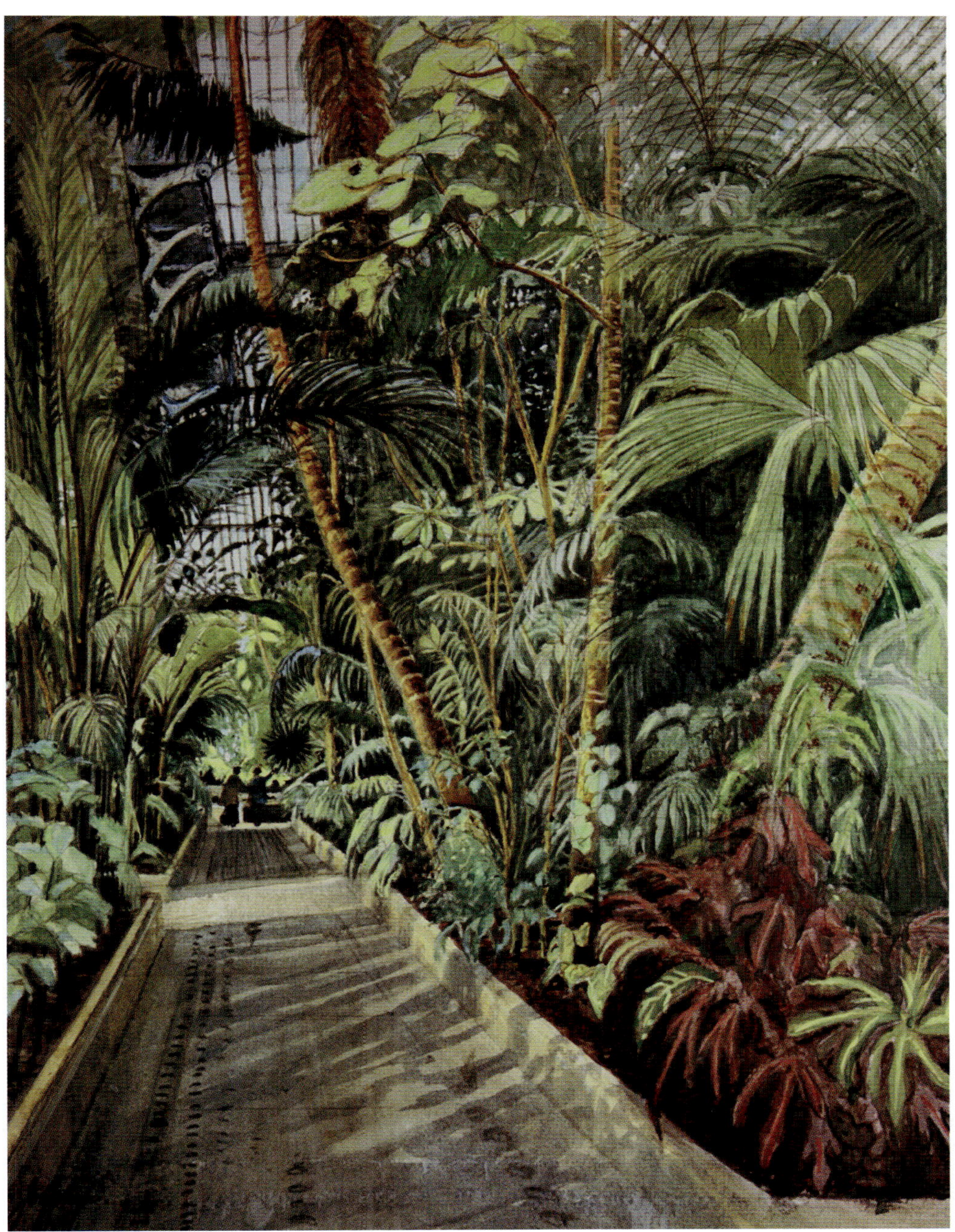

RIGHT John Doyle, *Palm House, Kew*, 2006, watercolour on paper, 56 × 45cm. PHOTO: MICK DUFF

Annabel Gault

A childhood friend, also a painter, showed me a catalogue of Annabel Gault's exhibition at the Redfern Gallery entitled *Recent Paintings*, November 2006. One look at the work and I was convinced. Most of the exhibition centred on work done in her own garden.

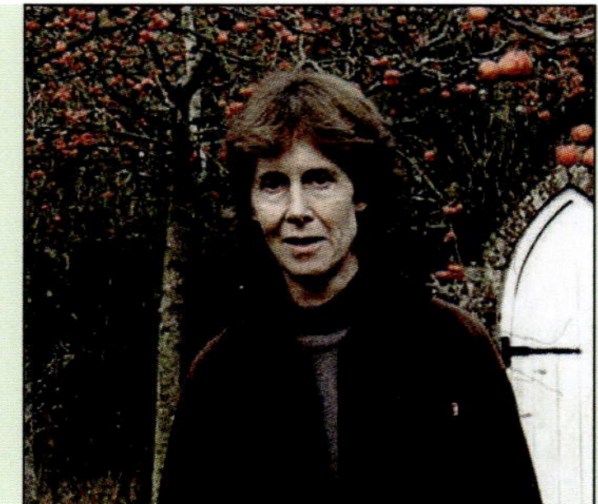

The Artist. PHOTO: KARIN SZEKESSY

As Annabel says, 'It is the familiar subjects you come back to, even though you try to go beyond.' It is her own garden in Suffolk, where she has been for twenty-five years, which very much dominates and has its own language. 'It doesn't really look as if it is planned, it has a wildness, but underneath there is a real structure.' Her paintings reflect all this.

Annabel comes from a family that is connected with the art world. Her father was at Camberwell School of Art for a year, her sister is a painter, her brother runs a gallery, and her own daughter has just finished at Goldsmiths. She herself studied at West Surrey College of Art for four years before doing a post-graduate course at the Royal Academy Schools.

At the West Surrey College of Art, the dominant ideology of the teaching was Abstraction as a result of Pollock, Abstract Impressionism, Pop Art and the rest of American painting at the time (1973–77). There was always the idea of going beyond what you can see and finding something deeper and more significant. Annabel's particular form of Abstraction was as simple as overlapping horizontal lines in gradating tones from black to white, although drawing continued as an essential background to her work.

The Royal Academy Schools were equally exciting. The obligatory first term in the Life Rooms was an interesting discipline. Students were left mostly on their own to enable them totally to immerse themselves in their work. Annabel pushed the theme of Abstraction further, the horizontal lines became fragmented and sometimes almost erased. She started working on watercolour paper with inks. Some of the pieces resemble old maps or land seen from a great height. She still enjoys this work but says, 'The trouble with art school is that you build up so many rules and inhibitions for yourself, you have to relearn that you can do anything, that there are no rules.' She feels that it can take at least ten years after leaving art school to find your own identity as an artist, and maybe a lot longer.

FACING PAGE Annabel Gault, *Garden in Early Summer*, 2006, oil on paper, 30 × 40in.
COURTESY: REDFERN GALLERY

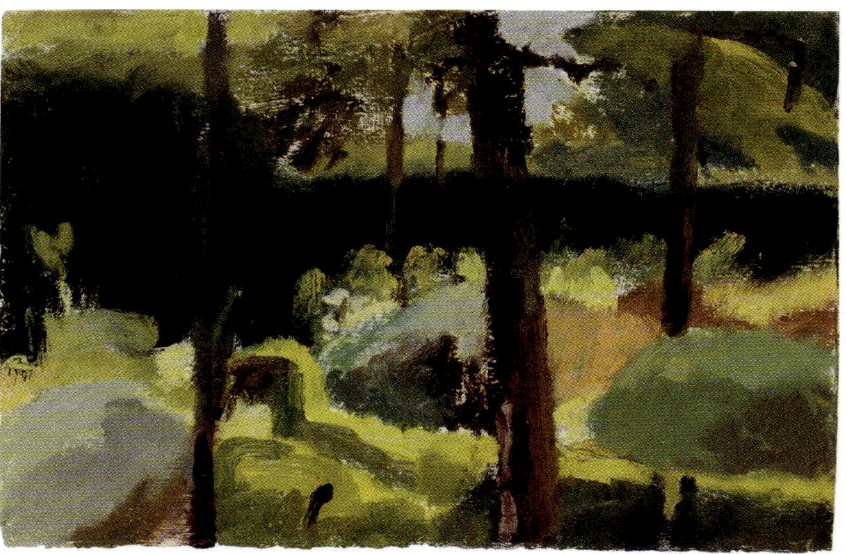

Annabel Gault, *Dark Hedge*, 2006, oil on paper 13 × 21in.
COURTESY: REDFERN GALLERY

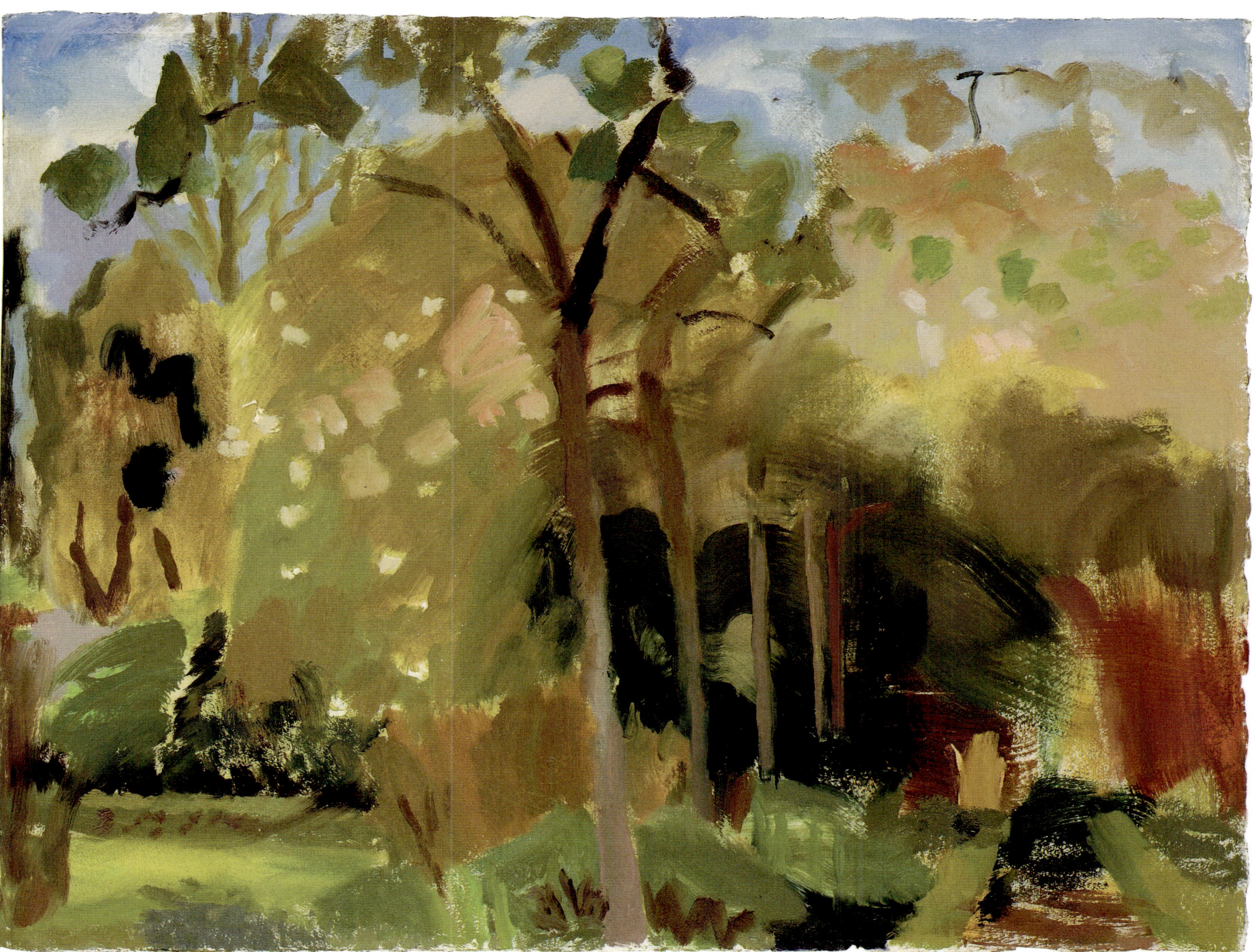

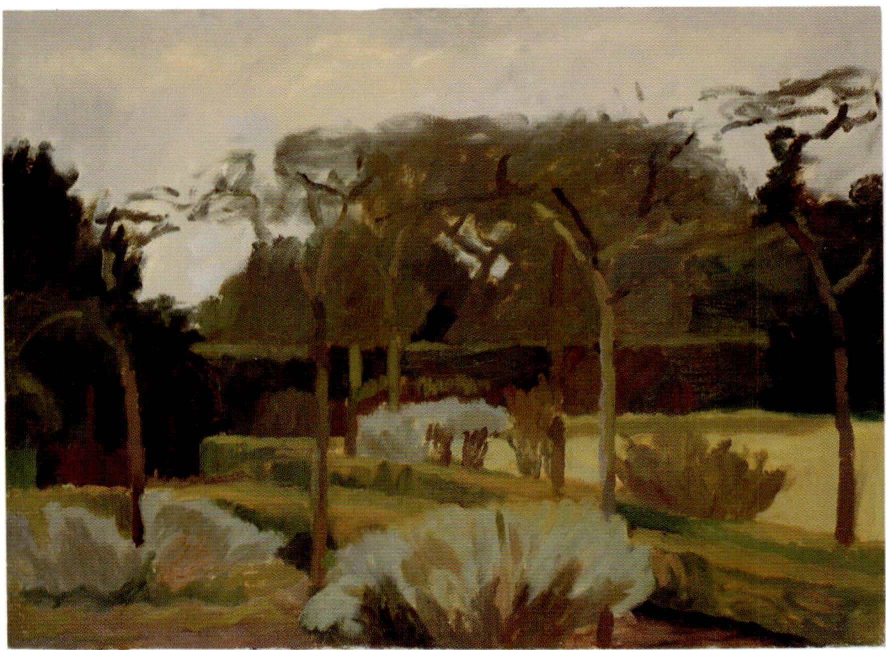

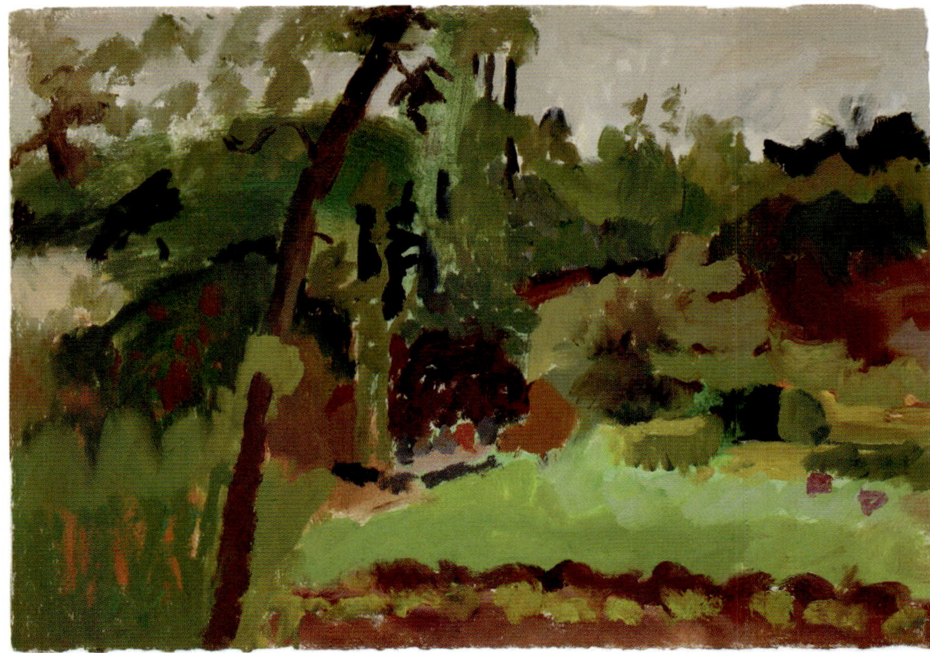

Annabel Gault, *Garden in February*, 2006, oil on paper, 35 × 48in.
COURTESY: REDFERN GALLERY

Annabel Gault, *Garden in May*, 2006, oil on paper,
21 × 30in. COURTESY: REDFERN GALLERY

She fought with Ruskin Spear but found Roderick Barratt helpful with his rare gift for teaching and encouraging students to develop their own ideas. Fellow students were also an important source of inspiration and understanding. The old building held great mystery with its dimly lit Life Room and long dark corridors.

She learnt from the Royal Academy Schools the everyday discipline and practice of painting. Annabel generally works from around 8.30 – 2.00 and then returns later for more work, but, 'I have to get that initial five to six hours' work in.' She generally works on heavy watercolour paper primed with three or four coats of Lascaux gesso (suppliers: A. P. Fitzpatrick) and primed cotton canvas. She consistently works outside, relishing the challenges of midges, rain and wind. 'It can be helpful to fight against something. The energy then feeds into the work.'

She continues to draw and will sometimes have long periods of only drawing. She uses charcoal and the drawings are as gutsy, as vigorous and as interesting as her paintings. She works on a large scale and will use drawing as an exploration of an object or idea, often working in multiple images.

Working outside is tough. Annabel takes all her oil paints and brushes in a heavy rucksack, boards with the paper fastened to them and a palette. The boards are propped on anything to hand and she lays the paints out on the earth and sits on the empty rucksack. She makes the chalky surface of the paper more fluent by wiping a turpentine-and-oil mixture over it. She works fast, 'fusing into a coherent whole the conventions of the sketch and the finished oil painting'. She conveys the impact of a place through a series of images. She goes back and back to a chosen place. These sketches are then displayed in the studio. She does

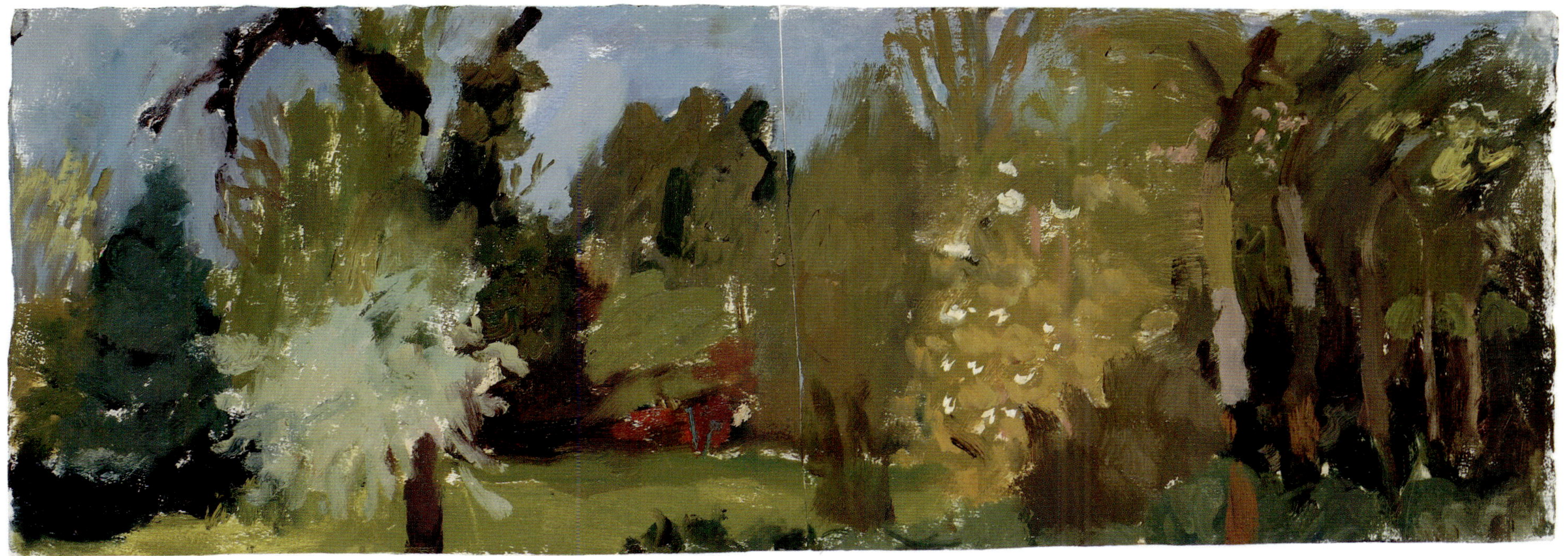

Annabel Gault, *Spring Garden*,
2006, oil on paper, 11.5 × 32in.
COURTESY: REDFERN GALLERY

not just convert the images but uses them as inspiration for much bigger canvases.

Annabel describes painting in America in May when it snowed so that she had to kit herself out as for skiing. On another occasion, she related working in her own garden on a February day (the coldest of the year) 'when the colours were purply grey, muddy and dark dark'. She spent so long outside that her bones hurt and she understood the meaning of 'chilled to the marrow'. On one trip in the Australian desert with seven other painters, she recalls someone crying out, 'All I want is my studio and Radio Four!'

Some of her influences have been the wise practical advice of the printmaker Valerie Thornton, the work of Howard Hodgkin and the sketches of John Constable. Her work bounces back and forth between the more figurative and the abstract and looser work. She tries to break new boundaries, to go somewhere else and to keep an open mind.

Annabel feels that for her a combination of studio work and the challenges of working outside keep her work fresh. She has now had fifteen solo exhibitions, taken part in twenty-seven group exhibitions and has work in various well-known collections. She is an artist who is continually questioning her ability to convey the relationship between the painting and the experience. Perhaps that is why she often returns to the familiar, her garden, which she loves. The Suffolk landscape may not be in conventional terms as beautiful as the Sussex countryside, where she grew up, but it has an informality and lack of pretension which complement her work. To quote one of her heroes, 'I paint life as I see it, feel it, smell it and think it, but above all see it.'

Angela Gladwell

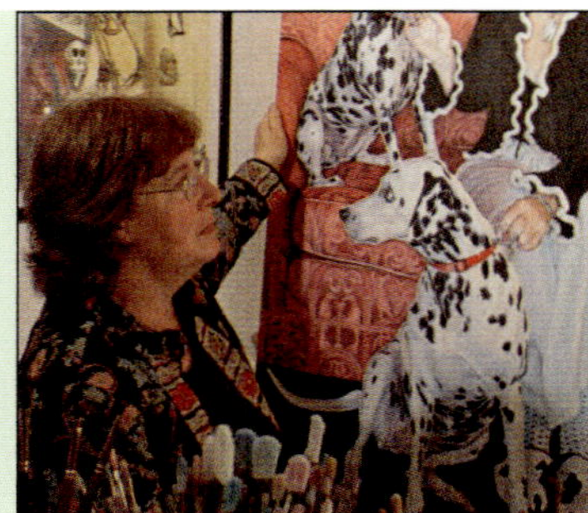

The Artist. PHOTO: MAX A. RUSH

The stained glass artist Kate Baden Fuller studied at the Royal College of Art at the same time as Angela and her husband, and she was responsible for introducing me to this accomplished painter.

Angela is a very skilled painter in both oil and watercolour and her work is constantly evolving. When the curator, Ronny van Dedem, organised the 2006 exhibition *Artists' Kew*, she must have been aware that Angela's paintings would be amongst the most interesting. Not surprisingly, she offered them one of the prime positions.

To have the technical ability to be such an adaptable painter Angela started young. It was at the age of seven that she was aware of Dürer's praying hands that hung outside her headmaster's office at primary school and she wonders if everything can be traced back to their effect. At sixteen, she started a four-year course at Walthamstow where she was too young to qualify for the NDD. Fortunately she was accepted by the Royal College of Art where she gained the master's degree.

This was when the Royal College was directly connected to the Victoria & Albert Museum, which enabled the students to have direct access to the artefacts in the museum. All the students had to do was to go through an archway in one of the college corridors – and they were in the museum. Angela liked that, and used the V&A most days. This period also included a three-month stay in Paris as the Royal College owned a studio there. Her particular interest during her time in Paris was painting water and its reflections, principally those of the Seine. Water and its reflections have been a recurring theme ever since.

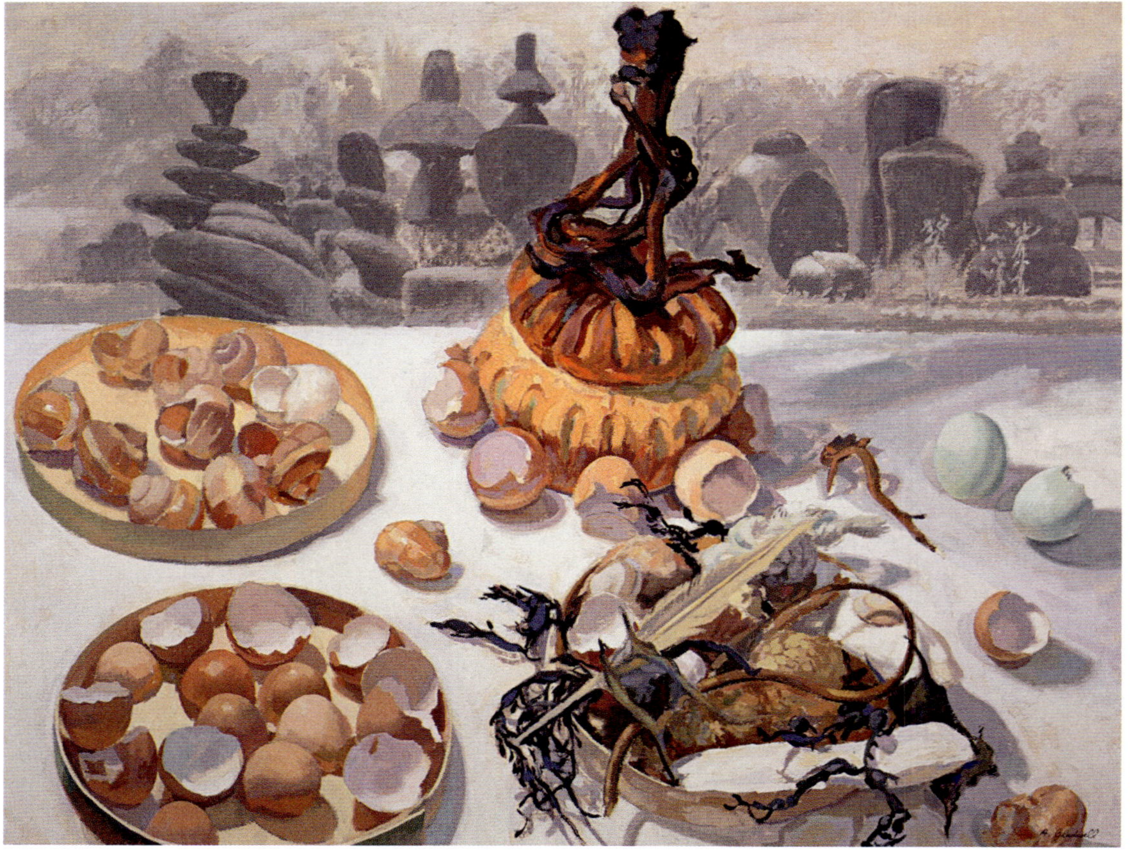

Angela Gladwell, *Egg Shells and Topiary*, 1988–2000, gouache on paper, 23 × 30in. PHOTO: MAX A. RUSH

At the time of her training the emphasis was on drawing and oil painting which 'is a wonderful medium for finding out what paint will do, so that when it comes to watercolour you find you understand so much more about paint.'

Having studied for seven years Angela felt it was time she earned her living in order to pay the rent and almost inevitably spent years teaching. It was 'initiation by fire', but she quickly rose up the ladder to run a department in Hackney for eighteen years and another department in Hastings for five years. With her extraordinary energy and dedication to painting, she continued to paint and show in a wide range of exhibitions (becoming a prizewinner in the Leeds Castle Open Landscape show). She has also had several solo exhibitions and her work has been included in many public and private collections including the Natural History Museum collection.

Angela gave up full-time teaching some years ago and now occasionally teaches on a part-time basis, allowing her enormous enthusiasm to be focused on her work.

She has several themes all working together. She doesn't make boundaries between them, believing that, 'It is all work, which is more important than categories or genres.' Her influences are equally diverse. 'I've got lots of art books, I wish I had more. I'm always finding inspiration in new directions.'

It is hardly surprising that she called one of her exhibitions 'a group exhibition by one person'. She says she 'goes back and forth through themes over the years ... and that work done a while ago is just as relevant now – ideas creep in from the past even when I think I'm doing something new.' Even so, eyesight changes as the years go by and in order to have access to the light for as long as possible she has her easels, chair and paint trolley on wheels, so that she can move from window to window or indeed into some other illuminated area. 'After all, the light is past its best after 2 o'clock in the afternoon in winter.'

For the *Artists' Kew* exhibition in 2006, she was initially chosen because of a recommendation from the Natural History Museum and it was suggested that she paint some of the wild life at Kew Gardens. However, when Angela set off for Kew six

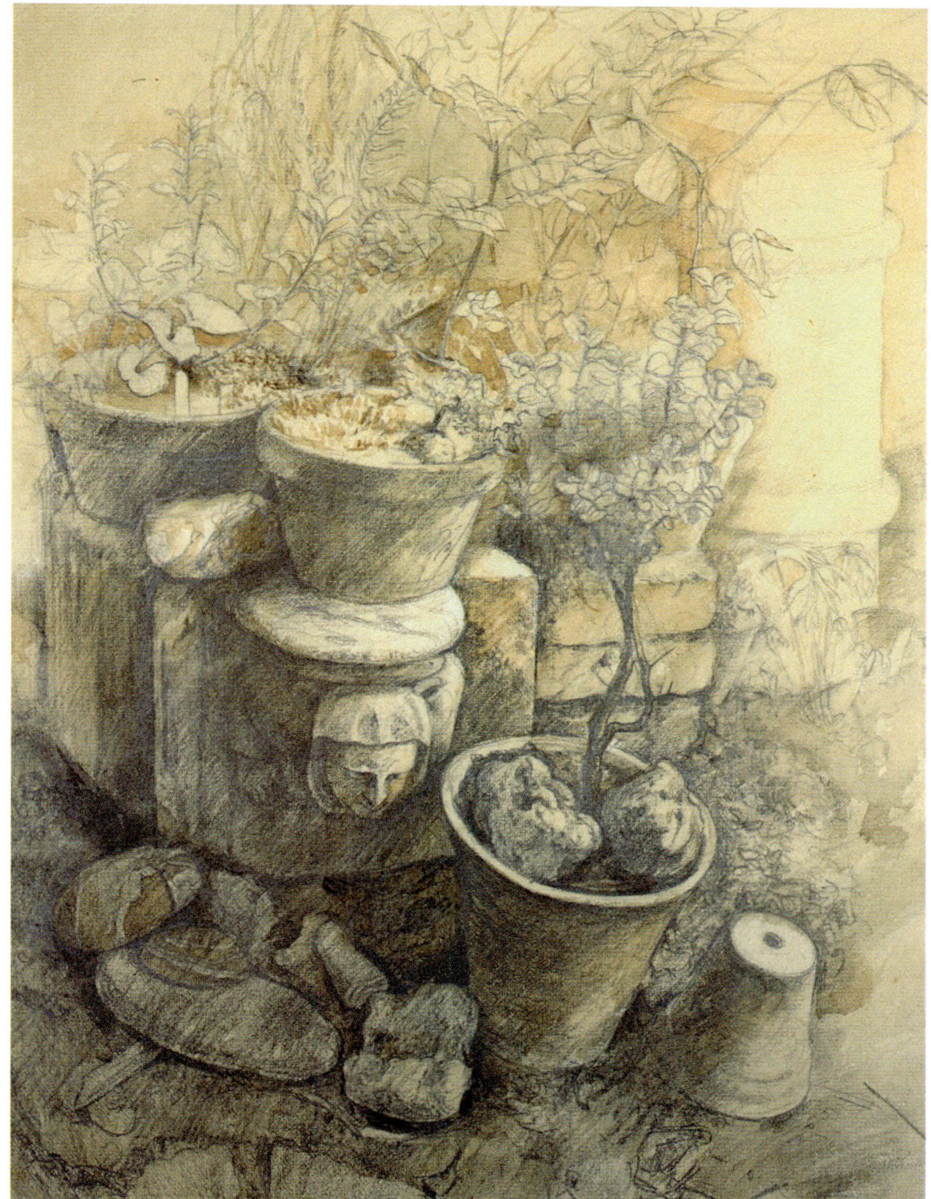

Angela Gladwell, *Garden Still Life*, 1980–88, pencil & watercolour on paper, 26 × 20in.
PHOTO: MAX A. RUSH

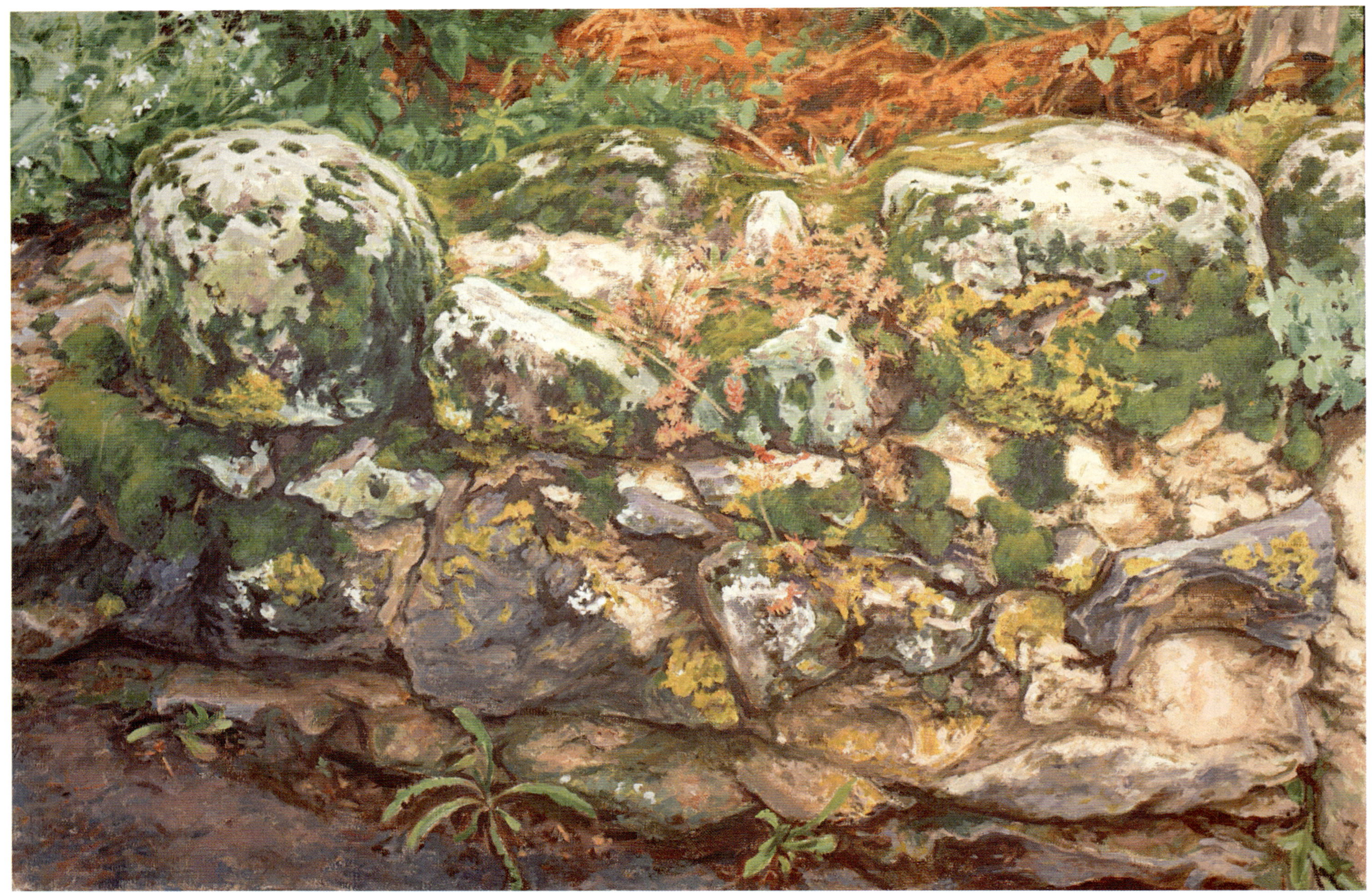

Angela Gladwell, *Big Moss Rockery, Massif Central*, 1988–2000, oil on very coarse canvas, 26 × 40in. PHOTO: MAX A. RUSH

months in advance of the show, it was winter and very cold indeed, and there was no wildlife in sight. While sitting in the café, she composed the idea for *Promenade*. 'I looked at these beautiful statues in the Orangery and thought that is what I'd like to do. Then when I saw the ruined arch I thought I'd put the two together as I've always liked stones and ruins. It would have been better if the arch had had more vegetation growing out of it, as in the past. I wanted to make the statues look as if they were taking a walk along the path that goes under the arch.' This picture turned out to be the one that Professor Sir Peter Crane, Director of Kew, bought for himself.

Another Kew painting was of Marianne North which seemed a suitable subject as Marianne had helped design, pay for and even conceive the idea of the Marianne North Gallery in the nineteenth century and was herself a most adventurous painter, as well as a great plant collector. So Angela took a friend down to pose as Marianne in the Cactus House. She also went to the costume museum in Bath to research authentic clothing for her model. The picture was painted in monochrome to emulate the sepia photographs of the period. The paintings were made with the help of photographs as, living so far from London, Angela could not work for any length of time from observation.

This is one of many theme shows that Angela has taken part in. As she says, 'In the past I have been labelled a surrealist, a landscape painter, a wild life painter, a natural history artist and, of course, a garden painter. People are very keen to have you categorised.' Angela has clearly been a most prolific worker talking of 'the mountains and mountains of stuff' she has had to do to get where she is today.

Angela talks of visiting the Royal Academy shows and being able to pick out from twenty yards away in a gallery the work of past tutors because it has changed so little. Her work is often diverse: the Levens Hall Topiary has an altogether different

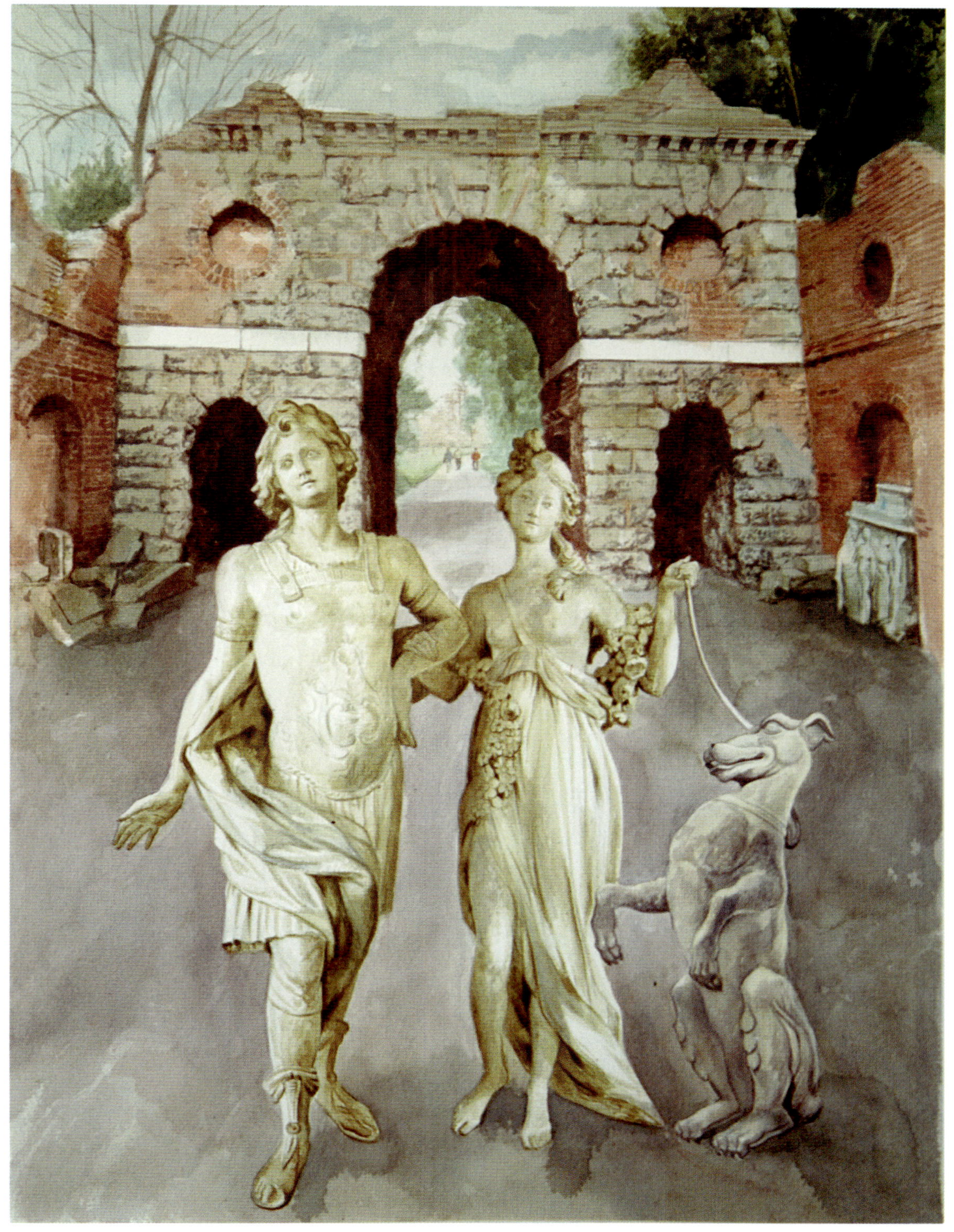

Angela Gladwell, *Promenade – Kew Gardens Statues*, 2005, watercolour on paper, 31 × 26in. PHOTO: MAX A. RUSH

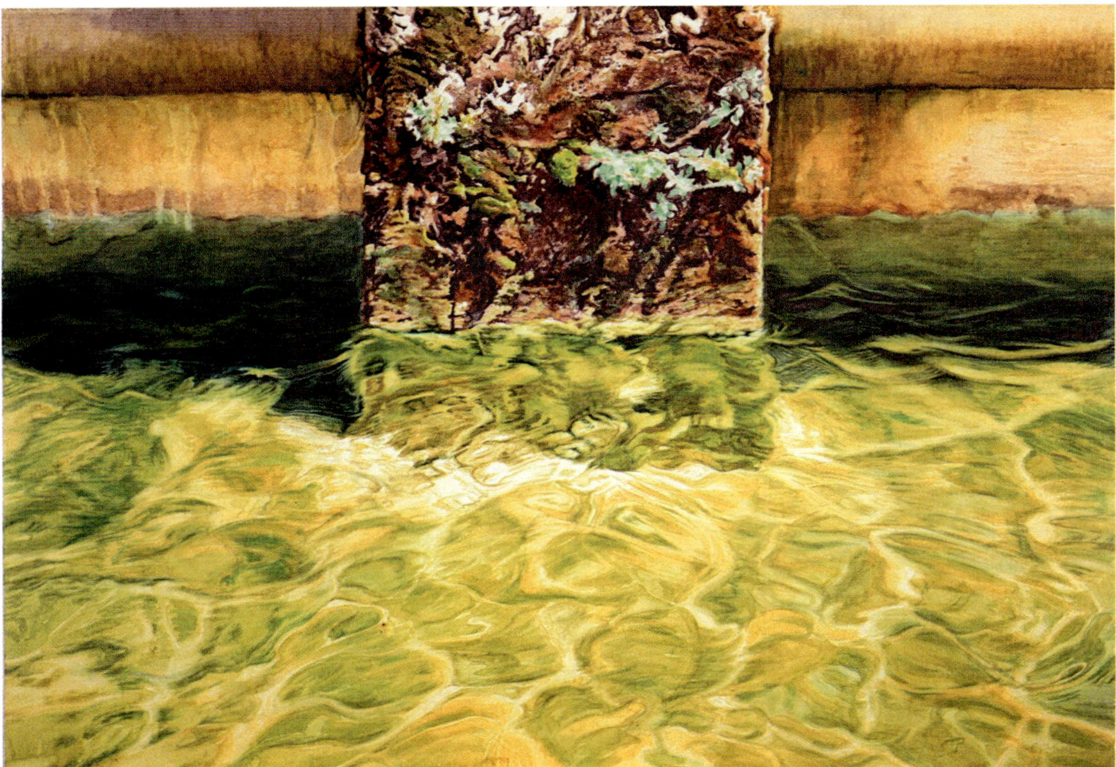

Angela Gladwell, *Green Water Fountain*, 1988–2000, watercolour on paper, 27 × 38in. PHOTO: MAX A. RUSH

quality from that of the statues from the Orangery at Kew. Her water scenes are full of pattern – there are suggestions of lichens and mosses, of surfaces etched, encrusted and bestrewn with natural history. Her work can be very tactile. Her French fountain picture is almost abstract in conception, without the intense detail of her other work. Here is an artist always able to surprise and delight with her exuberant and unusual work aided and abetted by vast experience

Jeffrey Hessing

A year ago I went to have dinner with Clive and Teresa Oakes in Tourrette-sur-Loup, France, not far from Nice, and there on the wall was a picture *Garden In Vence* by Jeffrey Hessing. The sweeping, swirling brush strokes and the delirious explosion of colour were most effective.

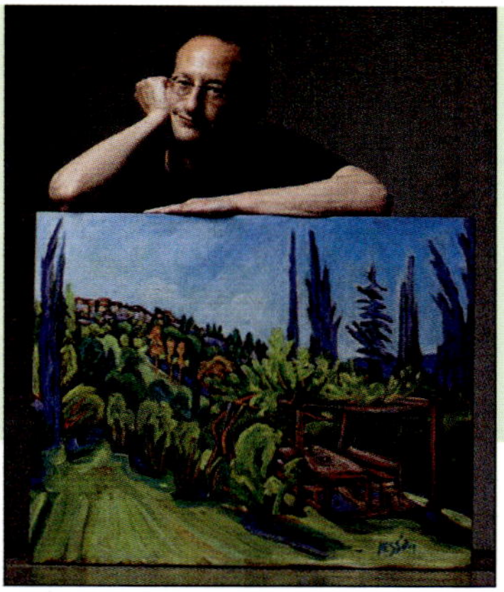

Artist in studio, Shanghai, China.

Jeffrey was brought up in Brooklyn, New York, as part of a middle-class family and says that 'from his earliest memory he knew that he wasn't going to be a normal person'. Originally he wanted to be a musician and singer but at the age of fifteen he 'basically shifted medium' and because he had always done a bit of drawing he began to develop the skills of an artist. It was one of his tutors at university, where he studied drawing and printmaking, who encouraged him to find an established artist for private teaching. 'I badgered the sculptor Leonard Baskin to take me on as a student outside the curriculum of the university.'

It was when Leonard Baskin went to Europe for six months and Jeffrey went to stay in his house that his ideas began to crystallise and he saw something of the direction in which his work could develop. This was partly because of his exposure to the collection of work in Leonard Baskin's house. There were drawings, paintings, sculptures, porcelain and glass as well as a private library of rare books, maybe in the region of 8000. 'It was amazing to wake up every day and to be surrounded by so many beautiful objects, from Tiepolo drawings to the works of the American Barbizon school, and it was this experience that made me sensitive to new directions.'

Leonard Baskin himself belonged to the post World War II tormented, introspective past and Jeffrey initially worked along in this popular direction, but then gradually decided he'd like to affect people by expressing a vision of a more positive world – the beauty of nature, the miracle of light – and this became his ambition. As he said, 'I gambled my whole life on being a

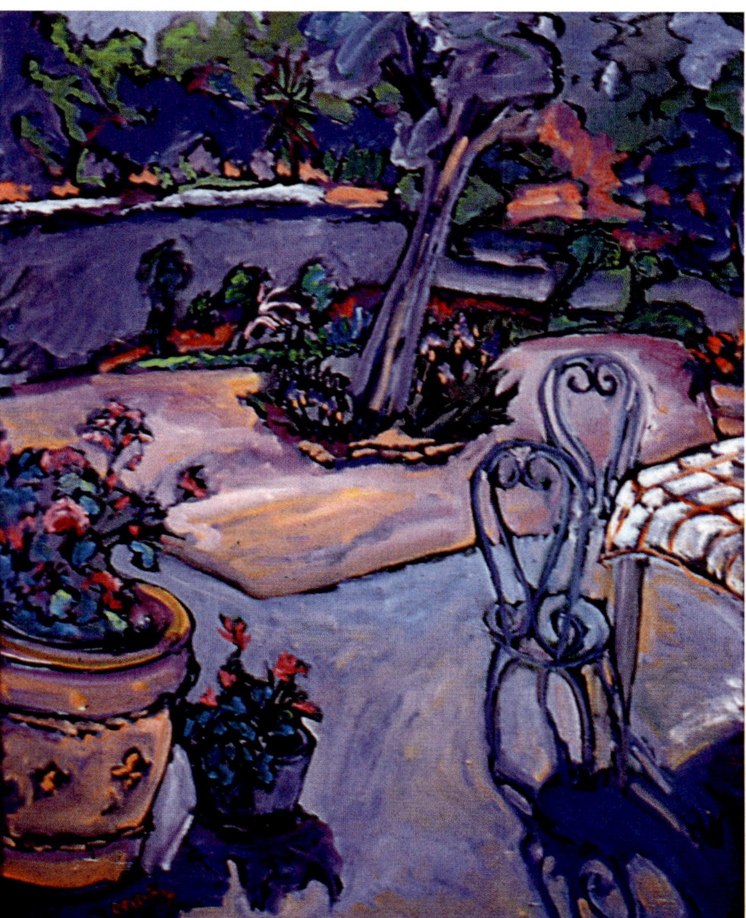

Jeffrey Hessing, *Artist's Garden, Vence*, 1999, oil on canvas, 100 × 81cm. PHOTO: JEFFREY HESSING

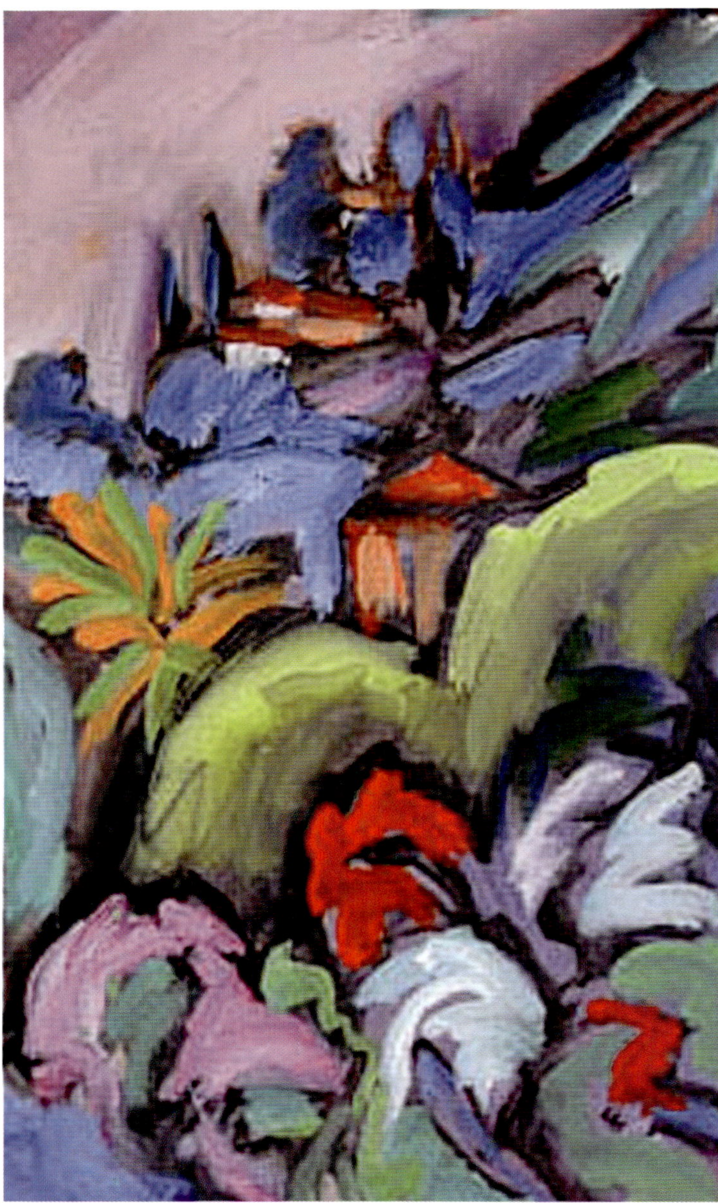

Jeffrey Hessing, detail from *Nature's Riot*, 2005, oil on canvas, 61 × 50cm. PHOTO: JEFFREY HESSING

figurative [representational] painter and assuming it would come back into fashion as, of course, it has.'

Once Leonard Baskin returned from Europe he helped Jeffrey plan his first trip to Europe, where he intended to travel and study. Initially he settled for three months in Florence and acquired a pass to the Uffizi Gallery where he spent two to three days a week studying and copying drawings and prints of the various Italian schools. For the rest of the week he visited other museums and galleries. This period was followed by a tour round other parts of Europe visiting cathedrals and museums, which included seeing for the first time a facsimile of a Constable sketchbook. 'I didn't have a formal training, I was basically self taught.'

After his tour of Europe, Jeffrey returned to live near Boston and, curiously, worked in only black and white for five years (using brush and ink). This was partly because of the Asian influence of the 'perfect line and perfect brush stroke – drawing is the basis of good painting'. The drawing period was followed by experimenting with watercolour and finally moving on to oils, which was when he began selling in New York. In some ways he feels his work has gone full circle as, after thirty years, parts of his oil paintings have a distinctly watercolour appearance where he has applied white spirit to the surface.

Jeffrey paints outdoors in front of his subject, and he found the weather in Boston 'disabled him in a sense' so he looked for a situation with a good climate and good culture – he was twenty-six years old with no money – 'creating a life that permits you to create can be the hardest part of being an artist.' Fortunately he acquired a residential fellowship at the Karolyi Foundation in Vence, near Nice, where 'even in winter it generally warms up by 11 o'clock and you can always wear enough clothes to keep warm, your fingers don't freeze, and with the help of umbrellas you can work in the rain.' It is in this area that he has based himself ever since, living in Vence for twenty-two years and in the port of Nice for about five years. Here he has a massive studio, where he sleeps and eats. He had to make two hundred telephone calls to find such an ideal space for the mass

FACING PAGE Jeffrey Hessing, *Cactus by the Sea*, 2004, oil on canvas, 89 × 116cm. PHOTO: JEFFREY HESSING

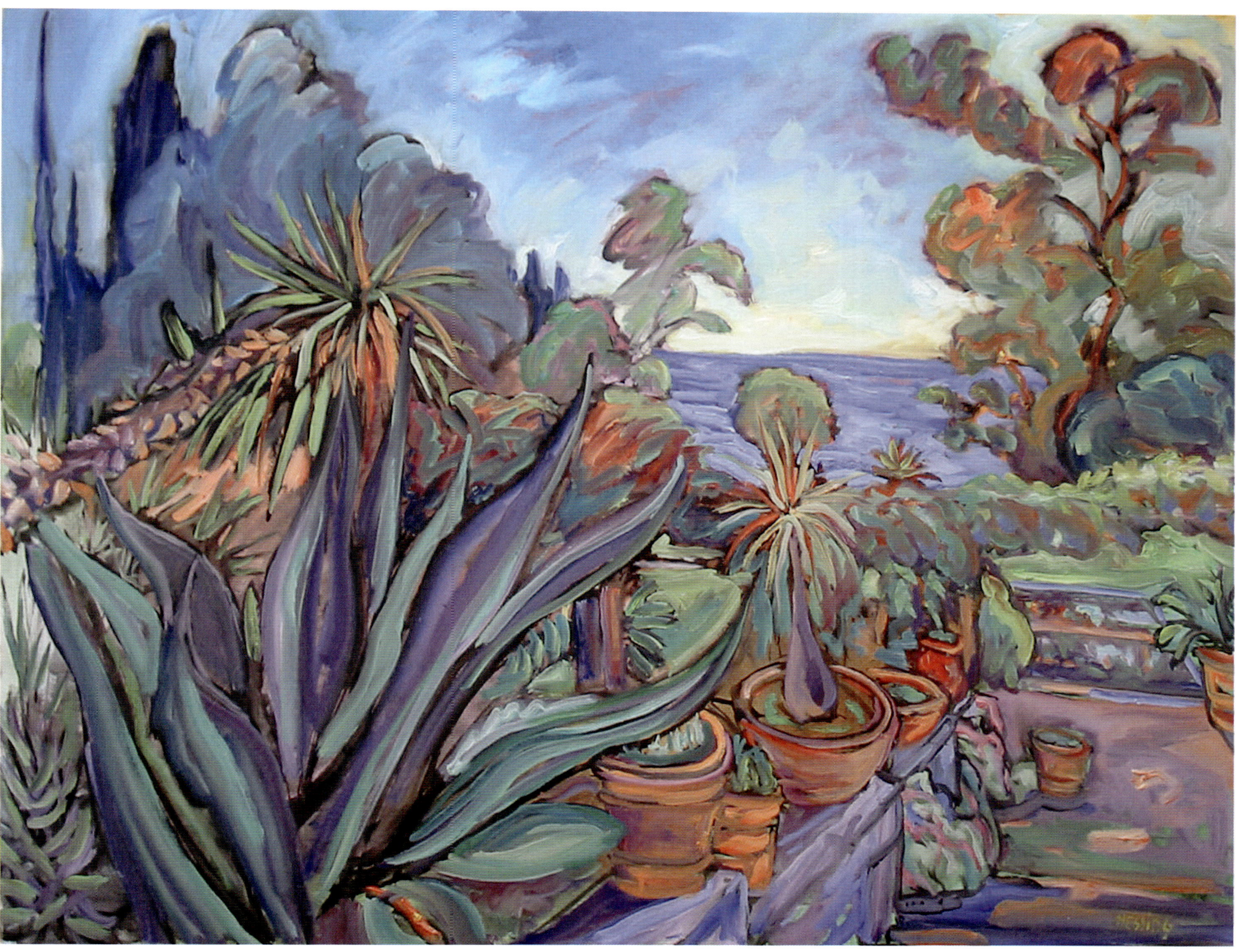

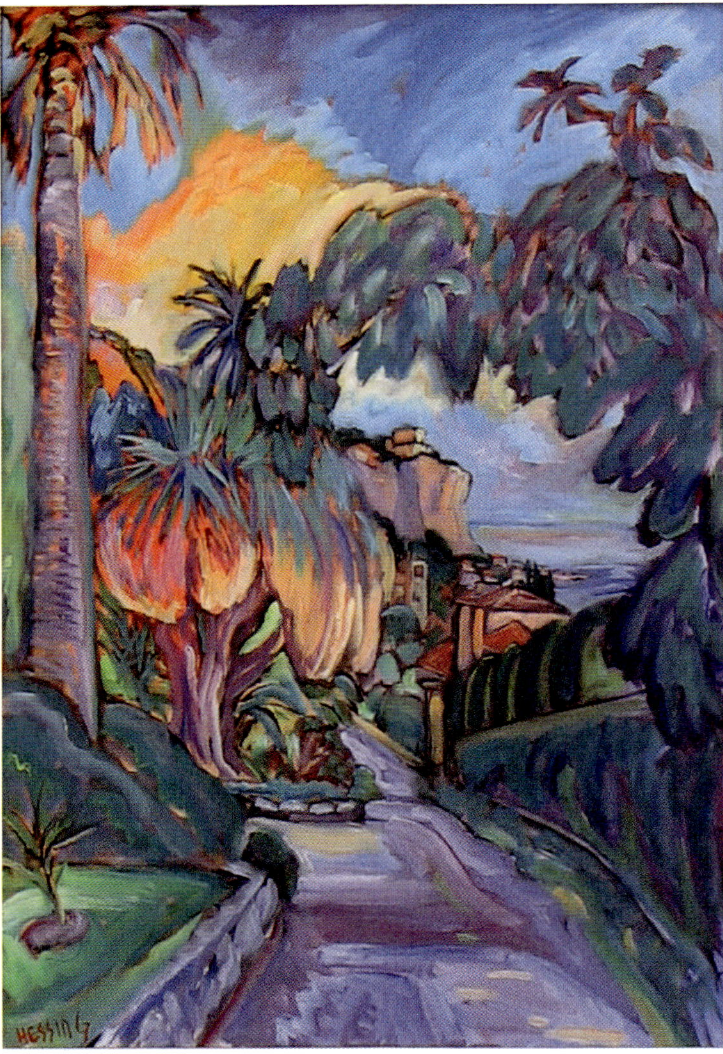

Jeffrey Hessing, *Road to the Sea*, 2004, oil on canvas, 116 × 89cm.
PHOTO: JEFFREY HESSING

of canvases and as a base for the places up and down the coast where he likes to paint. When at Vence, he had his own garden and access to about five other gardens where he has been able to come and go as he likes with his easel and paints, using the surroundings as his subject matter.

As a landscape painter it was almost inevitable that by working in this part of France he would become a painter of gardens. 'This area has been civilised for so long that much of the area takes the form of a garden.' This is in contrast to America where so many vast areas are wilderness. Over the years he has got to know the specific plants as gardeners often come over to him while he's working with comments like 'Oh, there's the agapanthus and make sure all the plants are represented'. Now he often uses the names of the plants as picture titles.

Recently Jeffrey had a show at the Jardin Exotique in Monaco using pictures he'd painted in three very famous gardens in and around Menton: La Serre de la Madonne, designed by the famous gardener Lawrence Johnston (who also designed Hidcote in Gloucestershire), Val Ralmeh, the botanical garden belonging to the Museum of Natural History in Menton (created in 1925) and Le Clos du Peyronnet owned by and created by the Waterfield family which was first established in 1915.

Otherwise Jeffrey has shown regularly over thirty years in Boston (every two or three years), and has a loyal following in New York, Florida and the West Coast. Other markets are ephemeral – Japan and Paris have been good but are fairly quiet now, and recently China has become an exciting new market. All this travelling creates problems of its own. 'I like the challenge of getting materials to where you want to paint – it's all part of the process.' In China he spent a week travelling with a Chinese painter (no language in common) and had no idea of how each day would proceed. At one time they climbed on horseback for two and a half hours to a height of 3500 feet to visit ethnic tribes where the men and women ate separately and where he witnessed the once-yearly ritual of slaughtering and cooking a pig.

Interestingly enough, Jeffrey uses only five or six colours: a turquoise blue, an ultramarine blue, a crimson red, a darker red, a cadmium yellow and, of course, black and white. (The light red is ground very fine at a windmill in Holland and has an invaluable, very dense pigment.) With these six colours he is able to create a great range of hue which reflects the sunny lifestyle of villas, which are often set high above the cliff faces on the coast between Villefranche and Menton.

He generally starts a new image by putting on a coloured wash in his studio – often using complementary colours – and then takes his canvas to the chosen site, probably in a friend's garden. He draws out the structure in black paint with a thick brush, 'reacting to the situation'. Some of the colouring is completed on the spot and some is finished off in the studio.

In his pictures there is a bombardment of colour which conjures up the image of bougainvillea, daturas, and even the profusion of indigenous birds like the hoopoe and golden oriole and butterflies such as the swallowtail and purple emperors. He makes the sky bluer than seems possible, and is continuing the tradition of the Fauves and other French painters of the 1920s and 1930s (Matisse, Chagall and Derain, to name but a few) who also found the Mediterranean coast so emotive and seductive.

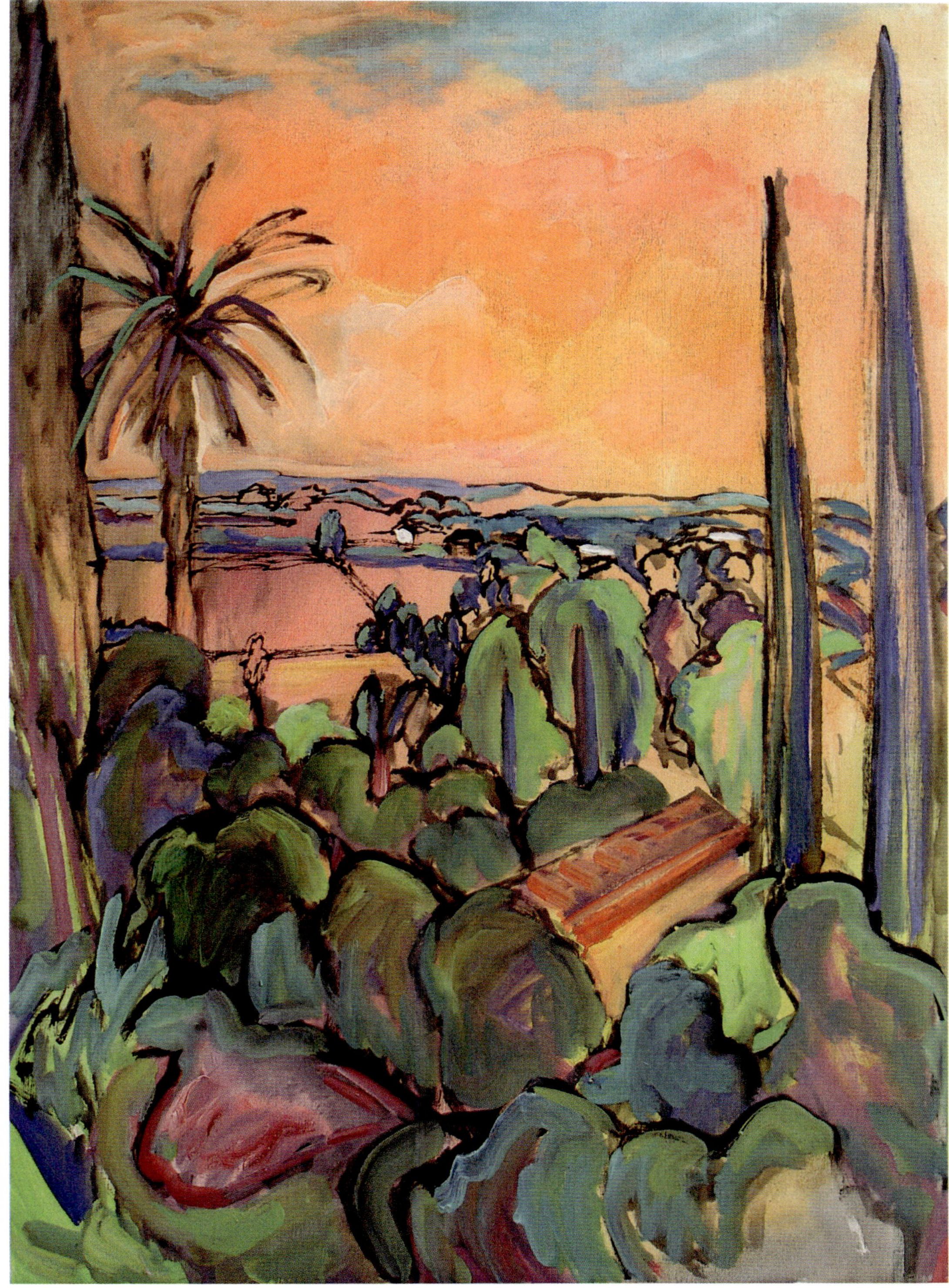

Jeffrey Hessing, *Morning in the Valley*, 2007, oil on canvas, 100 × 73cm.

François Houtin

I first noticed François Houtin's work at a twelfth-century convent in the Loire Valley which had been converted into a hotel. I saw his work again at the Francis Kyle Gallery, London, and realised how unique his horticultural fantasies were.

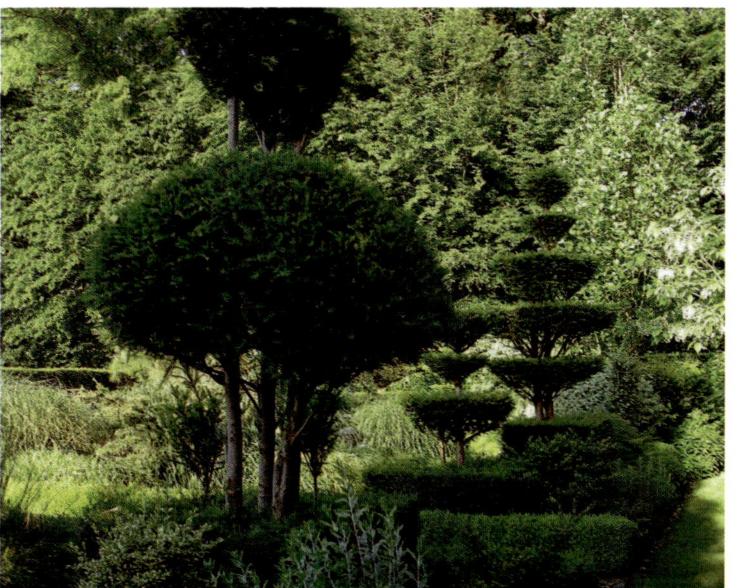

The Artist painting.
PHOTO: BÉNÉDICTE MONGROLLE

François began his connection with gardens when he studied landscape architecture in Paris in 1971. He went on to work for two well-known Swiss designers who not only designed gardens but also specialised in large-scale floral designs for events as diverse as a Rothschild wedding, an Hermès window display and even street decoration. Some of his landscape designs have been realised, one being a labyrinth garden in Castillon, Normandy. The garden is a succession of small garden rooms harmoniously separated by hedges, yet still having an individual theme. This widely diverse work gave scope for his vivid imagination and sense of fantasy.

However, after nearly ten years in this field, François decided that he would achieve more satisfaction by working on imaginary gardens. He re-trained in printmaking at a college in Montparnasse, quickly winning major prizes for his work. The compositions are obviously influenced by his knowledge of landscape architecture. Using the engraver's burin on copper-plate, he has published over four hundred etchings. These 'sequences' have included *Désirs, Délices, Délires* 1978, *Topiaire* 1980, *Cinq Jardins, Cinq Sens* 1982, *Fantaisies Romaines* 1985 and *Cabanes de Jardinier* 1999. The prints show how François has followed the Italian tradition of the Tivoli, Boboli and Bomarzo gardens, as well as the French and English style. He decorates these etchings with plants from the south – cactuses, cypresses, pines and palm trees – and with more flowing landscapes of wild flowers, grasses and topiary from the north. In all the images, he embellishes his practical knowledge of botany with eccentric detail and powerful imagination, often tortuous, sinuous and wavy. He is the printmaker-gardener, the draughtsman-nurseryman, the dreamer.

Alongside the etchings is a huge body of work using Chinese inks on paper and canvas. François frequently sketches out his ideas by using Chinese notebooks which fold out page after page. Recent sketchbooks showed the orchard as a theme: 'These are researches, but for me the sketchbook becomes a work of art itself.' When he uses watercolour (which is unusual

Jardins de Planbessin, Castillon, Normandy – gardens designed by François Houtin.
PHOTO: FRANÇOIS HOUTIN

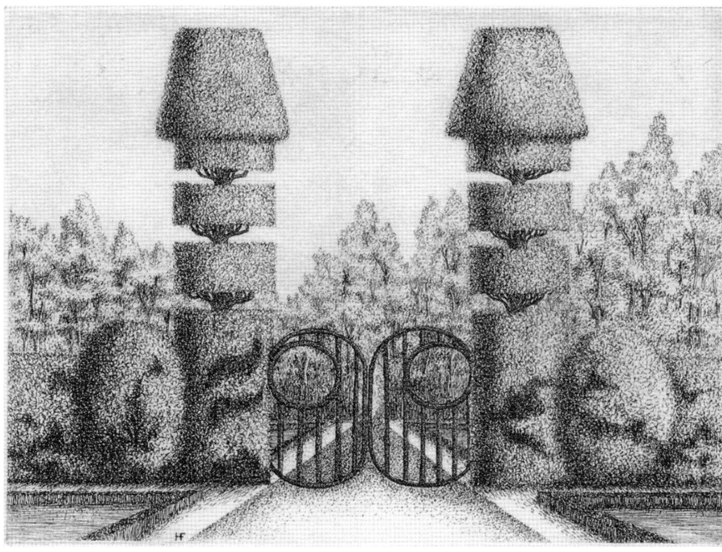

François Houtin, *Entrée Sud du Jardin des Délices*, 1978,
copperplate etching printed on Rives paper, 9 × 12cm.
PHOTO: JEAN-PIERRE DE KIMPE

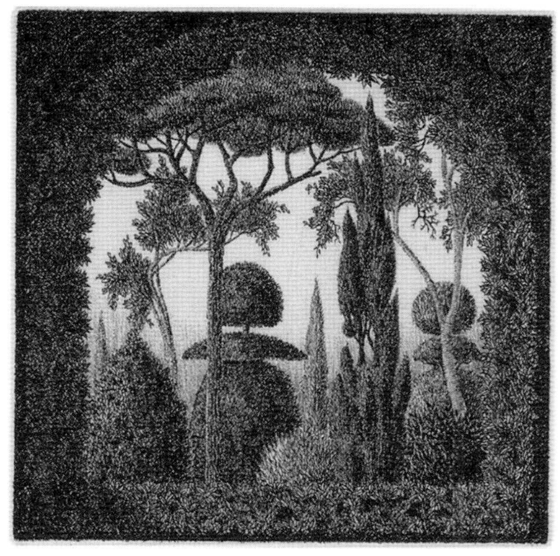

François Houtin, detail from *Regard*, 1985, copperplate etching
printed on Tiepolo paper. PHOTO: JEAN-PIERRE DE KIMPE

in his work as he says 'colour doesn't please me'), he can develop his fantasies and later transfer them to the Arches satin-finished paper that he buys in ten-metre rolls – necessary for his larger images which can have a height of two metres. These larger images are freer and more dramatic – tortuous, sinuous, wavy and serpentine.

He divides the Chinese inks into three separate pots at different densities, using a very light ink to outline the design. Then over a period of maybe a month to six weeks he will intensify certain tones trying 'to involve the individuality and personality of a tree so that there is a feeling of the fantastic.' He gives to horticulture a life of romance, with grottoes, gazeboes, ruins and labyrinths. However, from time to time he longs to work more with 'wild nature' and lesser-known plants 'to give the sense of the timelessness of nature. Roses, clematis and nasturtiums have more of a precise connotation and can conflict with this concept.'

It is not only the Flemish and Dutch engravers and painters who have been François' principal sources of inspiration but also the eighteenth-century architect and engraver Jean-Laurent Legeay, who was the teacher of Boullée and who created visionary suites of fountains. Almost inevitably he has admired Boucher and Fragonard.

François still keeps a studio in Paris, but recently he has done more work in Brittany. Here he has a vast studio with a ceiling high enough for his larger works and a smaller room for his etchings. The garden is not formally landscaped but contains trees with fantastic roots, creepers and twisting ivy that can inspire his fertile vision. It is not difficult to see the connection between pruning knife and etching tool, between branches and brushes.

He has exhibited in France, Belgium, Germany, Italy, New York, Chicago and London, often devising an exhibition around a particular theme. To give an example, it was while in England that he fell under the spell of English parkland and realised

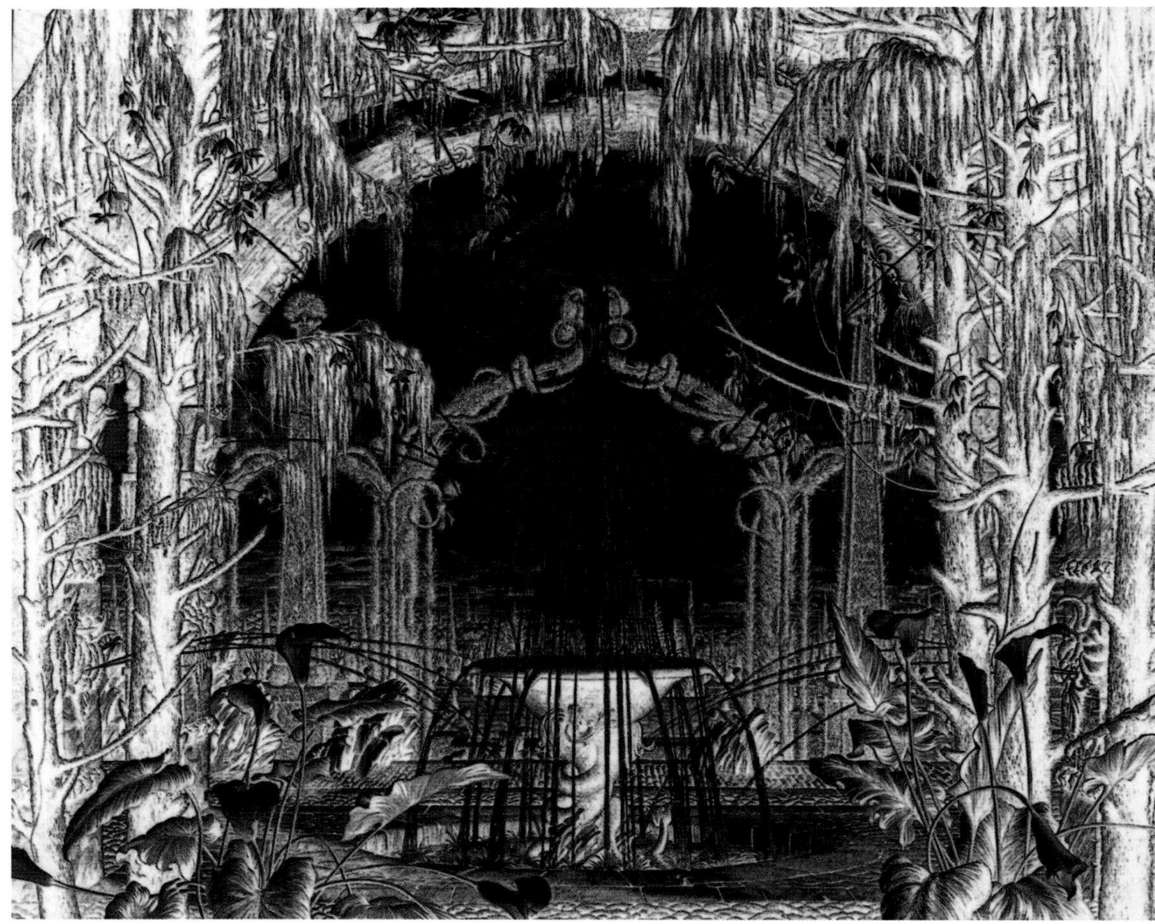

François Houtin, *Fontaine de Jouvence – arum lilies*, 1990, copperplate etching on paper, 114 × 146cm.
PHOTO: YVES LANGLOIS

FACING PAGE François Houtin, *Labyrinthe des Noms*, 1982, copperplate etching printed on Rives paper, 23 × 30cm.
PHOTO: JEAN-PIERRE DE KIMPE

'that for me the tree might become an essential symbol, the quintessence of the otherness of nature.' He is intrigued by oddities and there is an engraving which shows exactly this – an old ash tree with a birch tree growing out of it. 'Having noticed it, I studied it for about a day and then photographed it. I will work from nature and then add little pieces of landscape at will.' He allowed the tree to take centre stage, contort, become leafy.

Lately, François has been asked to portray the garden of Sir Roy Strong, where he will be working with elements of the garden and then translating them into his own style. It will be interesting to see the fusion of two such stylised works of art, the garden and the fanciful interpretation teeming with eccentric detail. Here there are arbours, labyrinths and architectural ornaments ready to be translated into a utopian world of mystery.

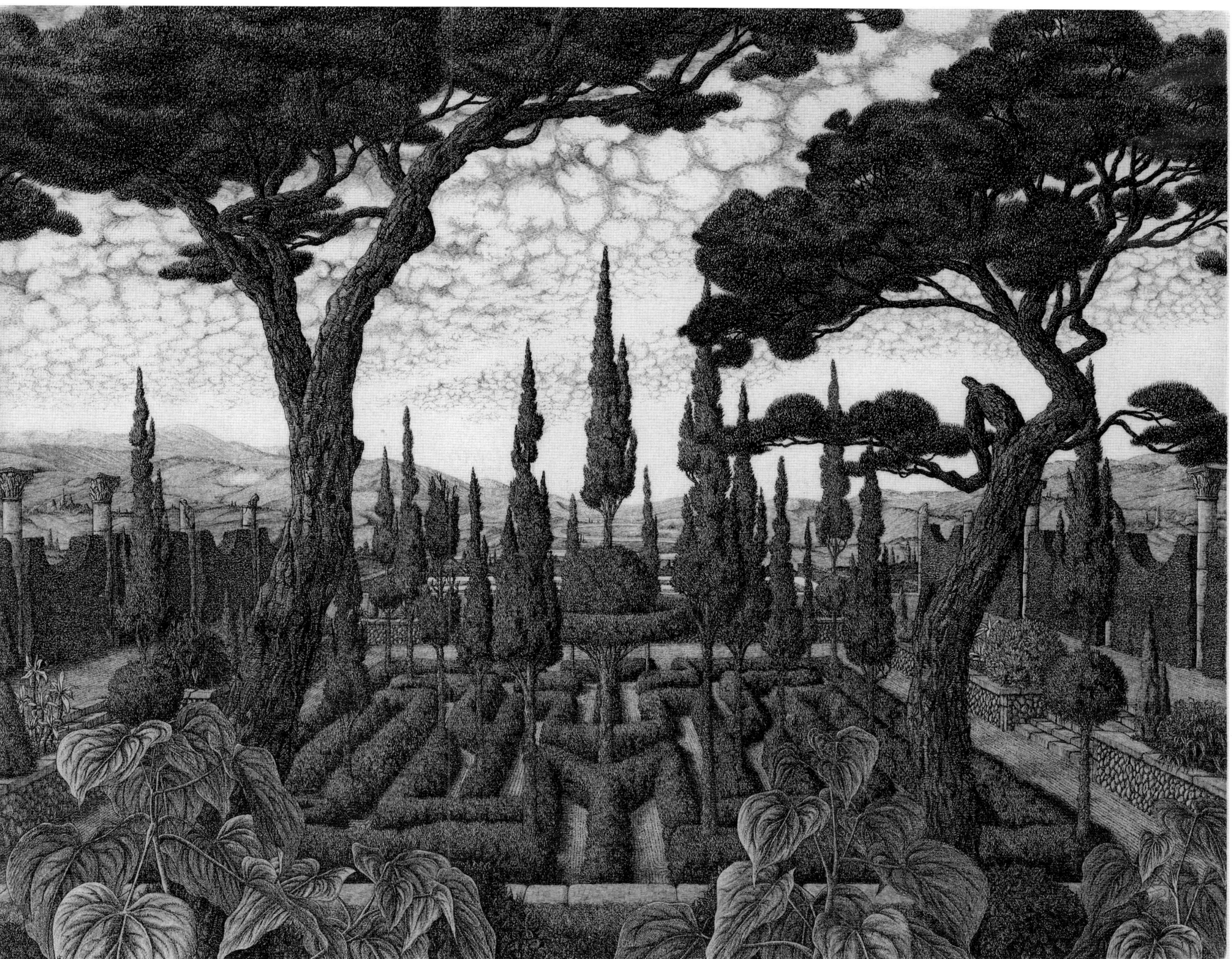

David Inshaw

I have had a postcard of *Our days were a joy and our paths through flowers* (1972) by David Inshaw on my studio wall for years and, like countless others, I have admired *The Badminton Game* at Tate Britain.

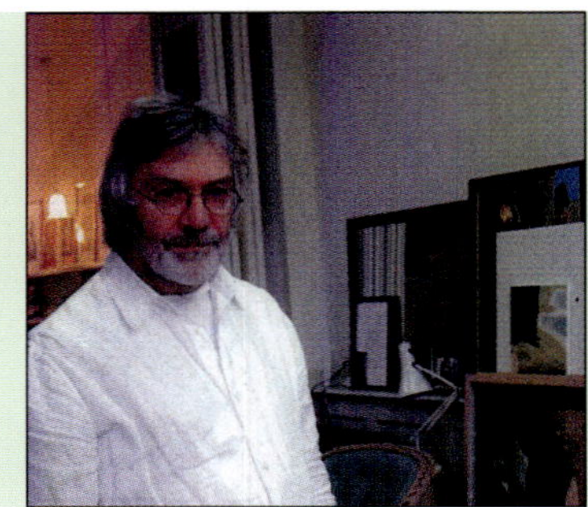

The Artist in his studio.

When you drive through the Wiltshire hills and surrounding countryside near Devizes, you begin to understand the extraordinary perception with which David has conjured up the atmosphere and particular impact of this landscape. David has described the landscape in Wales, where he once lived near the Black Mountains, as dramatic and wonderful but he could not 'find' himself in it. By contrast, his feelings for the Wiltshire Downs relate back to his childhood on the North Downs of Kent, where he enjoyed the sort of freedom denied to young people now – long summers spent picnicking, bird watching, camping and generally enjoying nature amongst the copses and dense woods around Biggin Hill.

His initial training was conventional enough, studying at Beckenham School of Art where he was taught basic drawing and painting skills. In 1963 he moved to London to go to the Royal Academy Schools. Here he was exposed for the first time to the influence of American Abstract Expressionist painters such as Jasper Johns, Rothko and others. He was excited by these pictures and began to think that this was the way forward for his own development. 'My degree show was based on Pop Art and American Abstraction in an attempt to be avant-garde.' This route proved to be disconcerting and unsettling, really a 'blind alley' as he cast about to find his true direction in painting.

In the early 1960s, the Royal Academy Schools were in a kind of time warp. The light bulbs were removed from their sockets at 4 o'clock in the afternoon to save electricity, the statues were painted black and the studio windows were covered with years

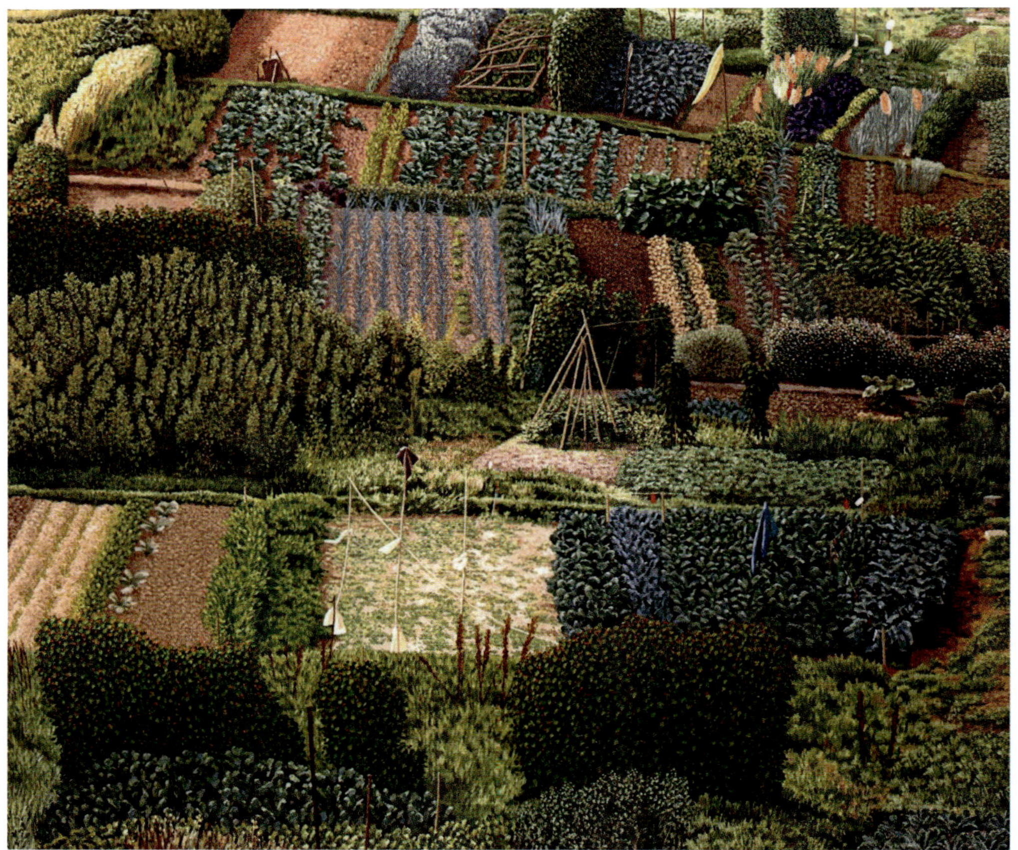

David Inshaw, *Allotments*, 1987–88, oil on canvas, 51 × 60in.

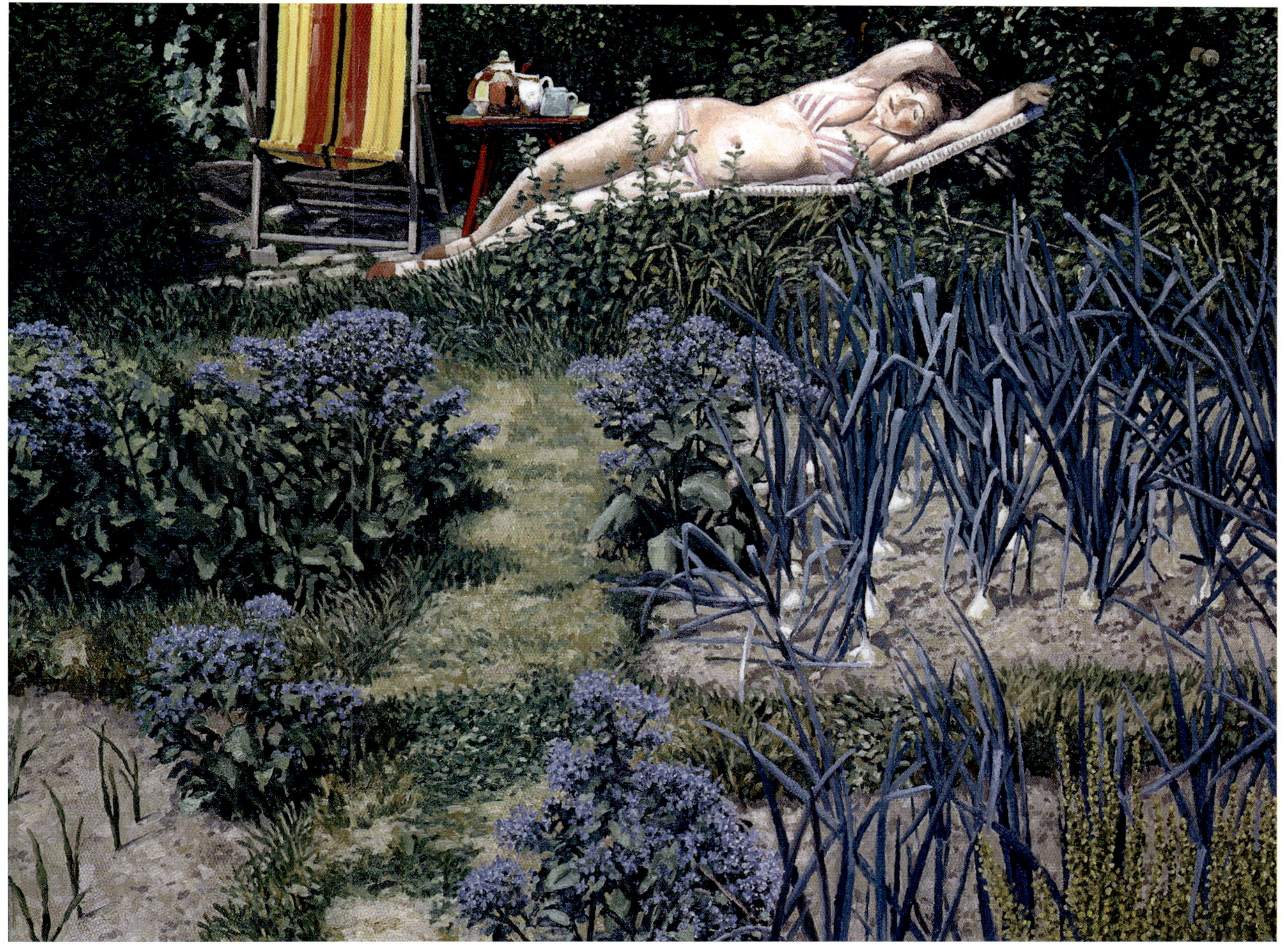

David Inshaw, *Figure in the Garden*, 1989, oil on canvas, 30 × 40in.
PHOTO: JULIA DIXON, COURTESY: TABRETTS FINE ART LTD

of grime! With the arrival of Peter Greenham, as Keeper of the Schools, windows and statues were cleaned and the studios became altogether lighter and the Academy began to catch up with all the great changes taking place at that time.

After graduation, David went to teach painting and print-making at the West of England College of Art in Bristol, where he stayed for about ten years. He formed a close friendship with the painter Alfred Stockham and the pair of them would go off every weekend to Dorset to explore the landscape. Reading Thomas Hardy's *Tess of the D'Urbervilles* had a profound effect on him – he was captivated by the idea that you could use landscape as metaphor for human emotions. 'This was a period of searching for the meaning of the relationship between man and nature.' This was also a time when he visited Montacute House in Somerset, where he became fascinated by topiary, formal gardens and towering trees. He was then painting with fine sable brushes, using tiny strokes in an obsessive and painstaking manner. In the 1970s he painted *The Badminton Game*, *Presentiment* and other pictures depicting scenes which have an atmosphere of arrested time, of mystery and of drama. These highly imaginary paintings were constructed from accumulated source material. Here was a visual language full of symbolism and fantasy – nature showing a sensual and at the same time an unsettling dimension.

By 1973, David wanted to get out of teaching. He realised that it was all absorbing and didn't leave enough time for his own work. All along, he had been sending paintings to exhibitions in the hope that 'something would happen'. In 1973, three of his paintings were featured in *The Sunday Times* colour magazine, and several galleries reacted to this. At first he was taken on by the Marlborough Gallery and then, at the suggestion of Peter Blake, by Leslie Waddington. This enabled him to retire completely from teaching in 1975. Over a twenty-year period, David had many successful exhibitions with Leslie Waddington and (later) his brother Theo Waddington. In 2004 he had a large show at Agnew's.

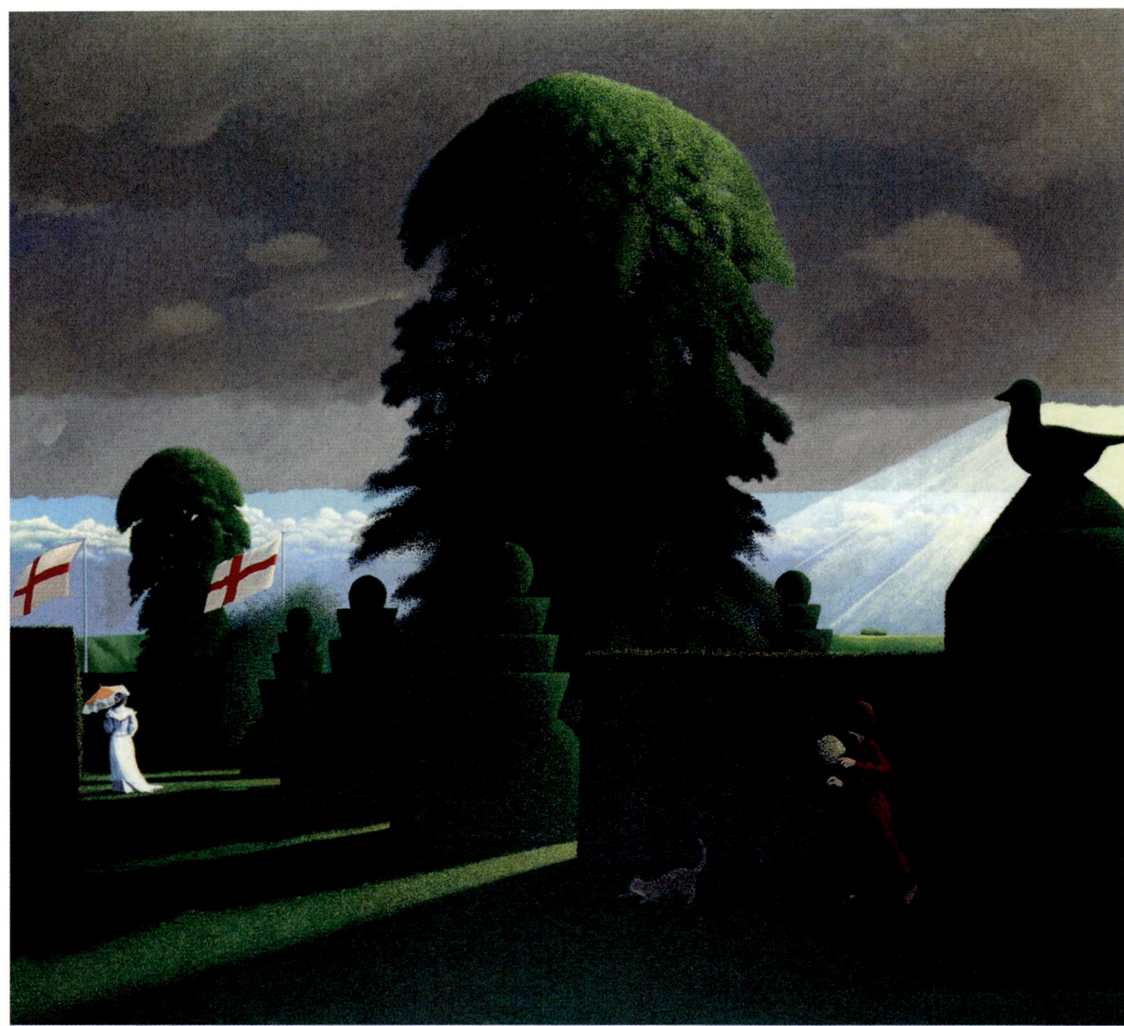

David Inshaw, *Presentiment*, 1973–78, oil on canvas, 51 × 56in.
PHOTO: JULIA DIXON, COURTESY: TABRETTS FINE ART LTD

FACING PAGE David Inshaw, *The Badminton Game*, 1972–73, oil on canvas, 153.4 × 183.5cm. COURTESY: THE BRIDGEMAN ART LIBRARY

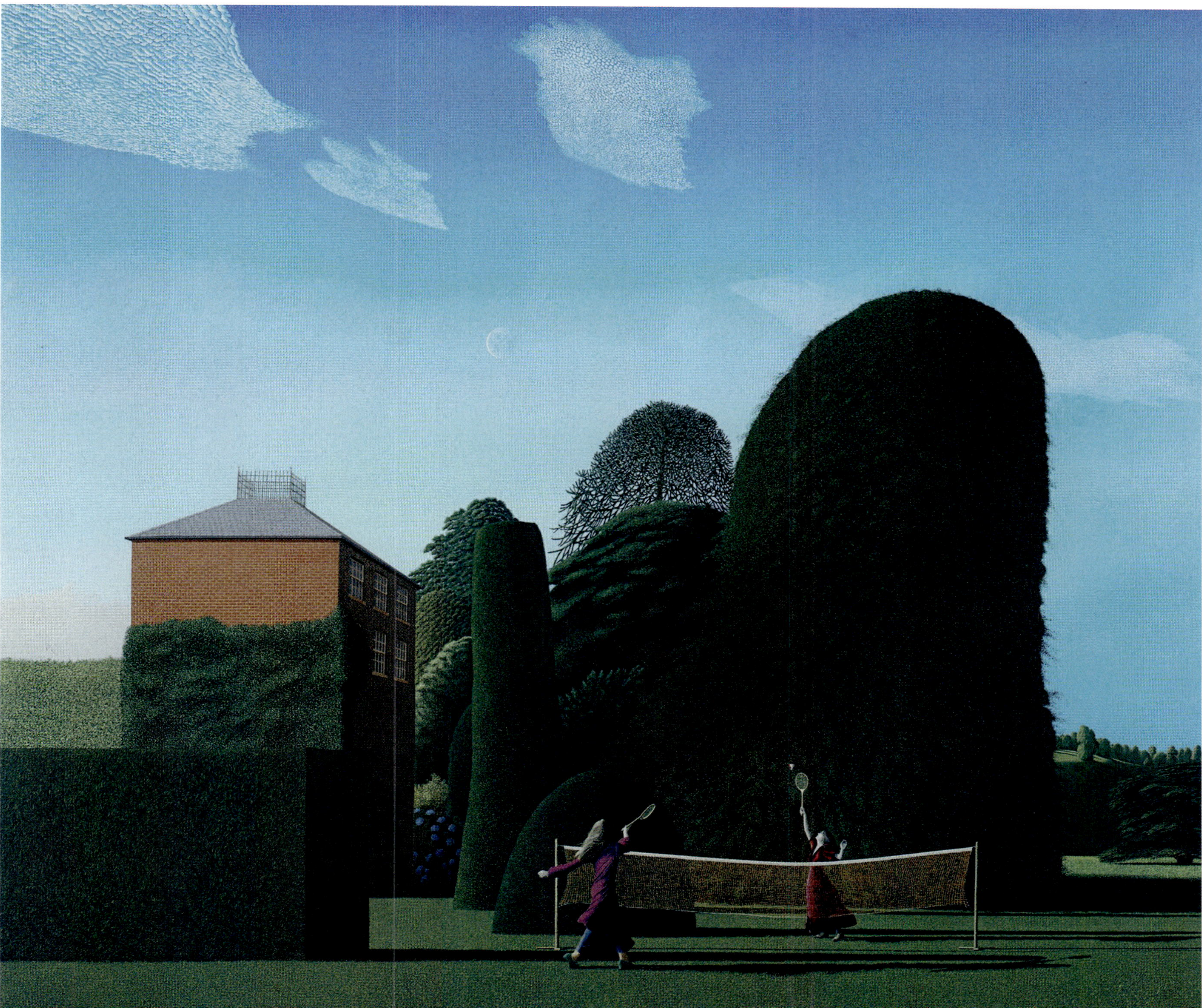

In 1975, David and like-minded artists working in a romantic English tradition formed a group to counteract the prevailing artistic trends. This was the Brotherhood of Ruralists. The group consisted of Graham and Ann Arnold, Peter Blake, Jan Howarth, Graham and Annie Ovenden and David Inshaw. Initially the group met four times a year (at each solstice and equinox), taking it in turns to act as hosts. The group felt that exhibiting together would make a stronger impact on the art world. In 1981, the Arts Council sponsored a huge travelling exhibition of Ruralist art, which went from Bristol to Birmingham, Glasgow to London. It was a powerful show that attracted a vast audience. Over the years the critics have made harsh judgements and been antagonistic towards the Ruralists, but they did not care!

The main theme of David's subject matter is still predominantly the figure in the landscape. He continues to add new elements to his repertoire. The pictures are painted more broadly than in earlier works, yet they retain the same air of tension between fantasy and reality.

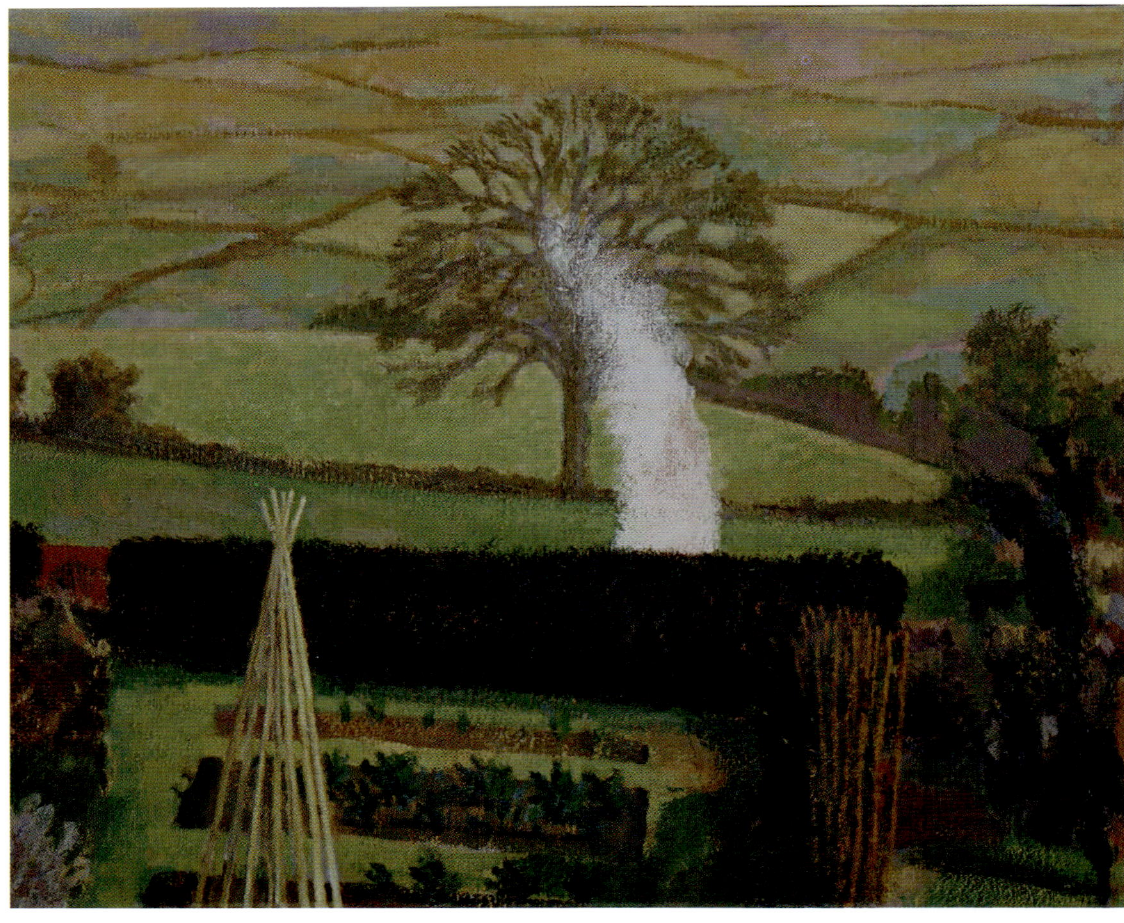

David Inshaw, *Garden, Bonfire and Landscape*, 1992–95, oil on canvas, 18 × 23in.
PHOTO: JULIA DIXON, COURTESY: TABRETTS FINE ART LTD

Ariel Luke

This is my own autobiographical entry. The stylistic influences on my work and my development as a painter were as diverse and happenstance as everyone else's. I was asked in 1982 to stay with Susie Henriques, who on the very day of my arrival inherited the most beautiful early Georgian manor house built in 1740 by Gibbs. The next day, she asked me to paint the house/garden.

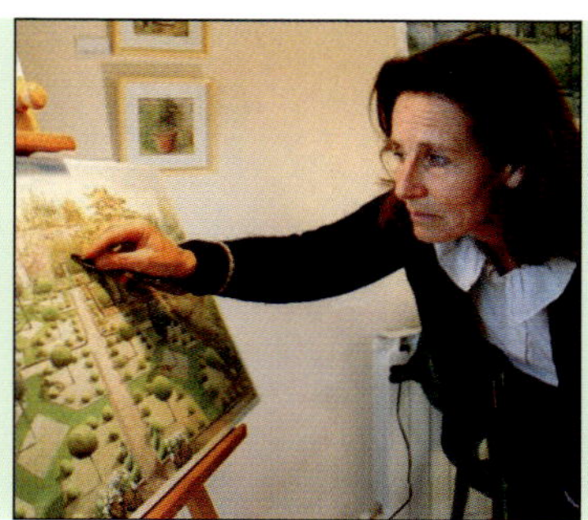

Artist painting. PHOTO: BRIAN GREEN

Until that time it had never occurred to me to use a particular garden as subject matter, as all my work had been conceived and executed in my studio, mainly depicting landscape in a rather minimalistic style. The garden of the manor house was very wild and unkempt so I was at a bit of a loss as to how to go about the painting. However, I remembered an early Florentine painting at the Courtauld Institute, London, which I had copied while studying at art school, using tempera on gesso, so I decided to do a small painting in this medium.

As a child I didn't imagine making a career out of painting, but at school I spent most of my spare time in the art room, principally because it was so warm and our art teacher had a personality to match. Then in the holidays I was often out sketching with my boyfriend and younger brother, with no particular purpose in mind except pure enjoyment. I did secretarial work at the Metropolitan Museum of Art in New York when I was nineteen, eventually enrolled for evening classes in life drawing while living in Canada and finally went to Wimbledon School of Art for four years.

The training at Wimbledon Art School in the late 1960s was predictably traditional. So I was grateful to a tutor, Peter Kinley, who, like his friend Howard Hodgkin, was very interested in Indian miniatures, for presenting a whole new approach to the design of an image. I adored Edouard Vuillard and was fascinated by René Magritte. At the same time there was the massive influx of exhibitions and work by the American Pop artists. This was an exhilarating time experimenting with various styles. At

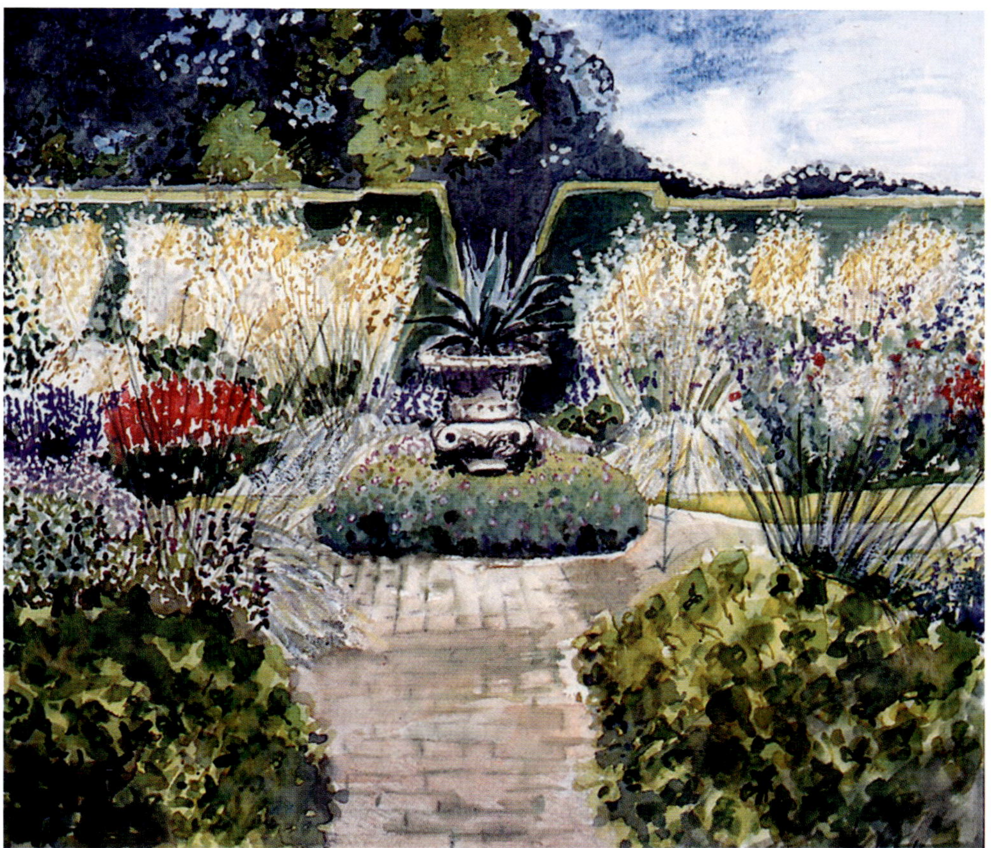

Ariel Luke, *Study of Garden at Glyndebourne*, 1997, watercolour, 11 × 13.75in. PHOTO: ROBIN BRIAULT

that time I made structures you could walk in and out of, painted big abstracts, one of which I showed at the Royal Academy, and used gesso and gold leaf for smaller images after the theme of the Indian miniatures.

On leaving art school there was a question as to how to continue painting and make some money at the same time. I started screenprinting at home when I had children to look after. I showed at about ten galleries in London and then in galleries in Australia, America, Hong Kong and Bahrain. This was fine in a way, but I was very conscious of the fact that the prints were catering for what I thought might be popular and therefore contrasted hugely with my own imaginative work.

It was in 1982, as described earlier, that I completed my first commission for a garden. Magritte's images often showed a painting within a painting – a picture showing the painting in progress all within the same canvas. I had often used the same device in my work. On this occasion, I asked a carpenter to superimpose one layer of board on another, the upper one with 'windows' cut for small vignettes.

The painting was small, and so dissimilar to all my other work that I rather forgot about it, but then Lady Vesty saw the picture and asked me to paint Stowell Park. From that time on, one commission has followed another and I have been painting gardens in France, Italy, Scotland, the Channel Islands and all over England ever since. Over the years I have painted nearly eighty gardens, some gardens such as Glyndebourne, Garsington Manor and Lord Carrington's Bledlow Manor being on the grand scale, and others – which I enjoy doing just as much – such as a little courtyard garden in Chelsea Square, or even a garden where there are weeds. Gardens are all an equal challenge in their own way. Painting in France and Italy has a kind of magic for me as the olive trees, cypresses and agaves are so sculptural and the vegetation is so different.

I myself have always been a passionate gardener. An interesting feature of my garden is a maze in the shape of an artist's palette, the outline made from yew. The five gardens within, in purple, pink, yellow, green and blue, symbolising the paint on

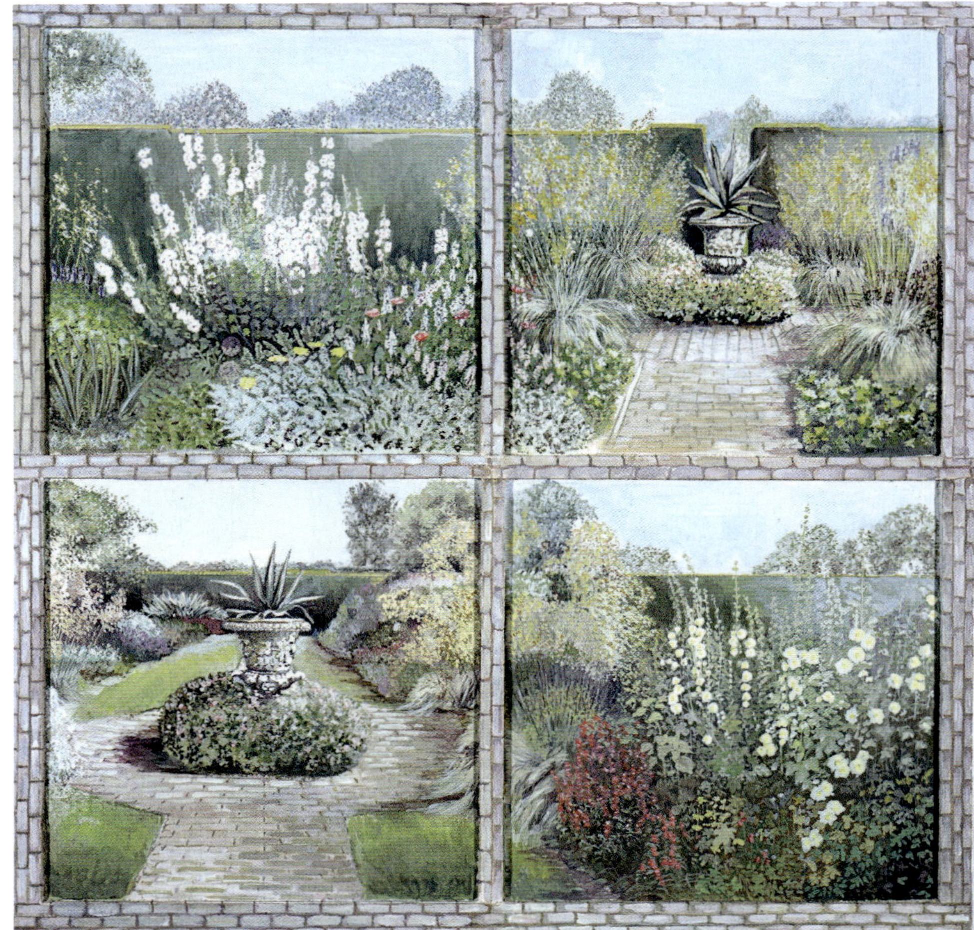

Ariel Luke, *Glyndebourne Garden with Urn*, 1997, tempera on gesso, 22.25 × 23in.
PHOTO: ROBIN BRIAULT

FACING PAGE Ariel Luke, *Yew Arches, Garsington Manor*, 1997, tempera on gesso 13⅞ × 18⅝in. PHOTO: ROBIN BRIAULT

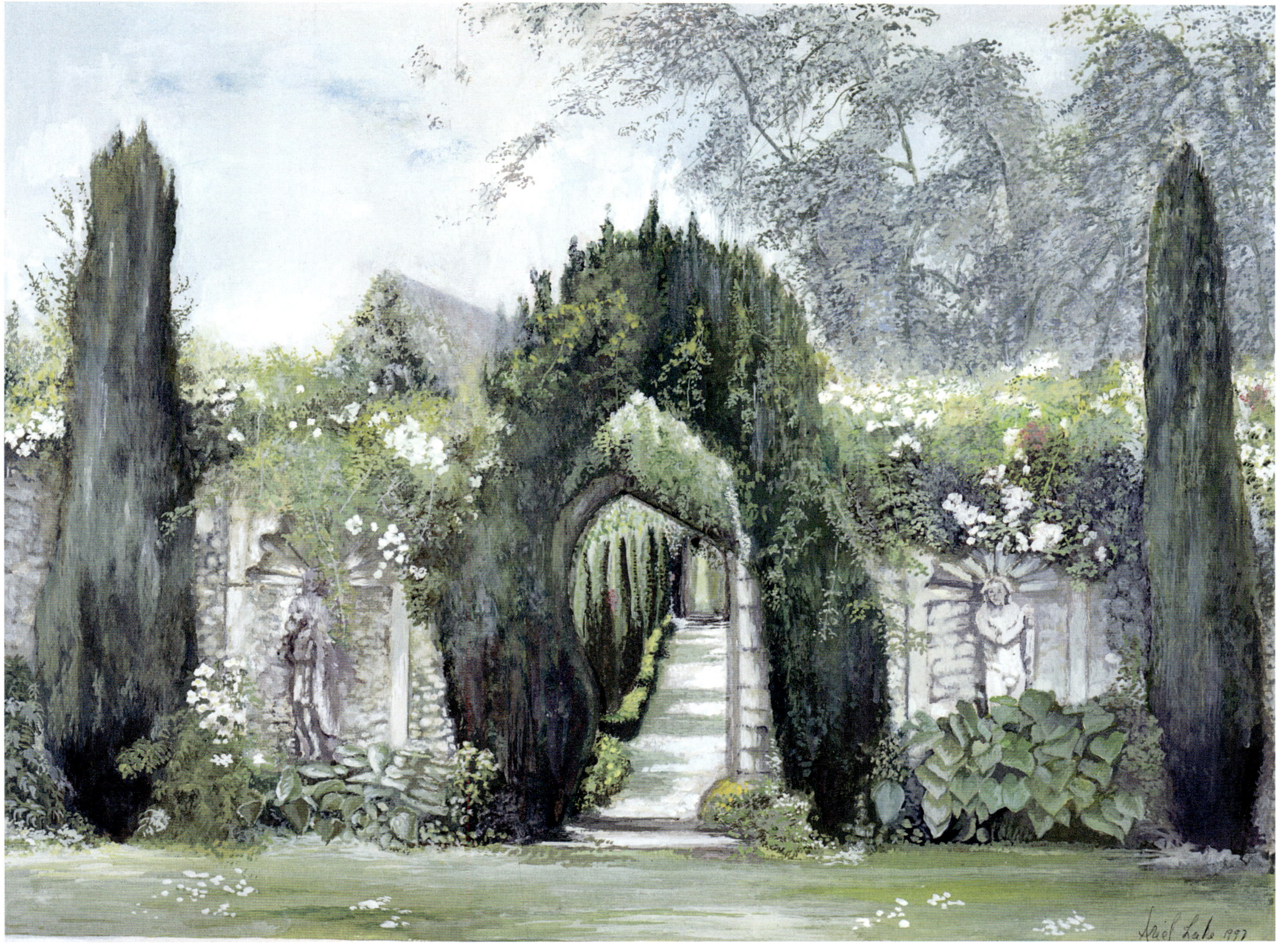

the palette, are separated by box. I grew all the 600–700 box plants from my own cuttings. If, when painting, I'm not quite sure of a particular shade of green for some foliage, it's helpful to be able to go outside and check with the plants themselves. I remember that, when painting the white border at Glyndebourne, I noted a white verbascum and thought, 'Well, I've grown that from seed and know exactly the form of the flower.'

When I began to receive commissions, I'd paint an area of a garden that I thought would make a good image. Then as time went by, I realised that if clients were to commit to such a project, they should have a better idea of what the final result would be. So now when I start a painting of this kind, I visit the garden and take a huge quantity of photographs. In my studio I make detailed pencil drawings as 'plans' that offer various options as to how the painting can look.

I have always felt that one of the reasons my paintings have been popular is that they generally include the raised border. There are four little views in the corners, two long views top and bottom, and two on the sides (if the painting is of oblong shape). As the wide frame/border is raised from the central view, there is a feeling of looking through into the picture. In any event the painting can be made up of nine separate vignettes or views which give a better feeling of the whole garden. When making the pencil 'plans', I try to balance out corresponding vistas. For example, it is preferable to have corresponding arches, vistas or doorways in each corner, and so on.

Once clients have looked at the pencil 'plans' and decided how they want the picture to look, I return to the garden and over a period of two to three days make watercolour studies of the features to be included in the painting. By studying the garden in this way, I can pick up little nuances/details which might otherwise be missed and are an invaluable part of the painting process. The studies are completed in the summer when the weather is more predictable (needless to say, I have experienced rain, wind and icy cold on some occasions).

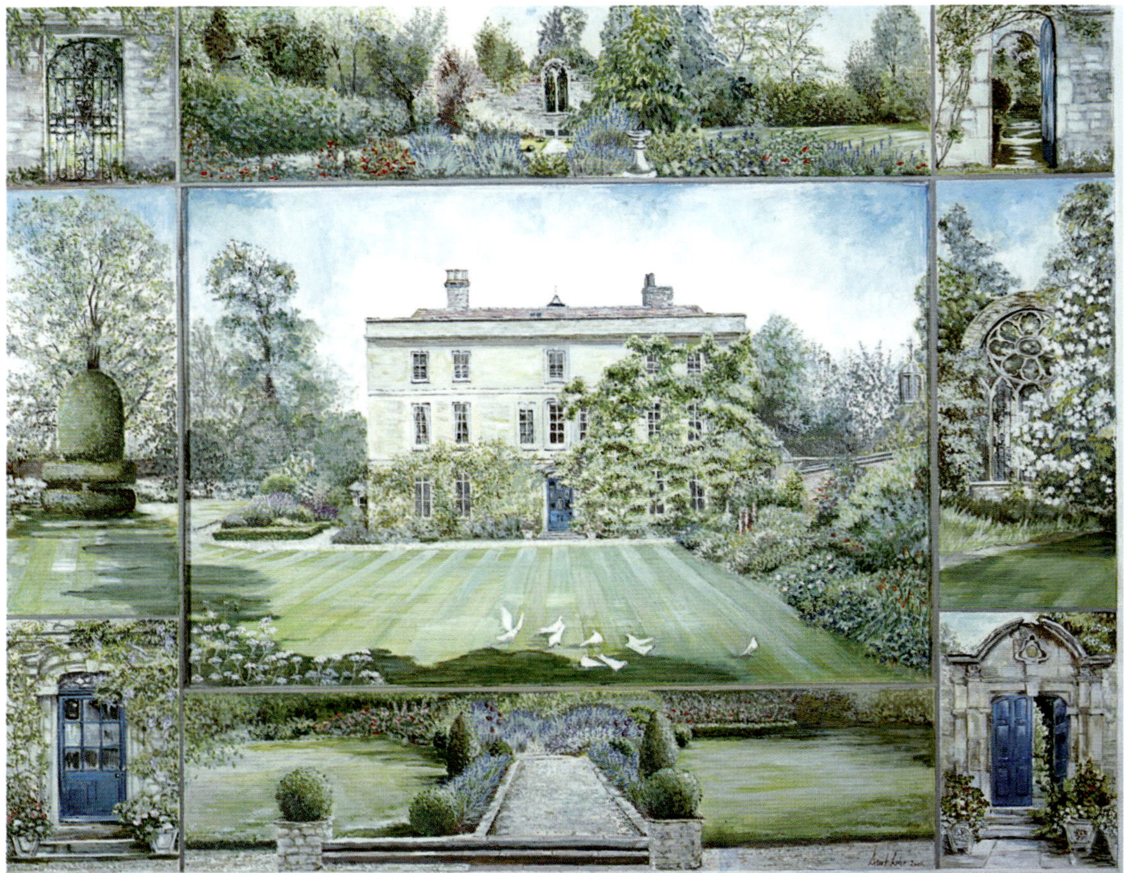

Ariel Luke, *Denton House*, 2003, tempera on gesso, 57 × 73cm.
PHOTO: ROBIN BRIAULT

After the panel with its raised border has been cut to size by a carpenter, the actual painting is completed in my studio. The process of sizing and applying gesso to the panel generally takes about a day. Tempera is a good medium to work with as the colours are mellow and soft and the paint itself very amenable and it seems sympathetic with plant life. The whole process takes about hundred and fifty hours depending on the size of the panel. Just occasionally I paint oil on gesso.

Once the painting is finished there is a vital process of discussion and criticism with someone who is straightforward and direct with her views and she may notice things that have eluded me because I've been so involved in the painting.

Mostly commissions come about through word of mouth. I started showing prints at the Lumley Cazalet Gallery in the 1970s and the Gallery gave me a one-man show in 1998 for my garden paintings. Otherwise my work has been on a stand at the Chelsea Flower Show and at the Courson Flower Show, near Paris; it has been part of mixed shows in the South of France as well as in the UK and occasional one-man shows. I also illustrated a set of stamps and First Day Cover for the Jersey Post Office on the subject of public parks and gardens.

Commissions to paint gardens and to paint purely conceptual work are very different. In the former there is more of a framework, whereas with the latter the thought process is inevitably more abstract and connected with personal experiences, moods and influences. I've no doubt that the two forms of expression benefit each other.

In my case, whatever the form of painting I'm involved with, I never stop making a mental note of leaf tones and shades; of the outlines and forms of trees, of how sunlight will change colours so vastly as the day proceeds and of the variation within a shadow – it's a whole new dimension to life!

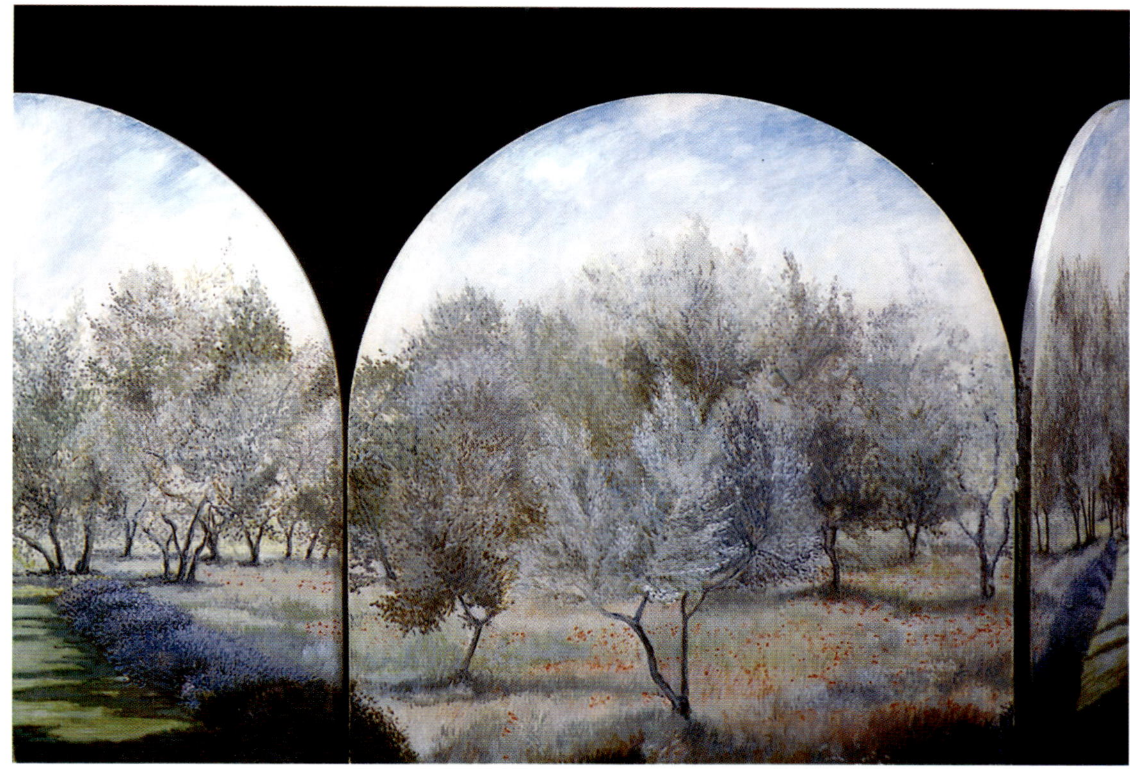

Ariel Luke, *Les Colles, France*, triptych, 2002, tempera on gesso, 15 × 30in.
PHOTO: ROBIN BRIAULT

Natasha Morland

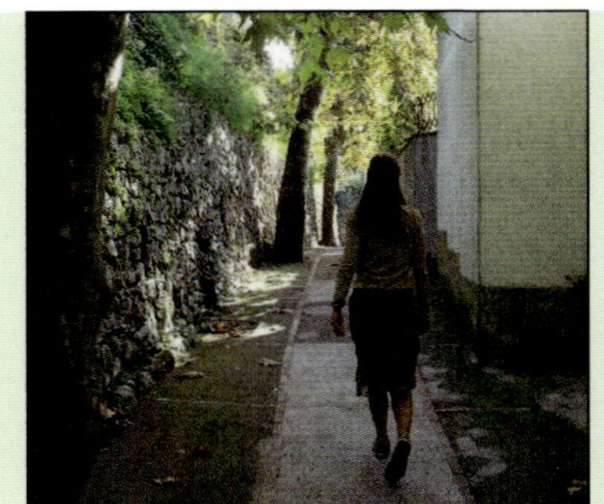

The Artist. PHOTO: BERNARDO GOZZI

Natasha's work first came to my attention when she advertised in the *Chelsea Arts Club Yearbook 2007* as a 'Painter ... Commissions undertaken, including houses and gardens'. When she sent me photographs of the paintings of Tyringham I was impressed.

Natasha describes her training as an artist as 'upside down in a way'. She was initially a furniture designer doing occasional freelance interior design. Then she was commissioned to illustrate a book which gave her enough money to take a year off for travelling, and on returning wasn't inclined to return to a nine-to-five job, 'but just wanted to paint, turning the sketchbooks from her travels into her starting point.' So she audaciously approached her bank manager with a painting and asked for a loan in order to work from a studio at 401½ Wandsworth where there are facilities for about thirty different artists. After about six months working and exhibiting from there she realised she was not sure 'what she was about as an artist' and decided to enrol at an art school.

She was at this stage tempted to study in Florence. She was attracted by the prospect of learning how to grind pigments and seeing 'what happens between one medium and another'. Even the prospect of spending a year just working in charcoal so as to gain a very thorough understanding of drawing appealed to her. When you look at her painting, *Getty Museum II*, created in California, you can see that she probably worked directly from her subject and that she used a representational style. However, with study at the City and Guilds of London Art School, her work has developed an altogether more fluid and atmospheric quality.

The London art college scene is 'far less about actual technical knowhow, this is something you more or less teach yourself, it's more about theory and conceptual art and being able to express your emotions.' For studies of Hyde Park, Natasha cycled each day through the park and, on arrival at her studio made sketches based on what she had seen. 'It was a kind of interesting memory because once you are not in front of the scene many more ideas tend to creep in. This is an environment whose artificial nature makes it a perfect breeding ground for the uncanny; everything has been put there, it is an unnatural habitat, a self-contained world within another world, like stage sets.' In the Hyde Park images the emphasis is on the strength and vigour of the trunks which convey an affinity with forests.

Natasha adopted a rather novel technique, using sheets and sheets of tracing paper placed one behind the other at a distance so that there is an actual physical depth to the image. The detailed pencil drawings on different sheets show through from one layer to another, giving a shadowy, misty, mysterious look.

In recent months, Natasha has been experimenting with pigments to find a way of handling paint which would produce a similar effect to that of the thousands and thousands of graphite marks made on the various layers of tracing paper. She has tried to repeat the slightly cloudy, mysterious effect which gives the pencil studies such vibrating energy. On her canvases she has been rubbing back layers of paint in some areas and using different kinds of glaze, thereby giving different intensities of light.

The focus on trees and trunks is hardly surprising as Natasha grew up in Westchester, New York State, and lived in a house that was about five miles from the nearest road and

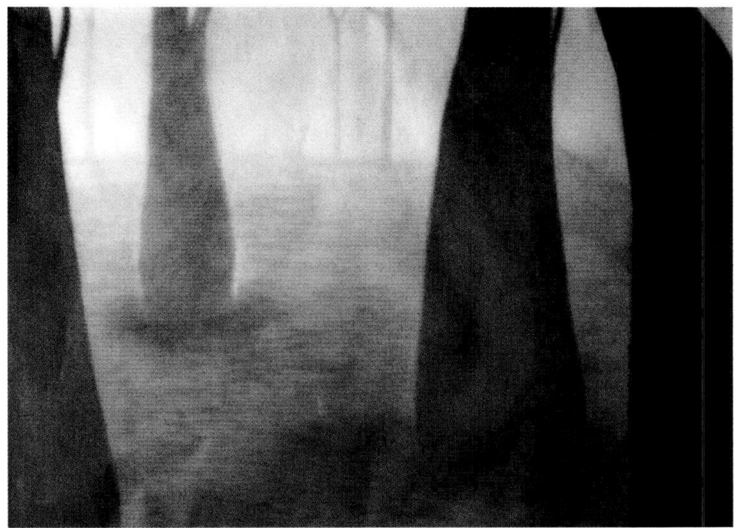

Natasha Morland, *Trace II*, 2007, graphite on 90gm² tracing paper (5 layers) mounted on board, 90 × 110cm. PHOTO: NATASHA MORLAND

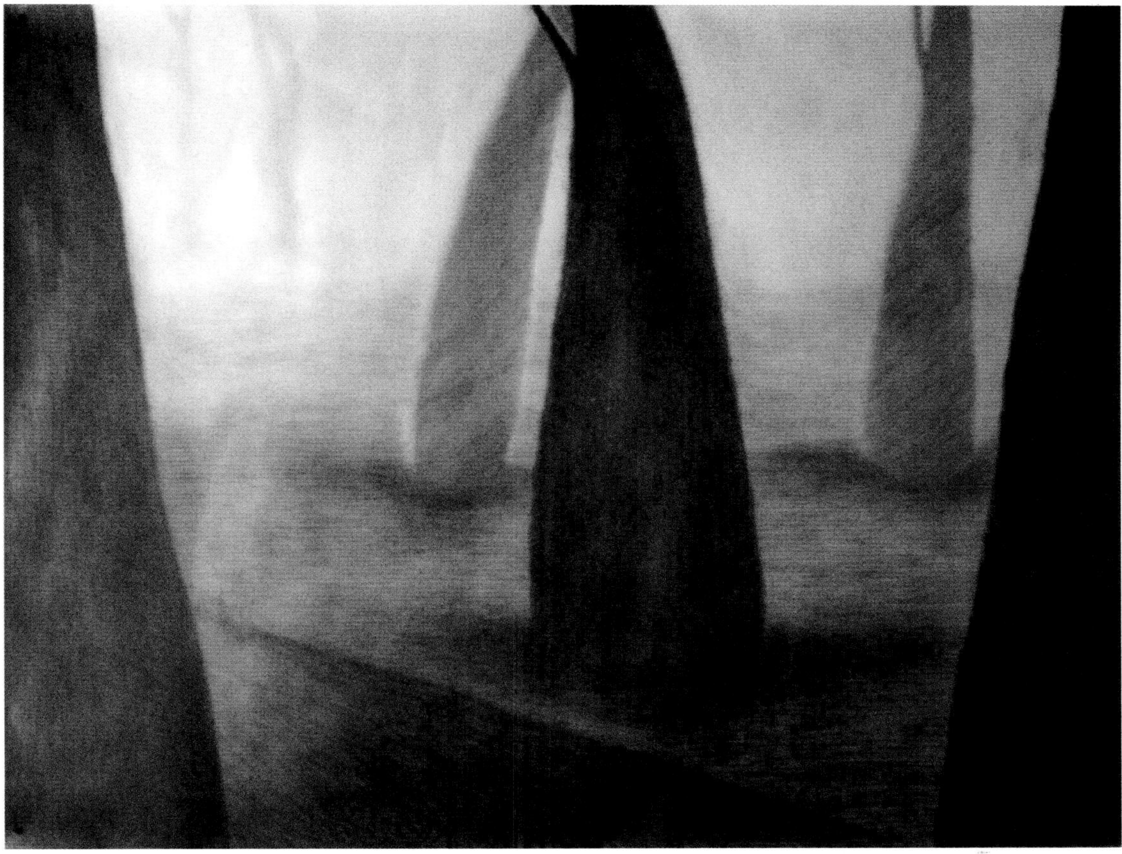

Natasha Morland, *Trace I*, 2007, graphite on 90gm² tracing paper (5 layers) mounted on board, 90 × 110cm. PHOTO: NATASHA MORLAND

very remote. She spent an enormous amount of time playing in the forest which for her presented two polar opposites. 'There was the potentially quite sinister aspect of the unknown, as opposed to a kind of peaceful sanctuary away from the unpredictability of people.' She has since won a travel award to go to the Sequoia National Forest in California where 'I spent days drawing and walking alone through gigantic groves, awestruck by the strong presence such trees commanded; they felt sinister and benign simultaneously.'

Most of Natasha's subject matter is landscape. Ideally she would like to sign up with a gallery for her landscapes while continuing with house/garden commissions. To date she has shown work in a group show at Sotheby's, art fairs, Gallery 54 and the Chelsea Arts Club. Her two diverse areas of work seem to work well together as the more recent of ten to fifteen garden commissions show a looser and more exuberant technique.

Initially she admired painters such as Hockney and Georgia O'Keefe, but now, when she is striving for a more painterly dream-like quality with more distinctive brushstrokes, she is looking at the work of painters such as Peter Doig, L. S. Lowry and Luc Tuymans to inspire her, 'painters who draw out the spirit of the subject matter ... and are hinting at deeper and potentially sinister issues'. Her interest is 'not to make her work like a photograph of what I originally saw, it's more about a combination of what I saw and what I felt when I saw it, and so I often make the images from memory. It is not necessarily a conscious thing, it's more a kind of subconscious

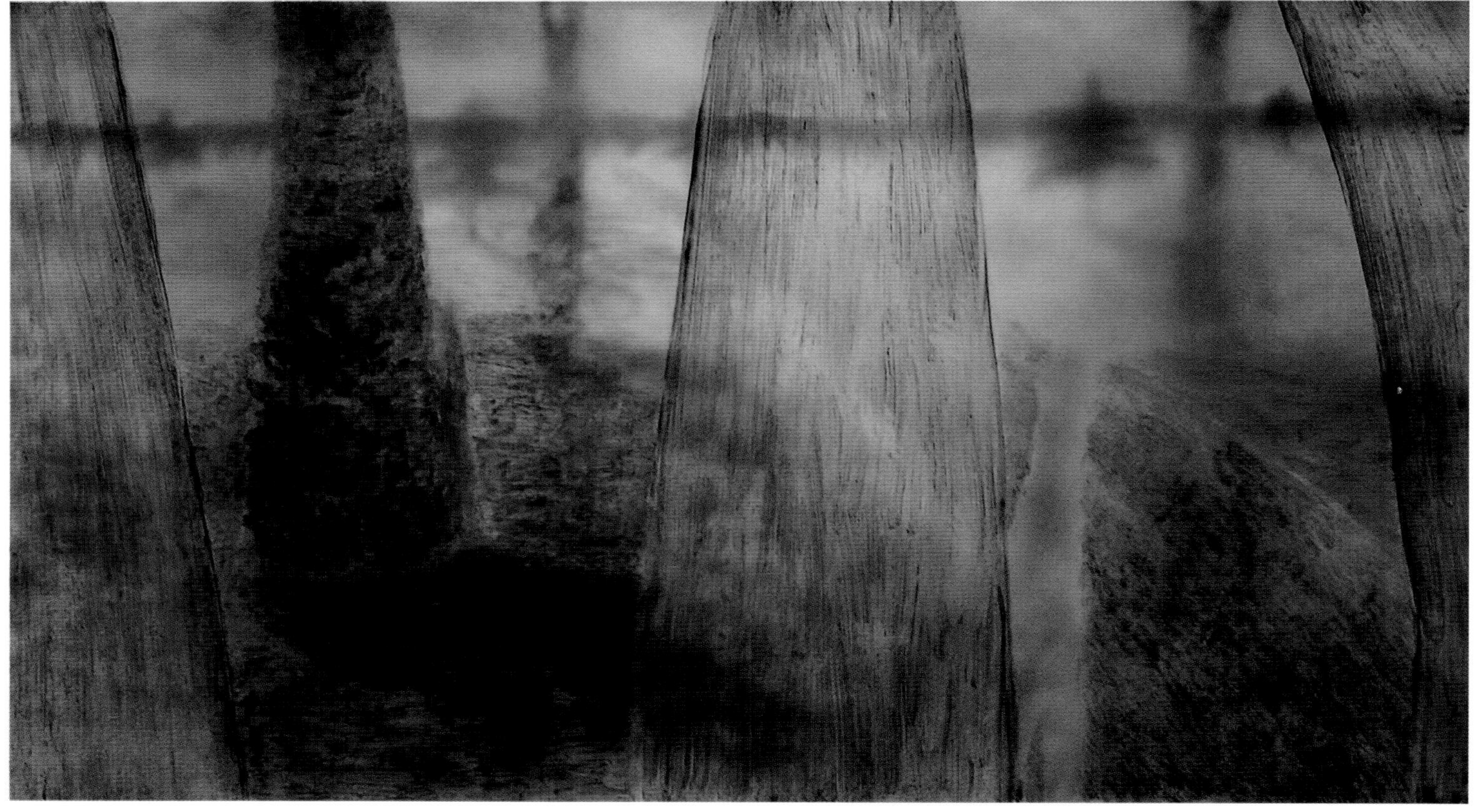

Natasha Morland, *Tree People*, 2007, oil on primed tracing paper (3 layers in a lightbox, 10cm in depth), 26 × 45cm.
PHOTO: NATASHA MORLAND

thing.' The paintings are an amalgamation of all the sketches and photographs done over a period of time, thereby not only achieving a painterly freedom, but honing technical skills at the same time.

It is this searching and experimenting with ideas about drawing and painting that add a vigour and charm to the garden paintings she has completed. 'After all, the public buy work because they like the way the images are presented, the creativity, the vision and the way light is presented – the way

of capturing something that moves you.' Of course, striving to make an image emotive and visceral is uncomfortable at times and 'in a sense you are making decisions based on what the paint did yesterday to the canvas.'

So here is an artist who is in her thirties and in the throes of intense, fresh innovation and development, but with a strong sense of purpose and dedication, whether she is involved in creative work of her own imagination or specific commissions.

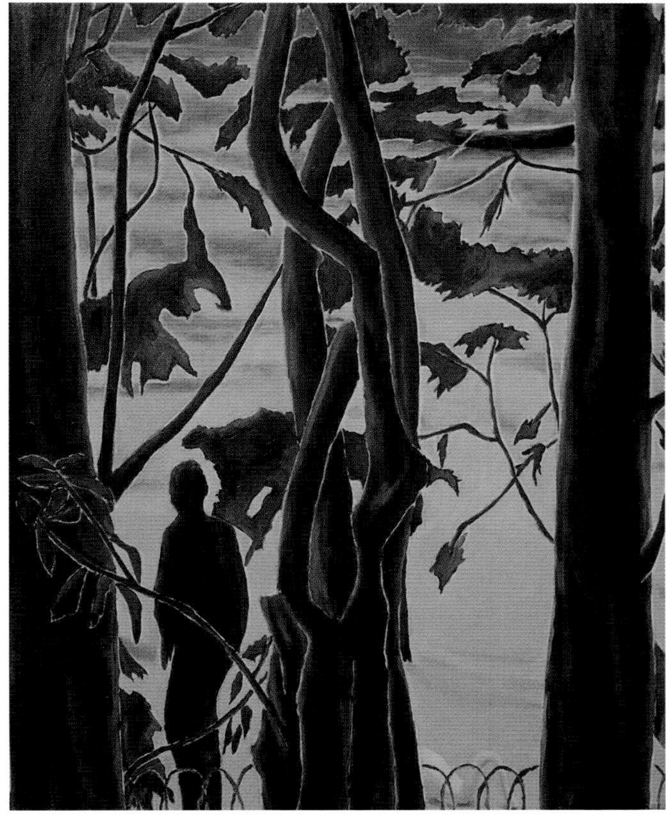

Natasha Morland, *Secret II*, 2007, oil on canvas, 43 × 35cm.
PHOTO: PAUL MINYO

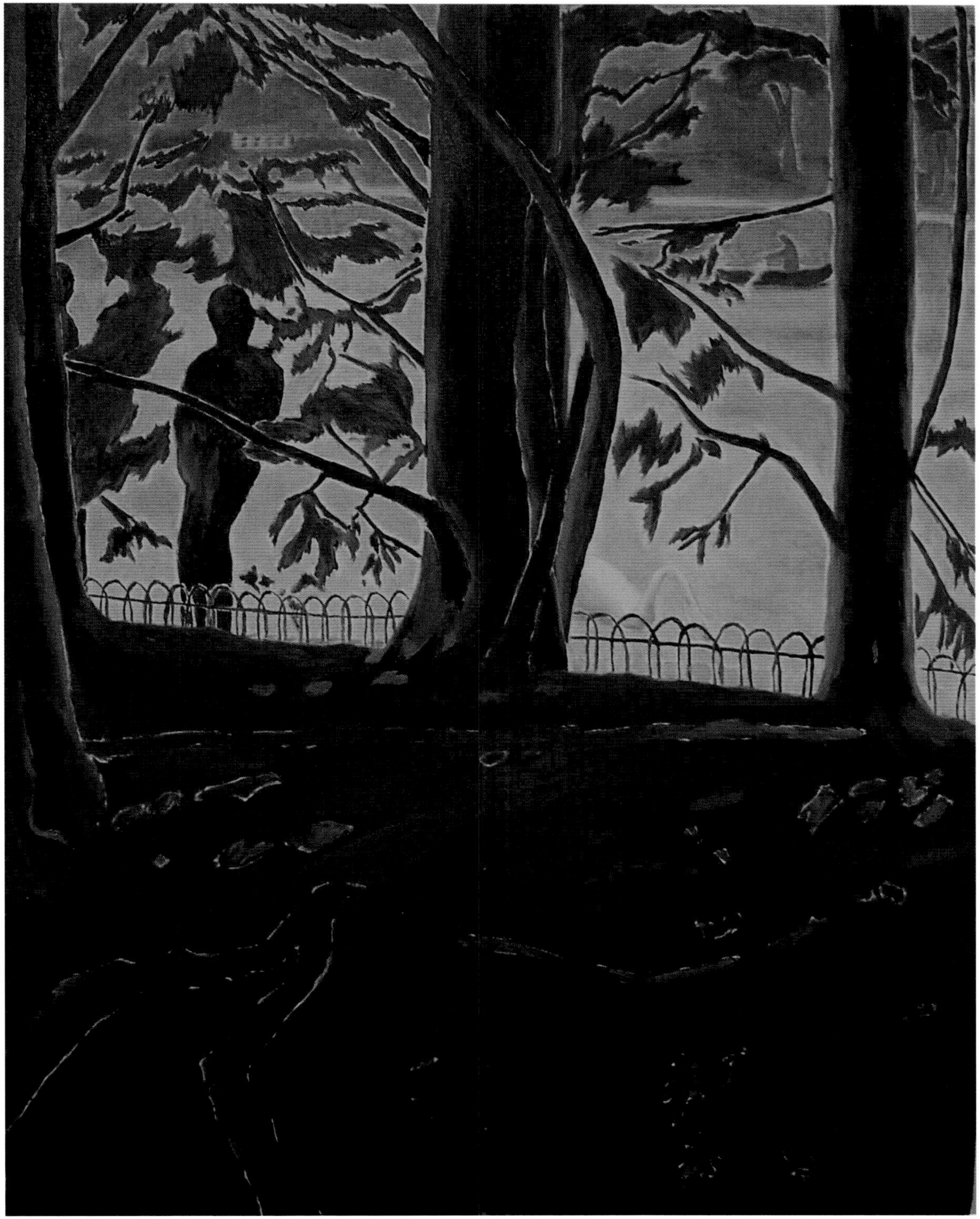

 Natasha Morland, *Secret I*, 2007, oil on canvas, 43 × 35cm.
PHOTO: PAUL MINYO

Jonathan Myles-Lea

Some paintings, once seen, you never forget and this is certainly the case with Jonathan Myles-Lea's painting of Sir Roy Strong's garden, *The Laskett*. It was the innovative 'bird's eye view' that intrigued me.

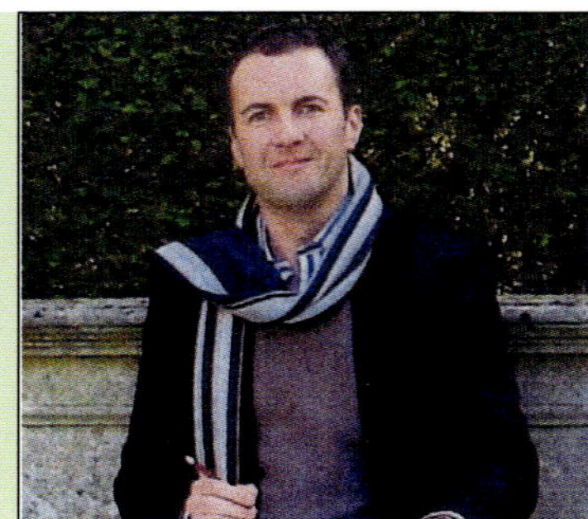

The Artist. PHOTO: SAREL JANSEN

In 1995 Sir Roy Strong asked Jonathan to paint The Laskett – the garden which he and his late wife Julia Trevelyan Oman had created some twenty years earlier. The painting was reproduced on the inside cover of Sir Roy Strong's diaries and to a certain extent is credited with having inspired the writing of *The Artist and the Garden*, published in 2000. This commission proved to be a breakthrough in many ways.

Jonathan was born in 1969 and brought up in the Lake District, and won an art scholarship to Malvern Boys' College. There he was inspired by Bill Denny, a very articulate art master who had trained at Goldsmiths. The emphasis was on craft and technical skills, which meant drawing from life and copying the work of old masters, rather in the manner of a Renaissance guild apprenticeship. He remembers being shown hundreds of slides of paintings from every period and hearing about the use of gesso in the manner of the fifteenth- and sixteenth-century Italian painters. (He taught himself how to make gesso by following the recipes of Cennino Cennini.) He later obtained an Honours Degree in History of Art and Architecture at London University.

Not knowing what to do next he went to live in and help restore a romantic Jacobean house called Plas Teg, in Wales, designed by Sir Robert Smythson in 1610 and owned by Cornelia Bayley, an antique dealer. He mowed lawns, restored floorboards and plastered walls among other things. Nearby there was another historical building, Bettisfield Park in Shropshire, a classical house designed by Sir James Wyatt and built in 1760. He became involved in recreating and replanting the original gardens and parkland using surviving plans from the eighteenth century. This period lasted a year and it was here that he painted his first landscape picture, which turned out to be the launching of his career.

Cornelia Bayley suggested that he paint a picture of Plas Teg and hang it in the Great Hall. There was a piece of wood blocking up one of the windows and, when a carpenter came to mend the window, Jonathan used the wood as the panel for the painting. The style he chose was influenced by early Italian Renaissance frescoes – Fra Angelico being one of his favourite painters. He wasn't so much interested in the atmosphere as the flat pattern, so that the house looked almost like a cut-out. Although he used only one brush and about five different colours, he was shocked to find, on completion, that it looked rather as if it had been painted in the seventeenth century – at the same time as the house was built!

Shortly afterwards Jonathan went to stay with a friend in Sussex, who suggested that he could make a business out of his painting. Although he was a little sceptical about the idea, he proceeded to place a small advertisement in *Country Life* magazine. He had five replies and, with his only picture, he set off to the various locations and in each instance gained a commission. The frame that he'd made for the Plas Teg painting was also admired – he's made his own frames ever since, thereby making sure that they are in sympathy with the pictures. He is adept at gilding, using red bole and leaf gold, and at burnishing

FACING PAGE Jonathan Myles-Lea, *The Laskett*, 1998, oil on canvas, 30 × 42in.
PHOTO: JONATHAN MYLES-LEA

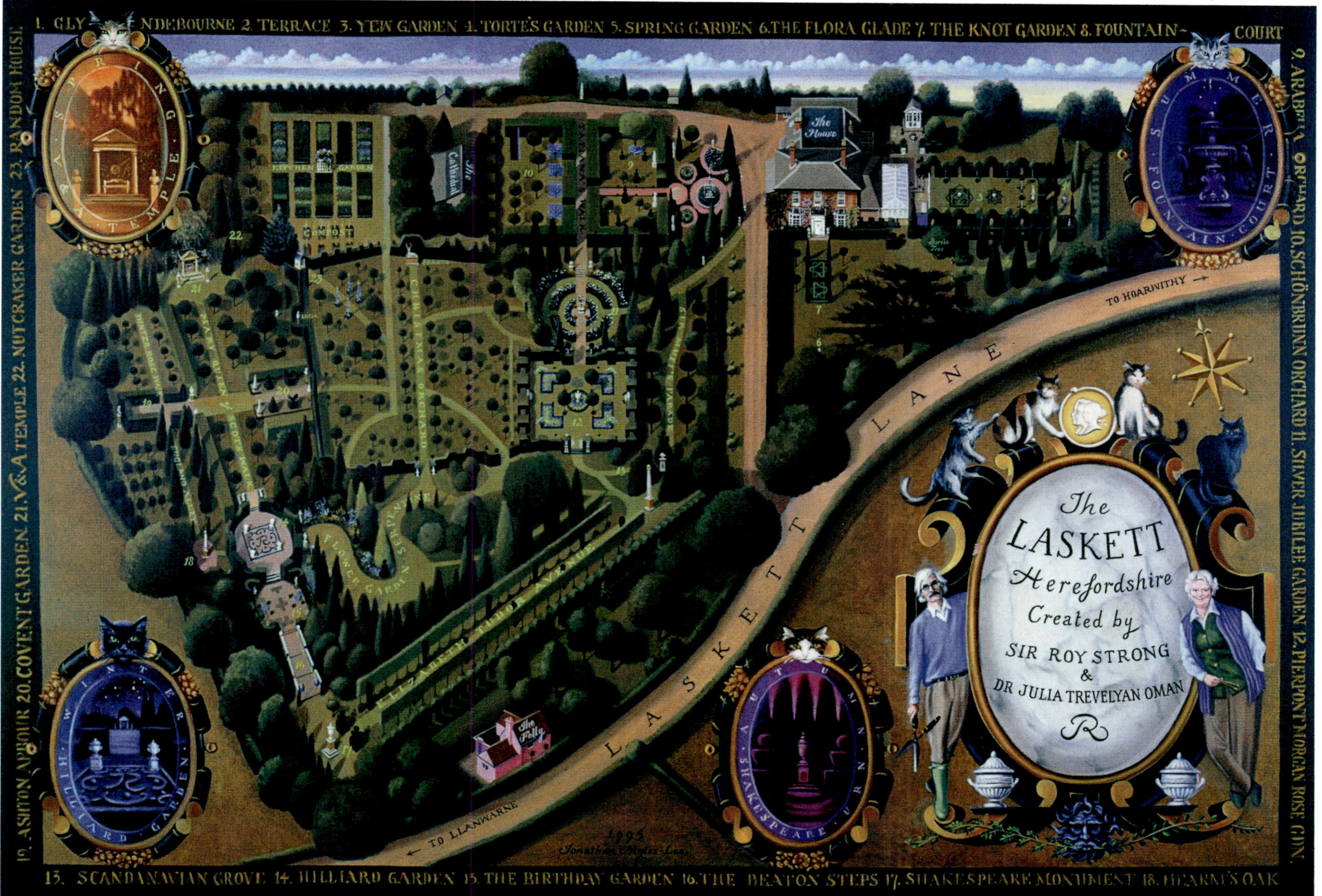
1. GLYNDEBOURNE 2. TERRACE 3. YEW GARDEN 4. TORTE'S GARDEN 5. SPRING GARDEN 6. THE FLORA GLADE 7. THE KNOT GARDEN 8. FOUNTAIN~COURT
9. ARABELLA ORCHARD 10. SCHÖNBRUNN ORCHARD 11. SILVER JUBILEE GARDEN 12. PIERPONT MORGAN ROSE GDN.
19. ASHTON ARBOUR 20. COVENT GARDEN 21. V & A TEMPLE 22. NUTCRAKER GARDEN 23. RANDOM HOUSE
TO HOARWITHY
TO LLANWARNE
TO LLANWARNE
1995
Jonathan Myles-Lea
SPRING
A TEMPLE
SUMMER
FOUNTAIN COURT
WINTER
HILLIARD GARDEN
AUTUMN
SHAKESPEARE URN
LASKETT LANE
The House
The Folly
The
LASKETT
Herefordshire
Created by
SIR ROY STRONG
&
DR JULIA TREVELYAN OMAN
13. SCANDANAVIAN GROVE 14. HILLIARD GARDEN 15. THE BIRTHDAY GARDEN 16. THE BEATON STEPS 17. SHAKESPEARE MONUMENT 18. HEARNE'S OAK

with polished agate. He then applies coloured waxes to achieve an antique finish. On one occasion a frame was mistakenly thought to be three hundred years old.

Stylistically, the commission for Sir Roy Strong in 1995 led to Jonathan's presenting a combination of plan and elevation in the same image. He depicted the garden from the air, as had been done in paintings by Dutch topographical artists in the seventeenth century. Jonathan also introduced what he called 'cartouches' which were framed scenes from the garden running round the borders of the picture. They show specific statues, a fountain, a garden vista and portraits of the owners – all details too small to see in the main picture. This device not only showed the layout of the whole garden but gave an insight into the inspiration and spirit of the design.

Sir Roy Strong labelled Jonathan's approach 'absolutely unique' and the support and enthusiasm he transmitted to his contacts and fellow garden owners were invaluable in extending Jonathan's reputation. Undoubtedly this led to Jonathan's introduction to Simon and Victoria Leatham, the owners of Burghley House, built in the late sixteenth century by Sir William Cecil. The famous park was landscaped by 'Capability' Brown and the house is undoubtedly one of the most important in Britain. The Leathams wanted a series of grand paintings of the house and gardens. The painting shown here exhibits a very rigorous symmetry and emphasises the geometrical layout of the site. As the area had never been surveyed, Jonathan paced everything out himself using the 'Myles-Lea foot', which is fairly accurate as he is 6ft 4in tall with feet to scale! He spent almost a week on the roof looking at the obelisks and the classical columns which are the chimneys in order to get these features correct in his picture. The plan he made was considered so detailed and accurate that the company re-leading the roof used his drawings for their own work.

He took eight months to complete the picture and, on the day that he was due to deliver it, he rang the Leathams to say he was not entirely happy with the painting, 'realising that the work might hang for another two hundred years or more', and asked

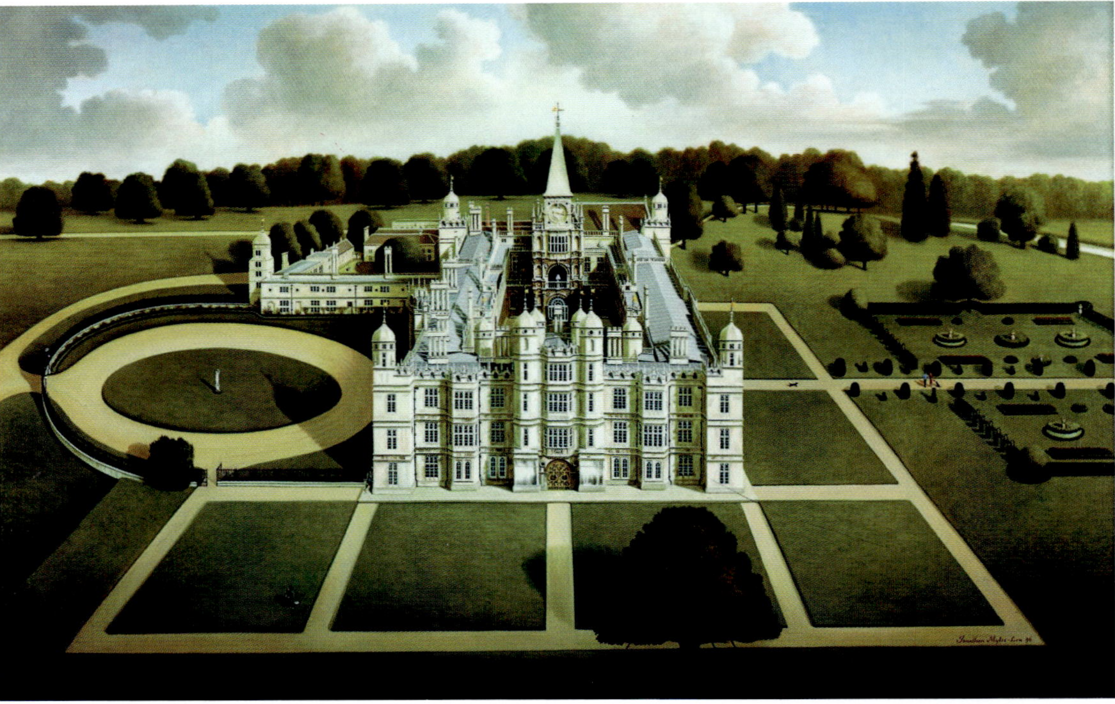

Jonathan Myles-Lea, *Burghley House*, 1996, oil on canvas, 30 × 48in.
PHOTO: JONATHAN MYLES-LEA

to be able to repaint it. This was a brave decision which resulted in him spending the next five months subsisting on a meagre diet of rice measured by a coffee cup and home-grown parsnips.

Jonathan was now an artist in demand and since 1997 a large project has been a series of views and line drawings of properties owned by the National Trust in Herefordshire and Worcestershire, then an extensive map of the wonderful Cliveden and another of Stowe gardens in the style of an eighteenth-century engraving.

His other important works have been to paint Gresgarth, Cumbria, for the garden designer Lady Arabella Lennox Boyd (1997), to paint both Daylesford House and Wooton Lodge for Sir Anthony and Lady Bamford (2000) and Wartnaby House for Lord King, the former chairman of British Airways (2001).

FACING PAGE Jonathan Myles-Lea, *Kasteel Wylre, Netherlands*, 2001, oil on canvas on panel, 48 × 36in.
PHOTO: JONATHAN MYLES-LEA

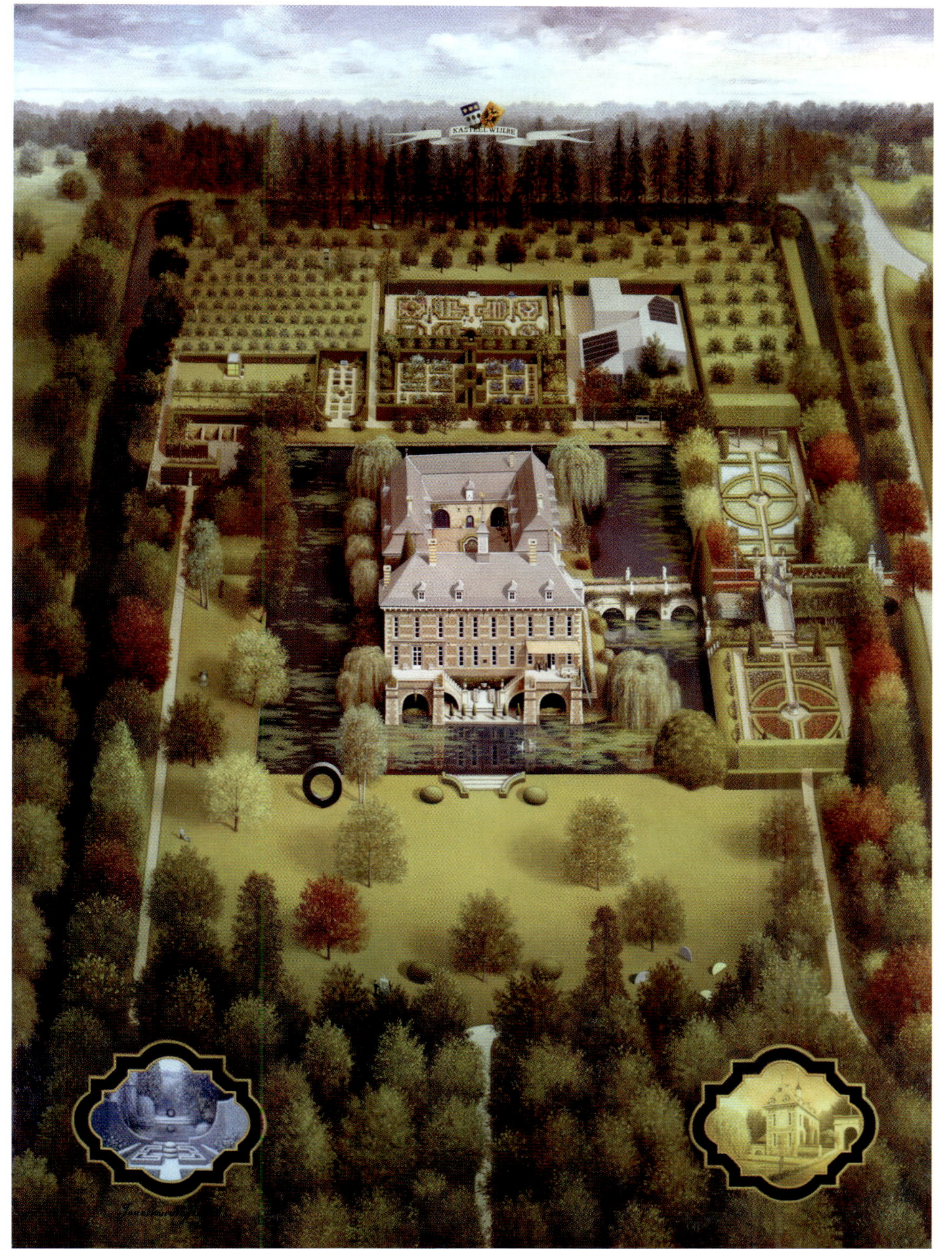

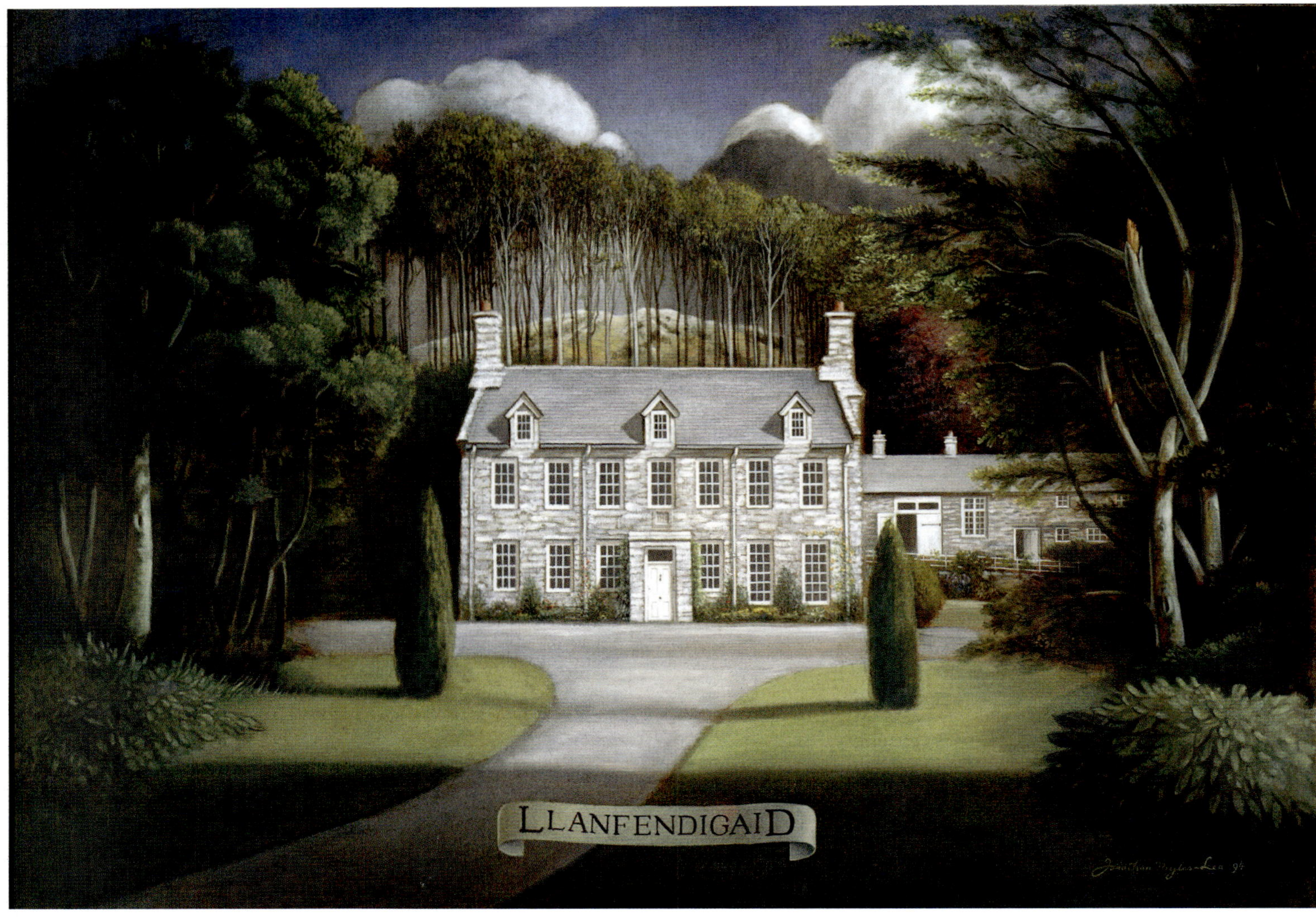

Jonathan Myles-Lea,
Llanfendegaid, Wales, 1995,
oil on canvas, 36 × 48in.
PHOTO: JONATHAN MYLES-LEA

Jonathan has also been in demand internationally. In the Netherlands he painted the Hof van Roosmalen and Huys de Dohm (both formal gardens with various 'rooms' in the English style), a moated castle on the Dutch/German border and another garden near Cologne. Finally, across the Atlantic he has painted a house and garden in South Carolina (belonging to a well-known fashion designer), and others in Florida and New York State.

He has now completed more than fifty commissions across the world, including, lately, one in Russia. This considerable body of work has inevitably meant that some of his pictures have been included in exhibitions, the most notable of which have been *The Artist and the Country House – from the 15th Century to the Present Day* at Sotheby's (1997), *The Writer in the Garden* at the British Library (2005), and *The Painting of the West Country House* at a museum in Bath (2006).

For these paintings a great deal of early work is done on site. It may include considerable interaction with the client for as long as a year. Jonathan sometimes photographs and makes structural drawings of the hedges and walls to determine their height and the material of which they're made in, say, November, and return in summer for the blooming of the roses and flowers. He can be quite extraordinarily accurate when depicting the planting. For instance, in the painting of a kitchen garden, the strawberries and raspberries and even their poles are in correct numbers. The seeds are in their trays and rhubarb forcers along the back wall with the sweet peas and potatoes in the right places. One of the gardeners in Arabella Lennox Boyd's garden was a bit aghast and said he 'couldn't believe it, oh, my goodness you have even got the artichokes in the right place'.

Much of this work is the result of the most meticulous preparation followed by exquisitely executed brushwork. The beautiful and delicate handling of paint is the result of a great deal of time spent studying at exhibitions and museums. 'There has been many a time when I have set off an alarm by leaning too far over protective rope while observing a particular paint-ing.' Recently he spent an hour standing in front of a Velasquez noting the colours and using the back of his hand as a reference from which to gauge the tones.

He has described plucking a hair from his head to paint a minute detail and frequently uses size oo as well as a wide range of other brushes. His paints come from a company, Old Holland, which was established in 1664 and supplied many of the Dutch old masters, such as Vermeer and van Ruysdael. He paints on a surface of linen which covers a panel and is coated with several layers of gesso, which he makes himself.

When he was making a map for the National Trust he looked at eighteenth-century engravings to see how tone was

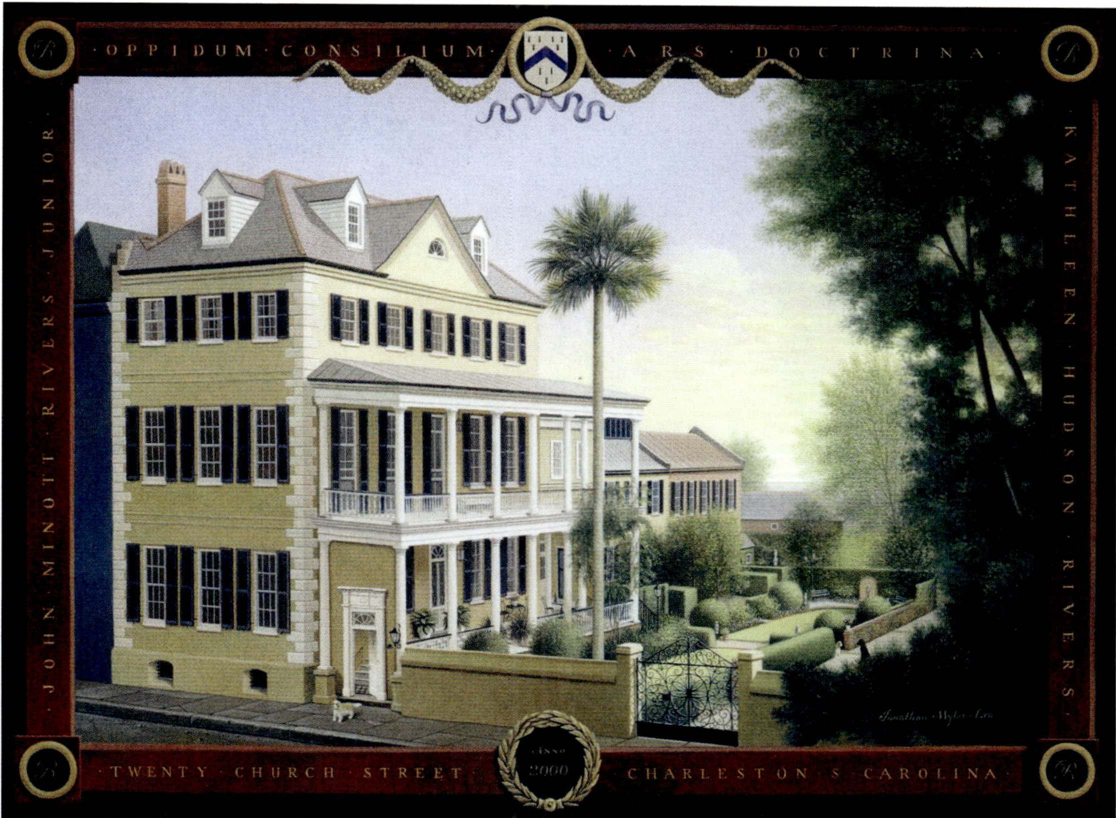

Jonathan Myles-Lea, *The Rivers' House, South Carolina*, 2000, oil on canvas on panel, 30 × 42in.
PHOTO: JONATHAN MYLES-LEA

created. He studied how the various tones were established by fine cross-hatching and by undulating lines interspersed with dots and dashes. He then absorbed this meticulous vocabulary in order to make his modern maps.

These paintings are absorbing to look at as well as being innovative and exquisitely executed. In all Jonathan's work there is a sense of timeliness and peace. It is no surprise that *Country Life* magazine gave him the title 'Living National Treasure' in 1997. Since then, Jonathan has completed a portrait of Highgrove house and garden for HRH The Prince of Wales.

John Pearce

Some time ago I went to see Francis Kyle at his gallery to talk to him about painters of gardens and he showed me the work of John Pearce whom I later met and talked to at the gallery.

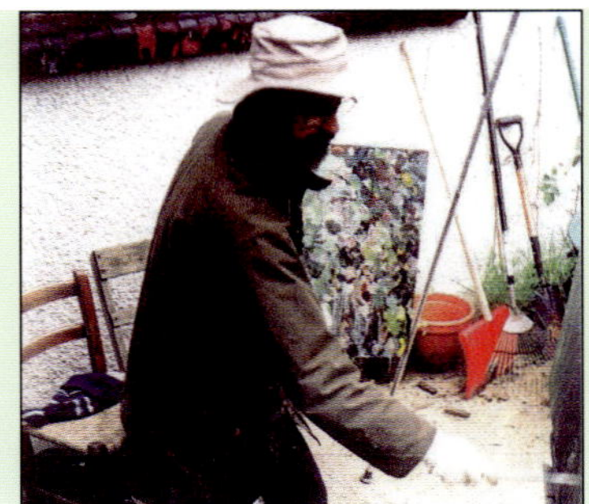

The Artist painting.
PHOTO: GERRY KEON

John was born 1942 in North London and has lived and worked from there ever since. He vividly recalls the bombsites, allotments and railway embankments of his childhood, so that it is hardly surprising that he finds 'wild nature very exciting, particularly when it is in a neglected state'.

Even when still at school, he went to evening and Saturday morning art classes. He then studied at Hornsey College of Art 1960–63. The college curriculum set aside one day a week for studying natural form (sunflowers and the like) and another day a week for outdoor drawing, which was unusual at the time. This appealed to John who often went to paint in the greenhouses of the college grounds. He won several awards including the College Sketch Club Prize.

In 1962 he exhibited with the Young Contemporaries, when David Hockney, Patrick Caulfield and other Pop artists were making their debut. His painting in a mystical ('Blake-like') style was quite different from theirs, but is said to have been praised by Anthony Caro at the Young Contemporaries Forum. John's style then was entirely symbolist (influenced by his work in stained glass) and not much like his present manner – except in its subject, *The Expulsion from the Garden of Eden.*

After art college he studied at Newcastle and later at Middlesex University, using his qualifications to teach but painting at the same time. He became very interested in education and there was a time when he was tempted to do a PhD, but decided against the idea when he realised it would affect the time he had to paint.

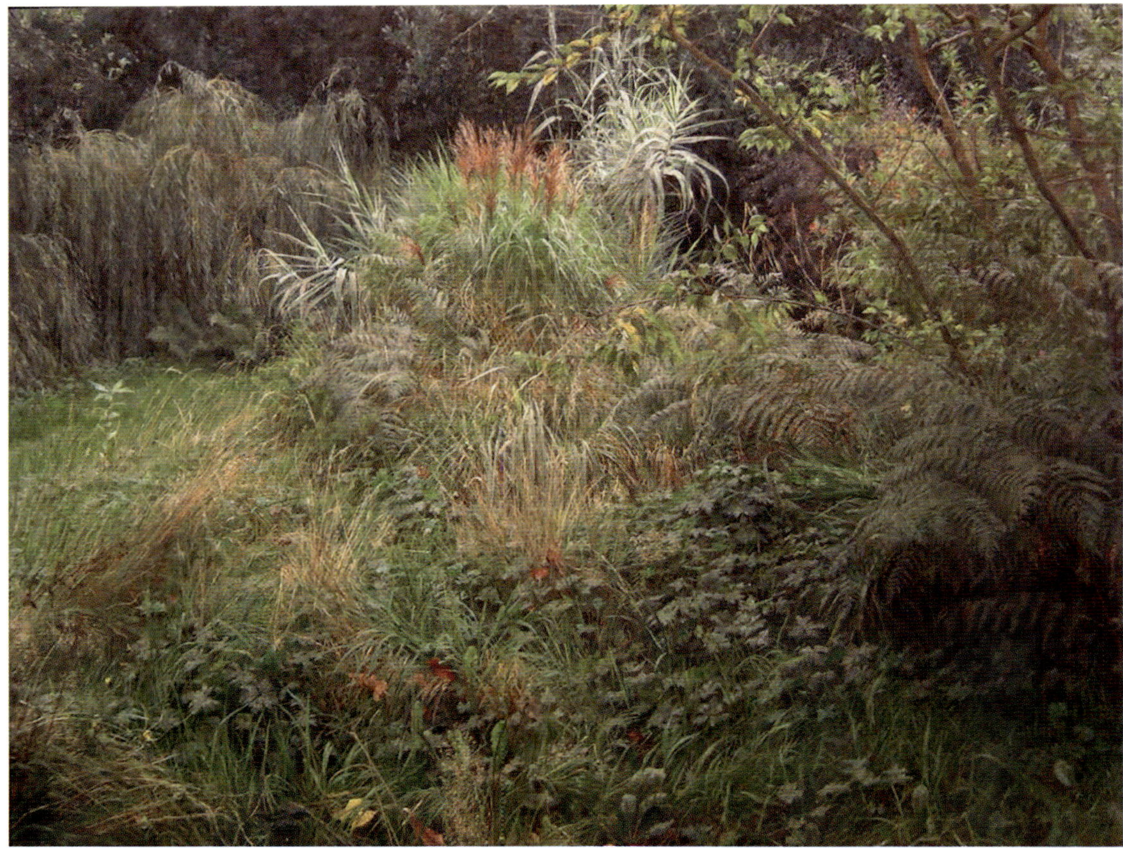

John Pearce, *A Half-wild Garden near Kenwood,* 2004, oil on canvas, 30 × 40in. COURTESY: FRANCIS KYLE GALLERY

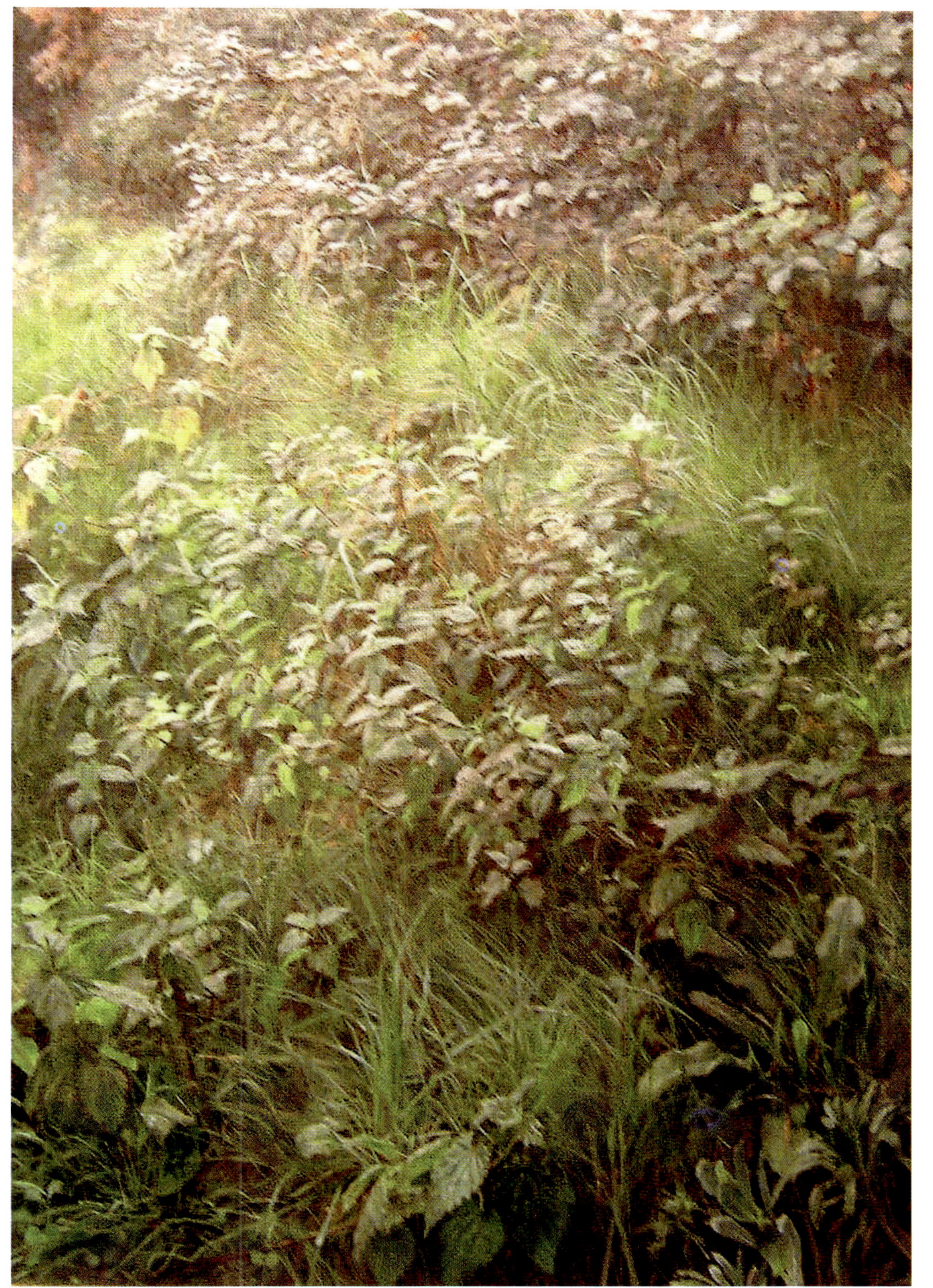

John Pearce, *Nettles in Long Grass*, 2006, oil on canvas, 32 × 24in.
COURTESY: FRANCIS KYLE GALLERY

While teaching at a Tottenham school in North London the pupils asked John to do their portraits. He enjoyed the direct interaction between himself and his subject – 'the reality of myself and what I was looking at' without trying to analyse or philosophise – and adopted a straightforward approach. He found himself becoming imperceptibly more realistic and visual, and this is a key factor in his present work.

In the 1980s, John began to have a measure of success, his work featuring in the *Spirit of London* exhibition at the Royal Festival Hall in which he was a prizewinner and the picture became part of the Permanent Collection at the Guildhall. He also showed at the National Portrait Gallery in the *John Player Portrait Award* exhibition. So, in 1984, he decided he could survive by painting full-time and put on a show that sold well. Around this time he had a couple of paintings in the Royal Academy Summer Show which sold immediately. Then followed a decade when he had a contract with the Church Street Gallery in Stow-on-the-Wold. In the 1990s, when his wife became ill and they had just bought a house near the sea in Normandy, he found himself under a certain amount of financial pressure, so once again he returned to teaching.

It was through teaching that he met up with a long-lost friend who introduced him to Francis Kyle. He has now been associated with this London gallery since 1998 and as a result been able to devote himself entirely to painting. 'It was a bit slow at first,' but it took off when the Francis Kyle Gallery had a theme exhibition *The Art of Memory: Contemporary Painters in Search of Marcel Proust*. Several of the place names in the area where John has his Normandy house occur in *A la Recherche du Temps Perdu*. He had six pictures in the exhibition and they all sold.

When the Tate Britain exhibition *Art of the Garden* took place in 2004 the vast majority of paintings shown were by artists from past eras. John was one of the few present-day artists and his work was featured in the section *The Secret Garden* where the emphasis was on intimacy and introspection. Martin Postle, in his article about this part of the exhibition, discussed the

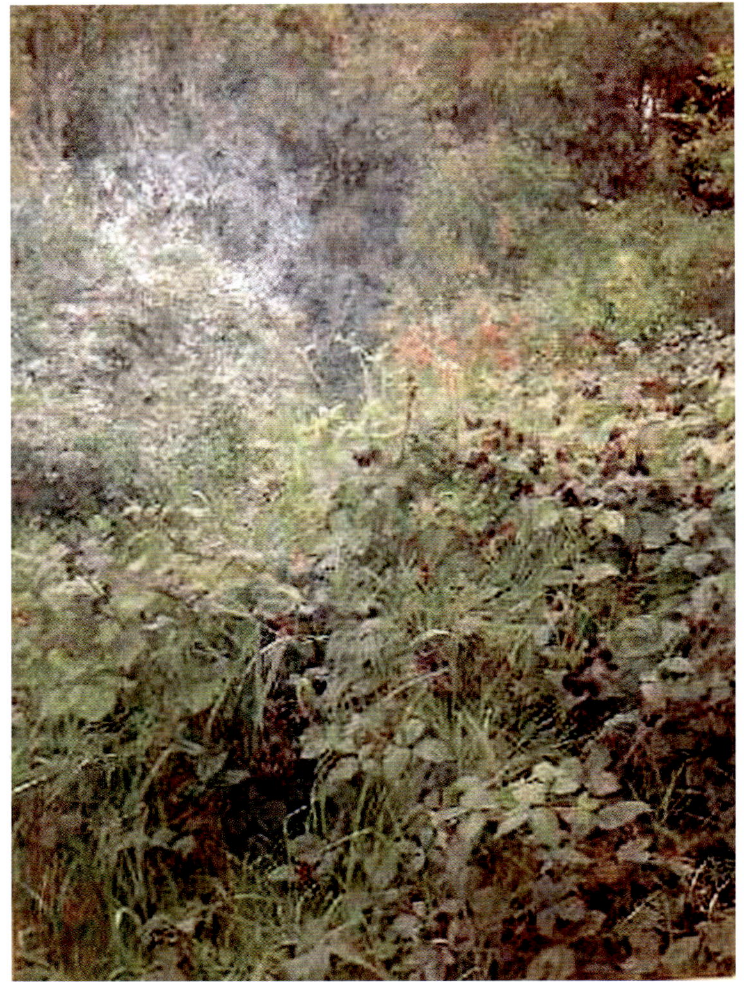

John Pearce, *Brambles in a London Garden*, 2001, oil on canvas, 40.5 × 30.5in. COURTESY: FRANCIS KYLE GALLERY

FACING PAGE John Pearce, *Poppy, Mint and Vine*, 2004, oil on canvas, 18⅛ × 24in. COURTESY: FRANCIS KYLE GALLERY

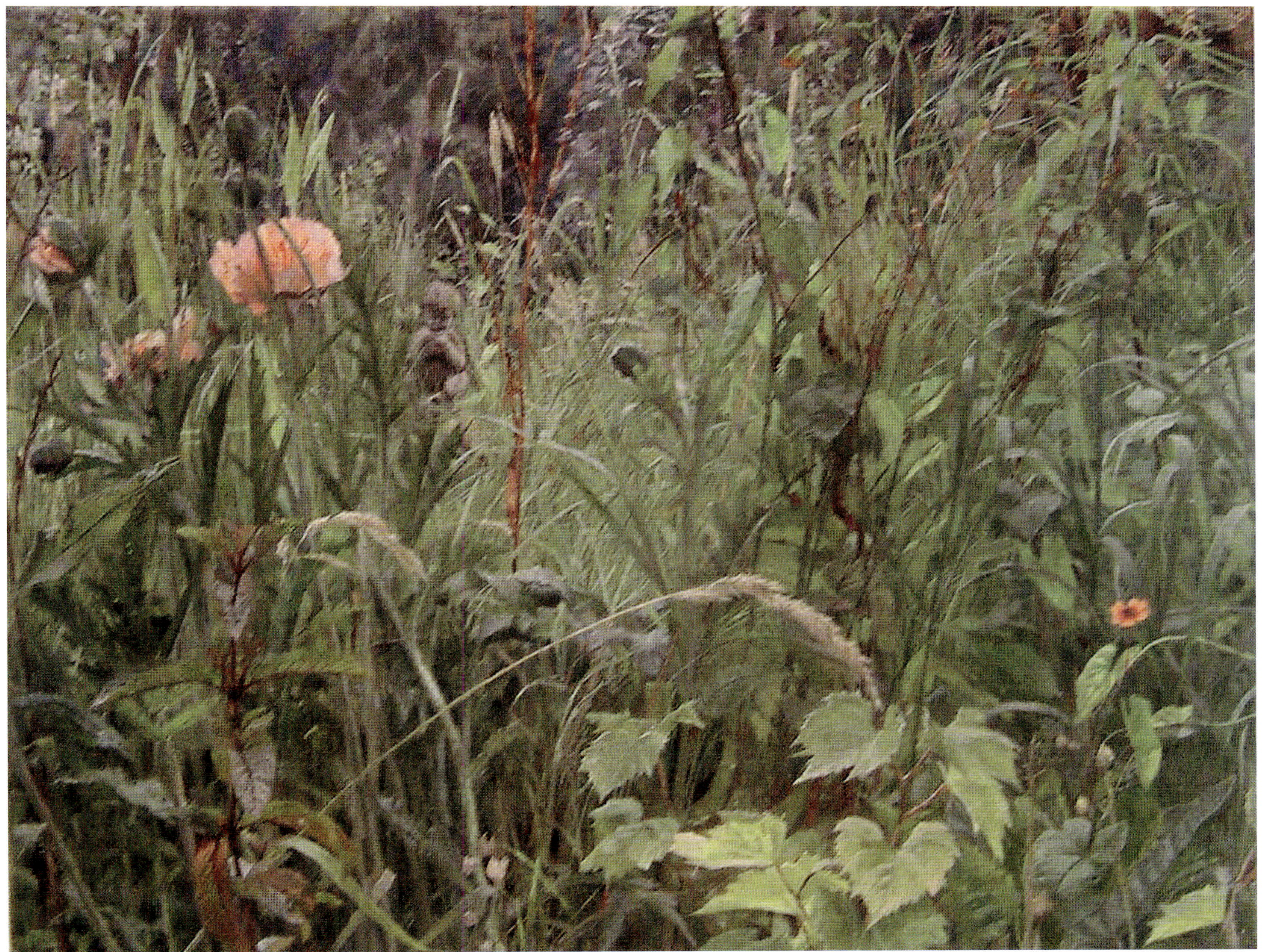

emotional attachment of the painter to the garden and how the garden provided a private world for the artist to retreat into. Two other painters whose work also appeared in *The Secret Garden* were Lucian Freud and Samuel Palmer, two artists whom John enormously admires. Lucian Freud talks of maintaining the drama in a painting by giving all the information he can. John has a similar attitude and interestingly enough both artists work entirely from direct observation, often excluding the sky so as not to distract from plant life and vegetation. 'Nevertheless, neither Freud nor I always exclude the sky. It is often seen indirectly, mirrored in the waxy shine on a leaf surface. This is particularly noticeable in Freud's *Two Plants* which the Tate purchased in 1980; also (on chestnut leaves) in my *Clement's Garden* (1987) and (on ivy leaves) in my *Interior, North London.*'

The unique feature of John's work is that he only ever works from direct observation on location in intimate proximity with his subject. On average, a picture will take six to eight weeks, though he has recorded taking five hundred hours. The approximate size is generally 4ft × 5ft 4in. In order to be able to work outside all the time, John erects a transparent awning over his easel allowing him to work in all conditions including the rainy light which prevails in Britain and northern France. During such a long period flowers come and go, leaves unfurl or fade and a clump of grass may grow rampantly or become limp with the effect of the sun. This is, in effect, what his paintings are all about. He does not purport to produce a single representation of a garden, the emphasis is on the process of observation. His subject matter is generally Victorian gardens in urban areas partly in a state of neglect. The favoured plants are brambles, bindweed, nettles, cow parsley and grass. 'Grass has something wonderful about the way it grows, what it does with light, its relation to the space around it and other plants and how it is affected by rain.'

John generally begins painting sometime during February, finding that the earlier in the year he gets to work the better. Although he never uses photographs for his pictures, he uses them to record the progression of a picture, during the days, weeks and seasons of its progress. Amongst these photographs are a few showing him wearing gloves, hat and heavy jacket for the more inclement parts of the year! He talks of 'standing in a stream flowing from a patio' or 'working on a sloping bank' and 'often starting at first light and going on into the dusk', constantly readjusting values over the whole picture – resourcefulness is clearly all important.

Essentially John works from background to foreground, building up interlaced layers of foliage. There are areas of intense depth and solemnity which move into areas of vivid brilliancy of light and shade. This has the effect of also implying movement through time. His style consists of observational drawings carried out in paint, thereby catching the animation and intensity of plant life in a passage of time. In Samuel Palmer's words, they are 'visions of little dells and nooks and corners of Paradise'.

Most of the paintings are in a colour range of pink to green with a wide range of cool greens and warm greens which can convey the effect of damp cobwebs or sunlit leaves. He has a very opaque green, oxide of chromium, which is essential to him as it helps the brushwork of overlapping foliage.

John writes quite detailed accounts of the progress of his work, and in these accounts are references to classical music and other painters he admires – Graham Sutherland, Samuel Palmer, Lucian Freud, Stanley Spencer and his favourite, William Blake. His comments are intuitive and discerning and give an insight into the more complex thought processes that are hidden behind these pictures. To quote John, 'The paintings seek, and are motivated by, a level of quintessential experience beyond thought.'

FACING PAGE John Pearce, *Interior, North London*, 1999, oil on canvas, 18 × 24in.
COURTESY: FRANCIS KYLE GALLERY

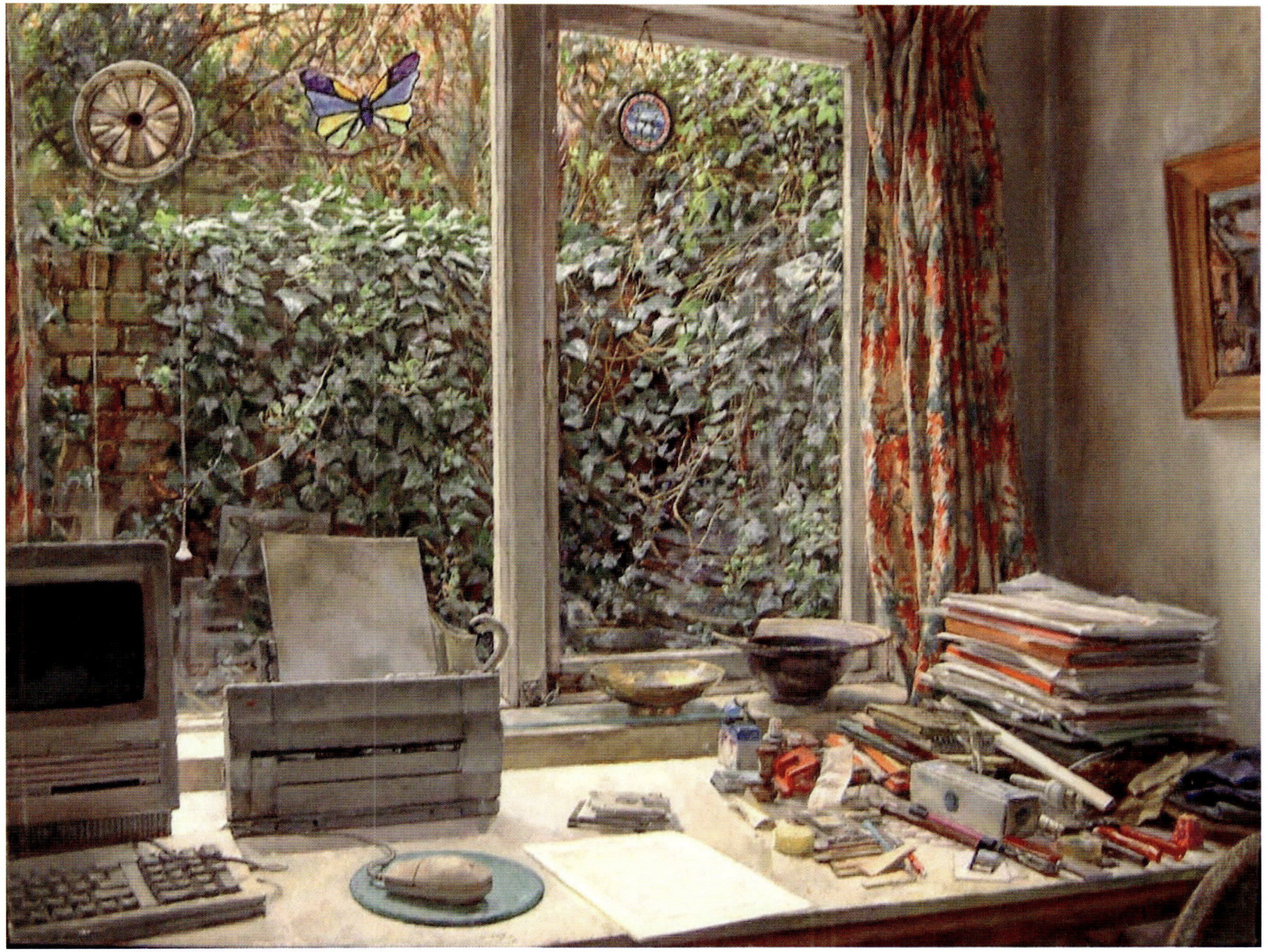

Ramiro Fernández Saus

In September 2007 my daughter, a sculptor, and I went to the British Art Fair at the Royal College of Art. I was much attracted to the work of an artist being shown by the Long & Ryle Gallery. Sarah Long then showed me a catalogue of the work of Ramiro Fernández Saus, and I was instantly captivated by the delightful humour evident in some of the pictures.

Ramiro studied painting at the Académia de Belles Arts in a small industrial town, once dominated by the garment industry, called Sabadell, not far from Barcelona, Spain. In his pictures you can sometimes glimpse factory chimneys pumping fumes into the air. Ever since graduating, he has had an impressive list of one-man shows and has taken part in many group exhibitions not only in Spain but also in London, Lisbon, Buenos Aires, France, Italy and Holland. He is now a well-known and respected artist in Spain and clearly gaining an international reputation elsewhere.

Sarah Long and Carolyn Ryle-Hodges first noticed Ramiro's work in 1989 when he won a scholarship to study for a year at the Delfina Studios in London. While in London, he became a friend of Craigie Aitchison (a member of the Royal Academy of Art) – two painters of different eras, each admiring the other's work. The Long & Ryle Gallery then included Ramiro in a group show of Spanish artists in 1990 and he has continued to have one-man shows there on a regular basis, gathering a most enthusiastic following 'who react strongly to his catalogues so that there is something of a rush to his shows.' There is clearly a close and constructive relationship between the gallery and the artist.

While Ramiro was studying in London he became very fond of the West Country, becoming captivated by the English trees. His paintings of this period were all green landscapes – incredibly beautiful, charming and inventive with a billowy, operatic quality to them – luxuriant, leafy landscapes.

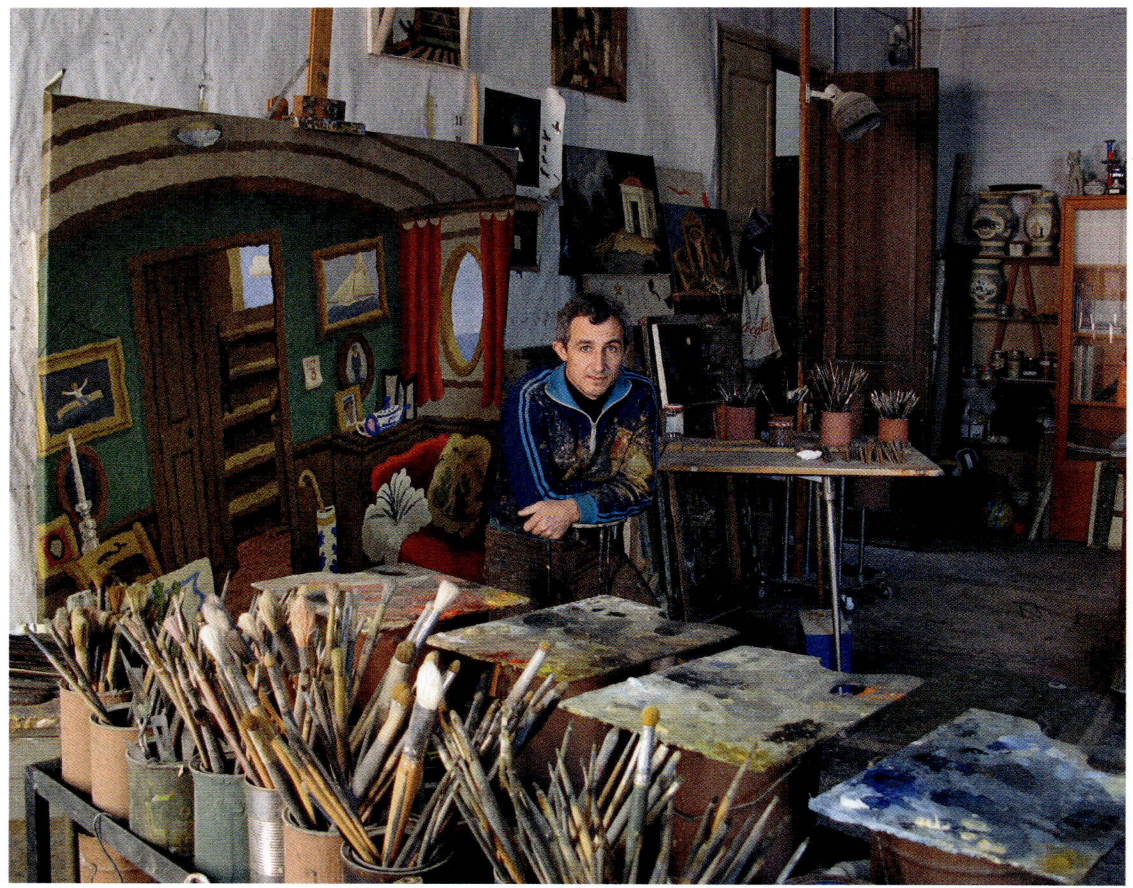

The Artist in his studio. PHOTO: FRANCESC ESTEVE

Since that time his shows have often been based on the idea of a journey, a new adventure. One of his shows was called *Travelling without Moving*. Ramiro is fully versed in the history of painting and there are indications of various influences, but it is his frequent visits to the American continent and the Caribbean that have provided the stimulus responsible for the tropical references and the naïve quality of his work. This is a self-sufficient world, an imaginary space where there are tigers, zebras and exotic coloured characters depicted in a very unique and personal manner. He himself often appears in the pictures and there are many other objects from his own daily life that make up this dream world.

It is interesting to look back at his paintings of the early 1990s and observe the subtle development since. At that time the brushwork was quivering, wavering and with less precise outlines, indicating his admiration for Delacroix and the German Neo-Expressionists, whereas now the outlines have an almost tapestry-like quality. He appears to paint to a certain line and then change colour to yet another line. This is evident in *The Roman Villa* with the distinct definition and wavy shapes of the trees. It's as if with increased assurance he has steadily clarified his brushstrokes – the shapes are simple, but there is a sense of trembling surfaces which give a jolly and seductive countenance to the images. Tree trunks are chunky, the grass is thick and hedges are wide.

His colours have also changed. Originally they were darker and more sombre conveying a romantic intensity and gloomy atmosphere. In the more recent work, as he has gained confidence, there are solid blocks of colour and altogether brighter tones. In *Happy Days* the roof of a factory situated in the background is a vibrant orange and the sky a luminous blue. The outline of the maze in *Butterfly Collector* is not a dark green but a rippling orange – no dappled reflections here! Other paintings contain some glorious reds and a mass of vivid colour which convey a feeling of bright summer.

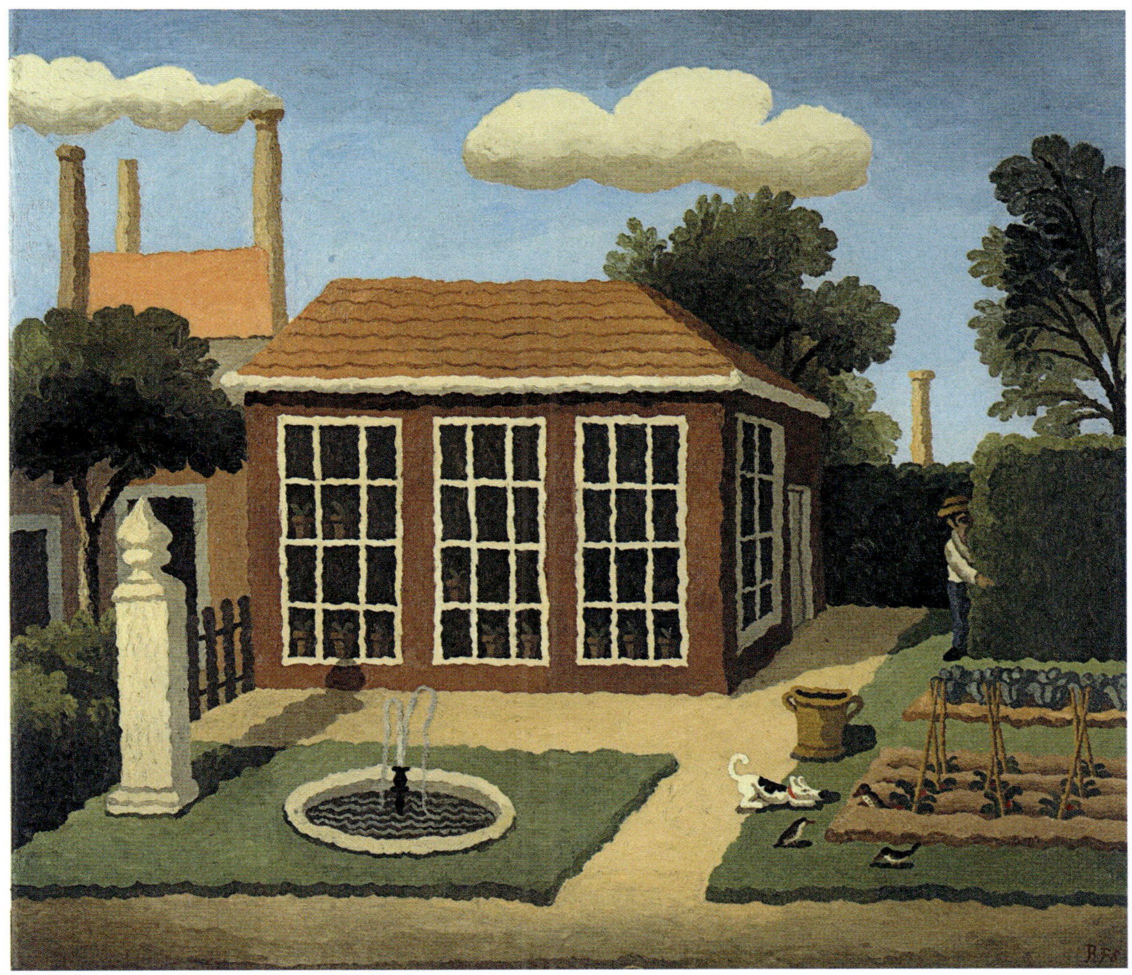

Ramiro Fernández Saus, *Happy Days*, 2006, oil on canvas, 80 × 94cm.
COURTESY: LONG & RYLE

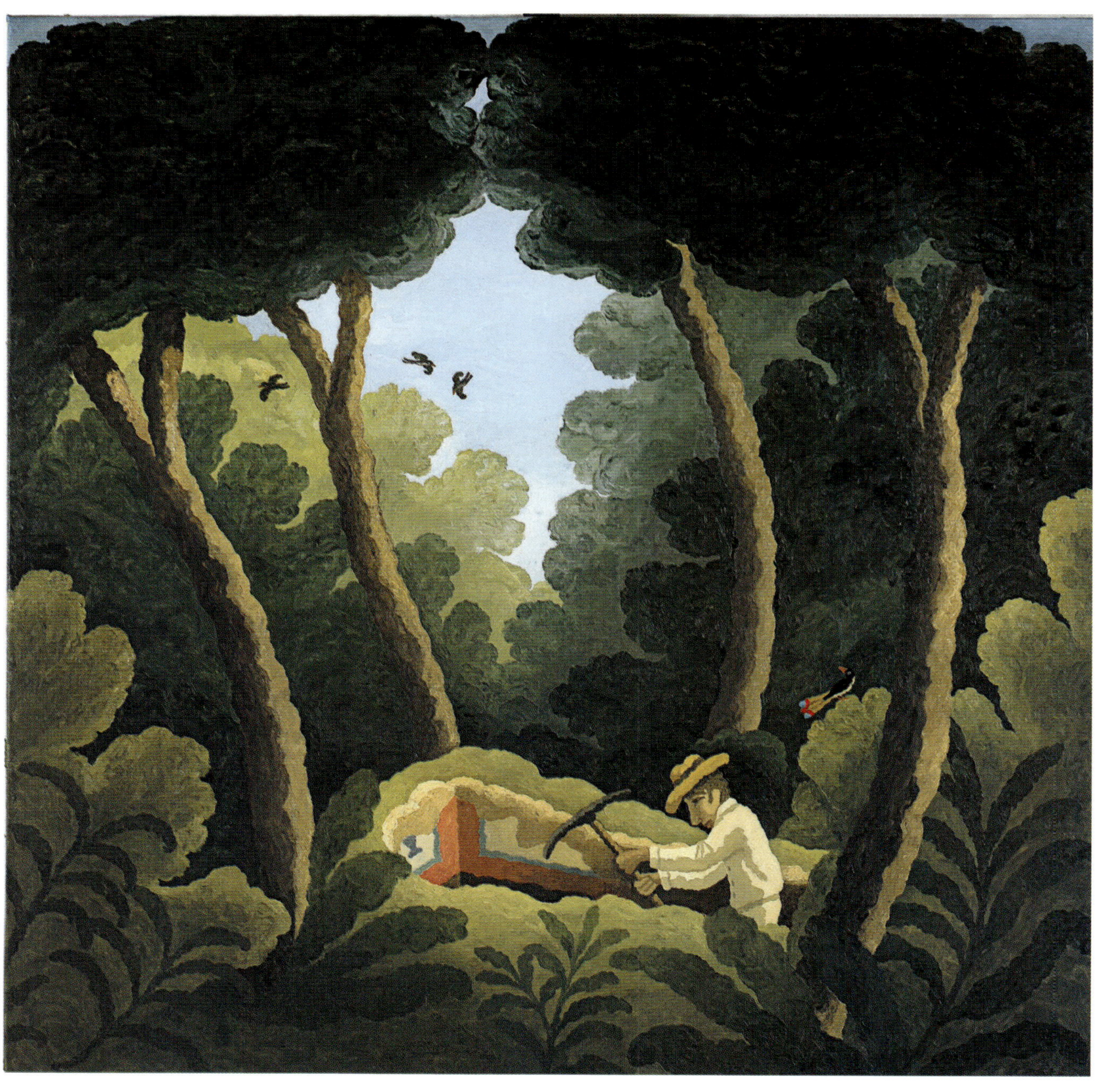

Ramiro Fernández Saus, *The Roman Villa*, 2006, oil on canvas, 172 × 176cm. COURTESY: LONG & RYLE

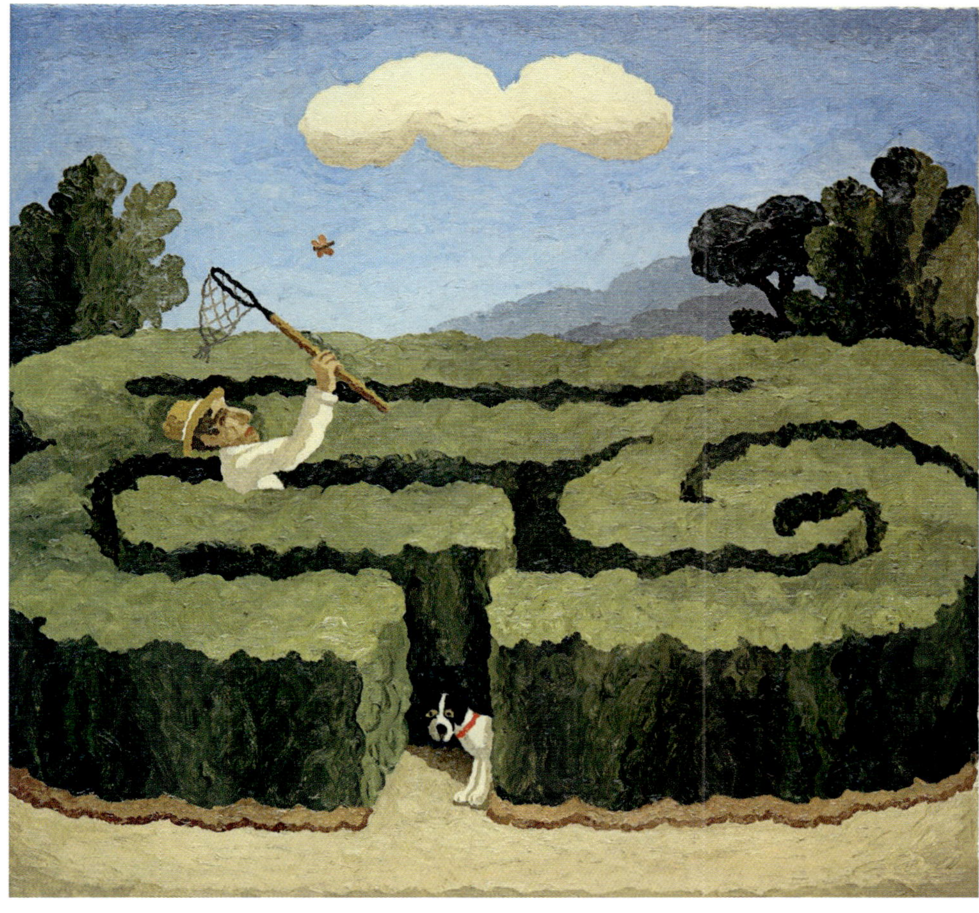

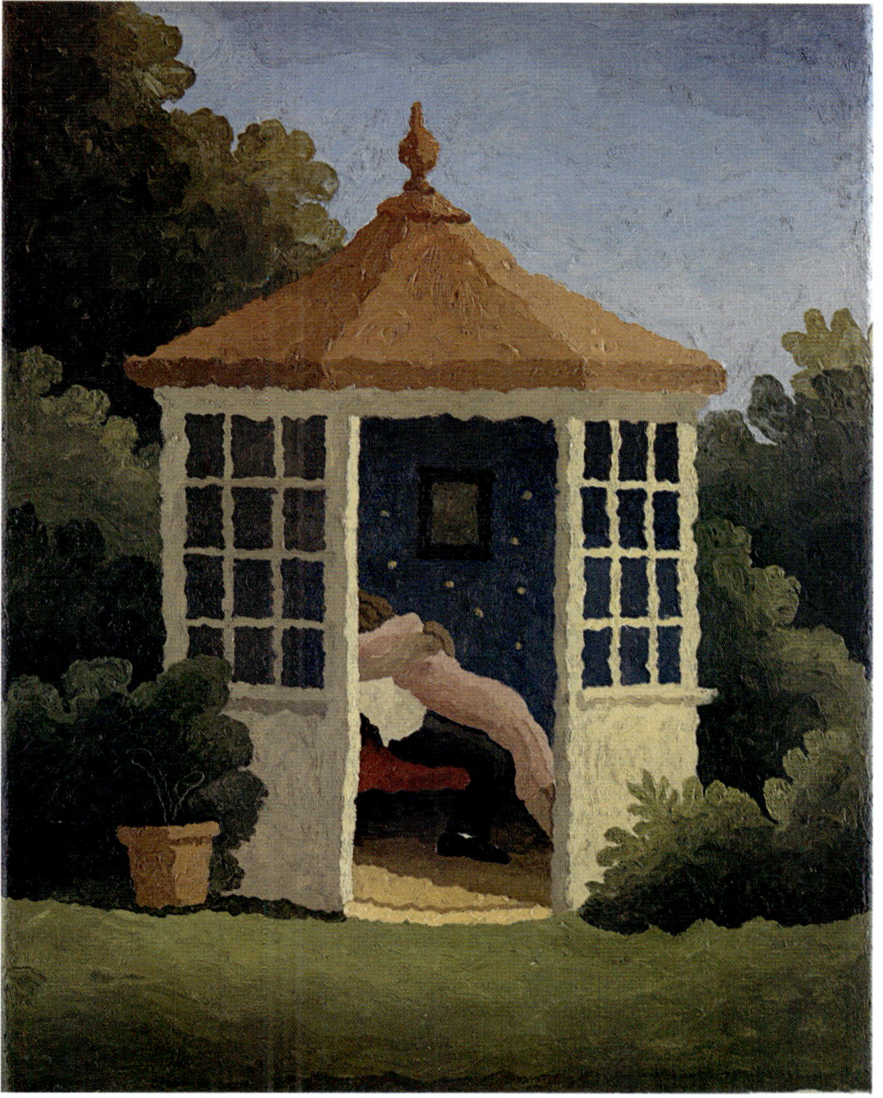

Ramiro Fernández Saus, *Butterfly Collector*, 2006, oil on canvas, 44 × 47cm.
COURTESY: LONG & RYLE

RIGHT Ramiro Fernández Saus, *La Joie de Vivre*, 2006, oil on canvas, 46 × 36cm.
COURTESY: LONG & RYLE

Ramiro's studio is a vast attic room which tapers off into a high tiled roof with small windows high above the rafters. There are countless pots full of sticky brushes, many tables, lamps and chairs of different heights, and inevitably paintings and sketches in abundance mingled with his ceramic sculptures. There are also his large, careful and precise oil sketches in A1 and A2 sizes where he outlines the colour changes in the manner of a stained-glass window. He most often paints at night and it is not hard to imagine him in this cosy world creating another exotic reverie. The studio is situated in Sabadell where there is still evidence of the textile factories, one of which belonged to the painter's family. He has exhibited at the Museu d'Art de Sabadell, once a rich merchant's house, and in his pictures he often includes some of the nineteenth-century trappings of the industrial bourgeoisie. The curtains have tassels, fringes and pelmets, the walls are covered with heavily framed works of art, even the same rich reds make an appearance. This is a very autobiographical world with interiors reminiscent of those that Ramiro grew up with, and similar to many that can still be found in Sabadell.

Simon Day wrote, 'Seeing Ramiro[' s work] for the first time I instantly started smiling.' In such paintings as the *Gardener* there is a charm that verges on the jolly. By keeping details to the minimum, he is able to convey a sense of a happy soul and there is no sign of cynicism or frustration. There is a warmth and sense of romance – a couple kissing under a moonlit sky in Italy or in a garden gazebo. There is always the presence of cats, a dog, a monkey, which the painter once owned, and, of course, the tiger which comes and goes in many a scene. Other objects which make an appearance are books, ceramics and, indeed, his own paintings. All this conveys a contented domestic world where life seems pleasurable and serene. There is an interaction between the exteriors and interiors. Night skies full of stars come into the bedroom, leafy, luxuriant landscapes

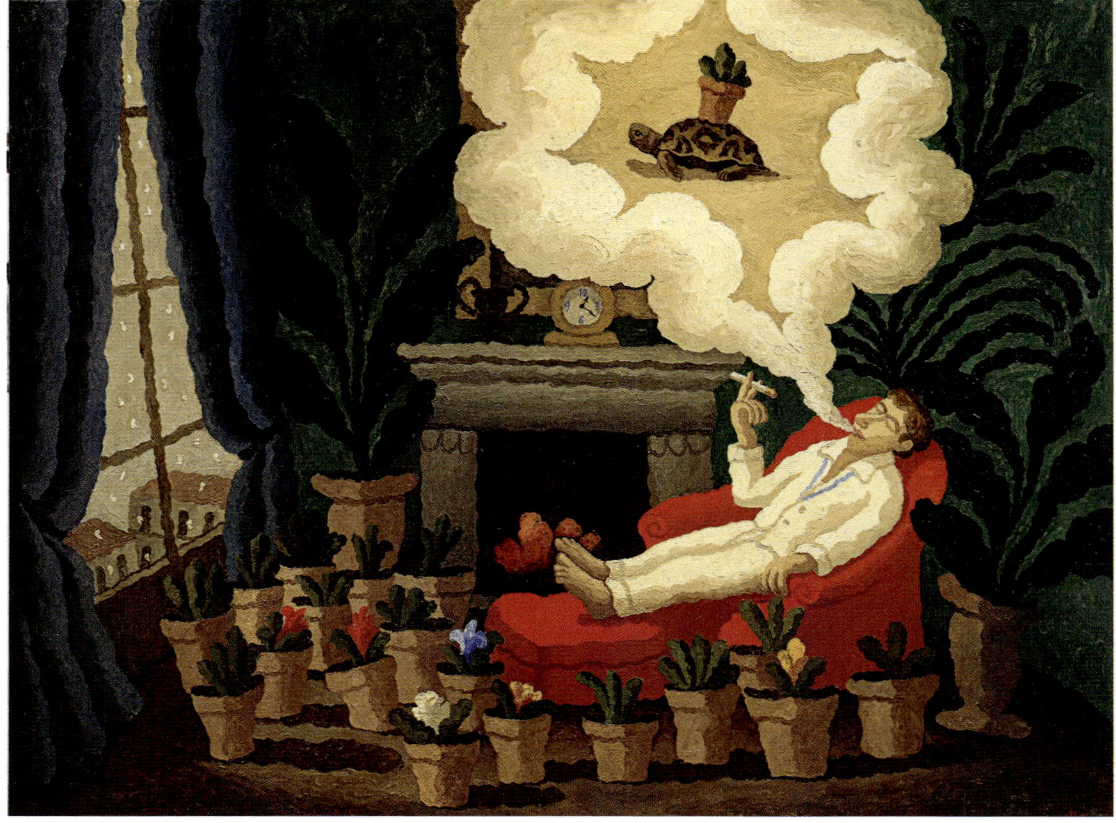

Ramiro Fernández Saus, *Les Paradis Artificiels*, 2005, oil on canvas, 120 × 158cm.
COURTESY: LONG & RYLE

decorate entire walls and often large windows are open to shapely clouds. Even so there is always an underlying robust structure which enables Ramiro to communicate an idea clearly. One of his recent exhibitions was entitled *Joie de Vivre* and another *The Garden of Eden*. Certainly the atmosphere appears relaxed and the spaces peaceful, but as Sarah Long says 'he is always coming up with completely new ideas so it's hard to know what he will do next.'

John Shelley

John Shelley's work came to my attention as a result of the exhibition *Art in the Garden* at Tate Britain in 2004. It interested me that we had both studied at Wimbledon School of Art with the same principal, Gerald Cooper.

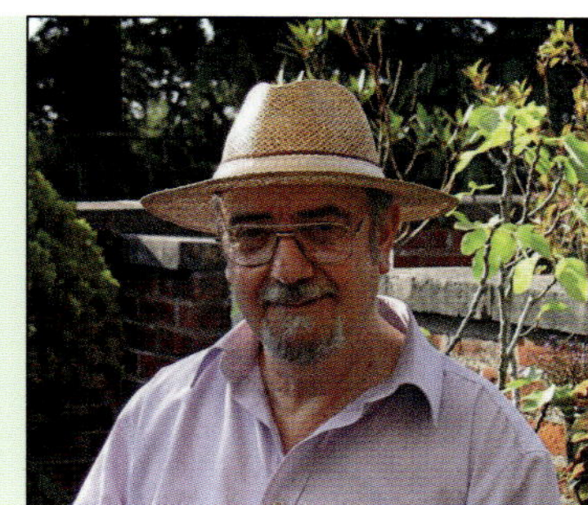

The Artist. PHOTO: ANGELA WILLIAMS

John has lived and worked virtually all his life in Surrey allowing his imagination to transform his observations into a kind of earthly paradise. The sun shines, the windows are open and the flowers bloom as if freshly opened. It comes as no surprise that Stanley Spencer and Samuel Palmer are two artists he greatly admires. Stanley Spencer had in many ways the same work ethic, for he also lived and worked virtually all his life in and around a similar environment. In fact when Shelley was on a student trip he met Stanley Spencer painting in the churchyard at Cookham. 'He was nice and offered me a Spangle.' Both painters depict the imaginary garden of the mind. Even the figures, often dressed in white, have an elusive detached quality about them.

It's interesting to discover that John developed this nostalgic vision very early on in his career, but then he also started out to train as a painter at a young age. At school he had a master who extended the hours spent studying art to fifteen per week, very unusual at that time and virtually unknown today. So it was relatively early when he chose to be an artist regardless of the fact that there was no particular family interest in the subject.

His school art master arranged for John to be interviewed for Wimbledon School of Art at the age of fifteen, where he stayed for five years. The course followed the traditional routines of that period – drawing from plaster casts, life drawing, portraiture and some imaginative painting. The principal, Gerald Cooper, recognised his talent and very much encouraged him to follow on to the Slade and Royal Academy Schools

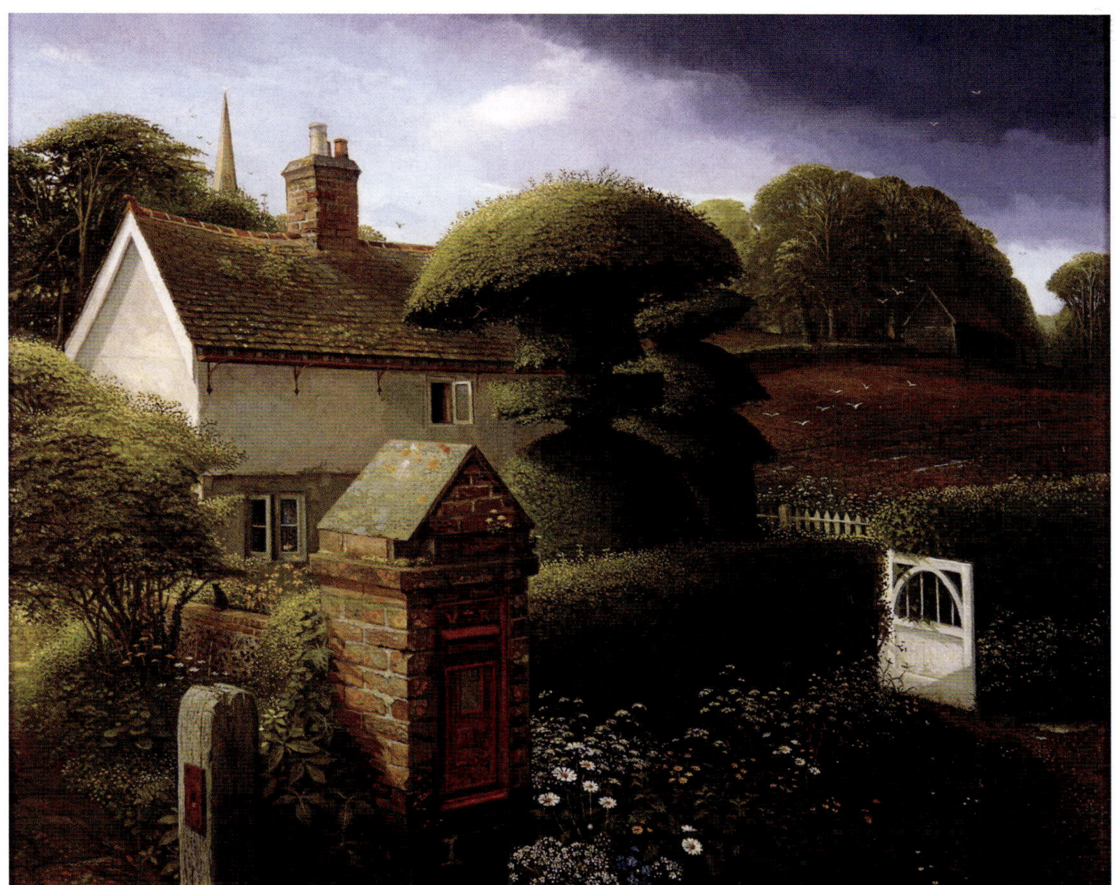

John Shelley, *Post Box Cottage*, 1989 , oil on board, 24 × 30in. PHOTO: HARRY SNELLING

although he only completed a term at each. 'I had a good time at Wimbledon and remember it fondly' and Gerald Cooper 'knew I would succeed', as indeed he did by winning the David Murray prize for a landscape picture at the Academy Schools.

This period was followed by consistent showing in the Summer Show at the Royal Academy from 1968–80 and again from 1988–92, where his work sold immediately, on every occasion. In 1968 the Tate Gallery acquired the entirely invented painting *Annunciation*.

At that time the bookshop owner, Christina Foyle, noticed his work and gave him an exhibition. This was followed by five years of showing at the Trafford Gallery, 1970–75, where he consistently sold out – in these five years he only had one picture returned. Since then John has been showing at Mandell's in Norwich (for thirty years). From here certain families have consistently collected or commissioned his work. Among these are the Roux brothers who originally hung one of his pictures at their restaurant Le Gavroche. At the time of writing, a gallery in London's Albemarle Street is negotiating a one-man show.

A first look at John's work makes it easy to suppose that images are of specific locations. In fact, they are taken from a variety of sources, both real and imagined. A cottage or church may be loosely modelled on a particular observation but the actual composition is created as the painting evolves. Shelley does not use photographs or draw on location, but makes small, loose pencil compositions in order to select an initial design for the picture. Then he makes adjustments and changes as the work progresses. In some cases the background may be changed years later.

Certain flowers appear again and again, mainly those that bloom in summer – Michaelmas daisies (asters), chrysanthemums, rudbeckias and heleniums. The plants themselves look vigorous, upright, well watered and in their prime. In one of Mandell's catalogues, John was described as being able to 'capture in pictures that very special pastoral, almost surreal vision of the English countryside, which had its birth with the visionary works of William Blake, Edward Calvert and Samuel Palmer.'

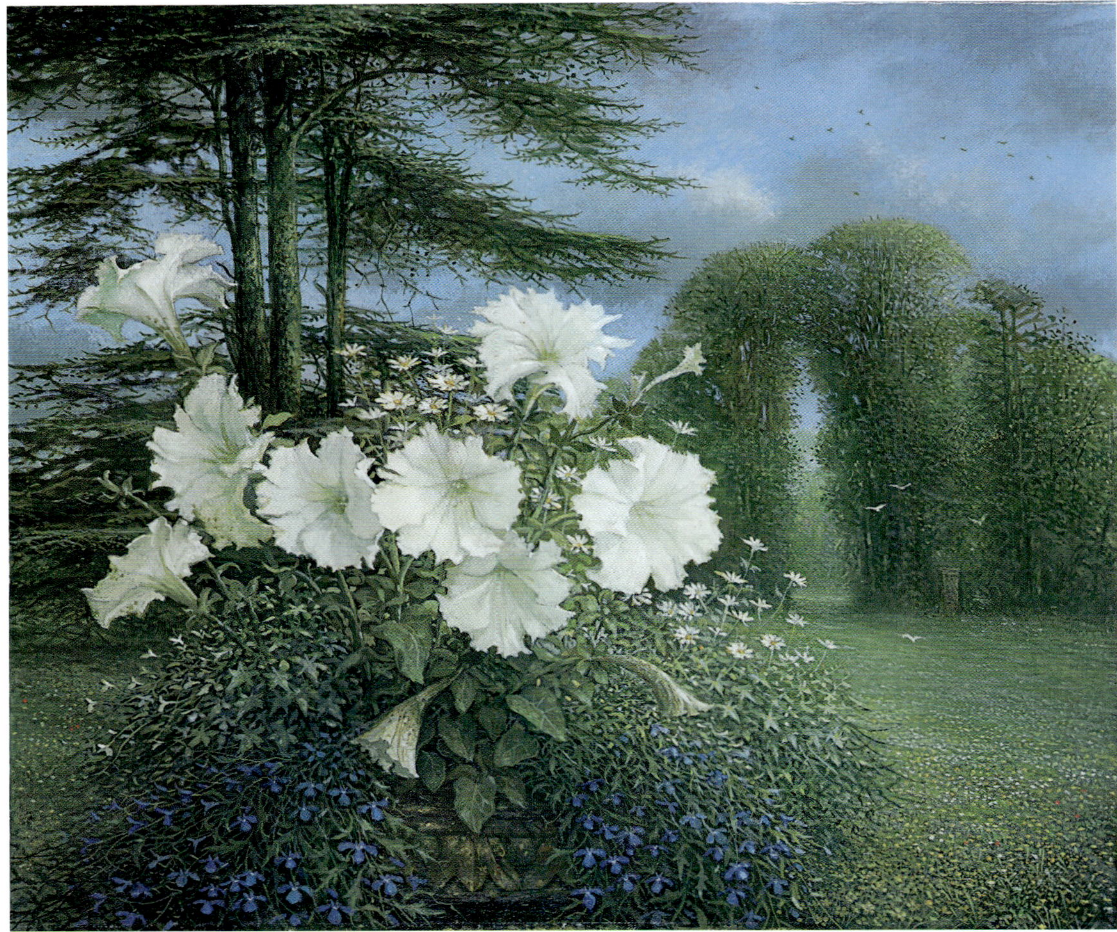

John Shelley, *In a Garden*, 1997, oil on canvas, 20 × 24in.
PHOTO: MILES WINTER

FACING PAGE John Shelley, *Manor Garden*, 2004, oil on board, 18 × 24in.
PHOTO: MILES WINTER

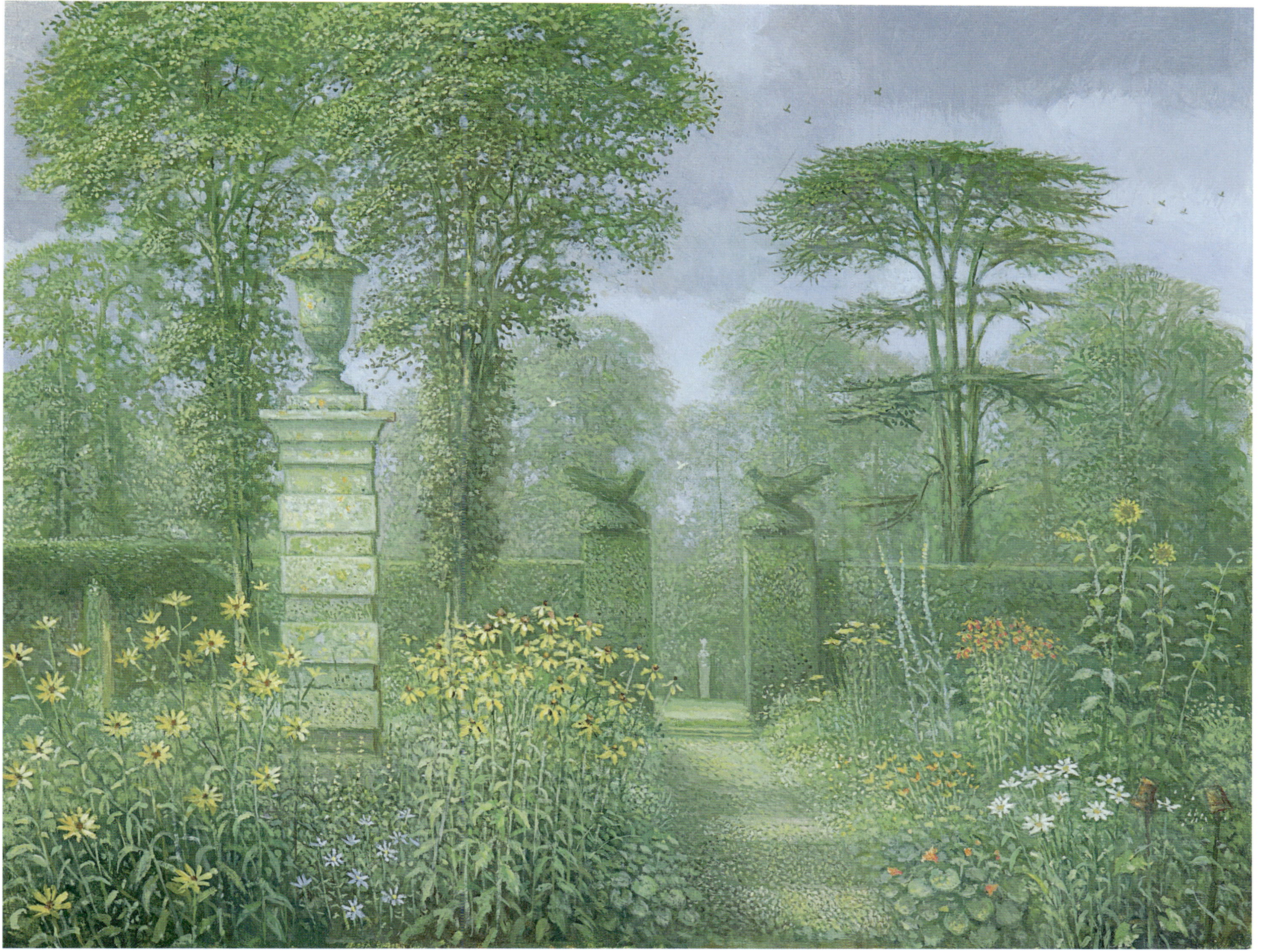

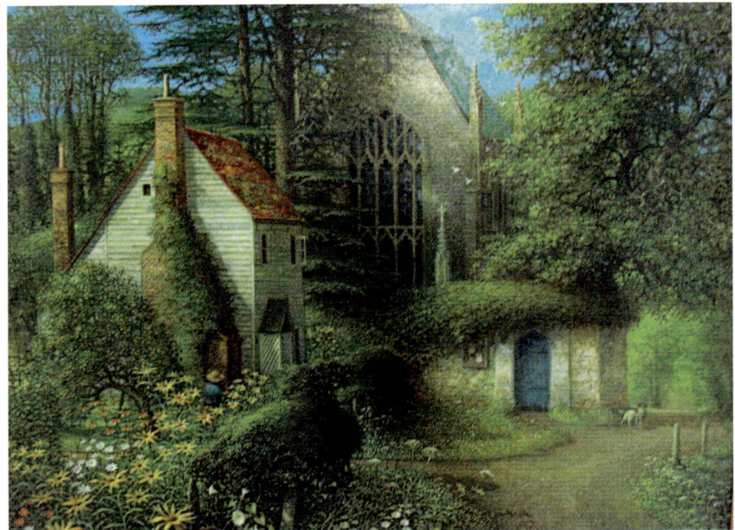

John Shelley, detail from *September Afternoon*, 1995, oil on board, 28 × 36in. PHOTO: ANGELA WILLIAMS

RIGHT John Shelley, *Kentish Garden*, 1986, oil on board, 28 × 36in. PHOTO: MILES WINTER

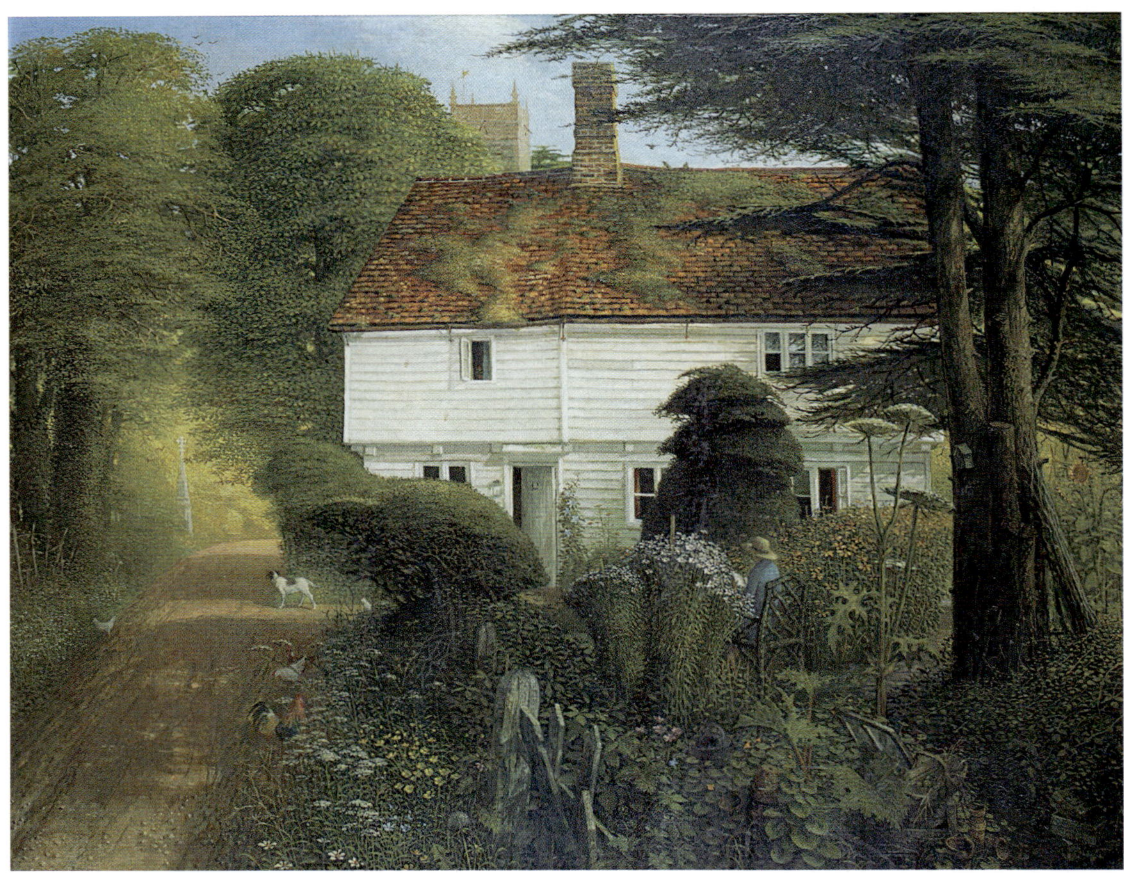

John paints two to three pictures a year, taking two or three months for each. They are executed on hardboard (a popular surface in art school days of the 1960s), and varnished with a mixture of matt and gloss after about six months 'but the longer you can leave a painting before varnishing it the better.' He starts a new work with enormous enthusiasm and 'goes like a train', painting very much in the manner that he devised years ago at art school. He is sufficiently self-assured about his work to act as his own critic. The paintings depict an idyllic refuge and show a calm stability at odds with this rapidly changing world. There is a consistent soft and atmospheric sunlight crossing these charming images.

Dick Smyly

The Oxfordshire-based garden designer Justin Spink is responsible for introducing me to Dick Smyly. He gave me a small brochure showing an unusual talent reminiscent of the English School of the eighteenth century.

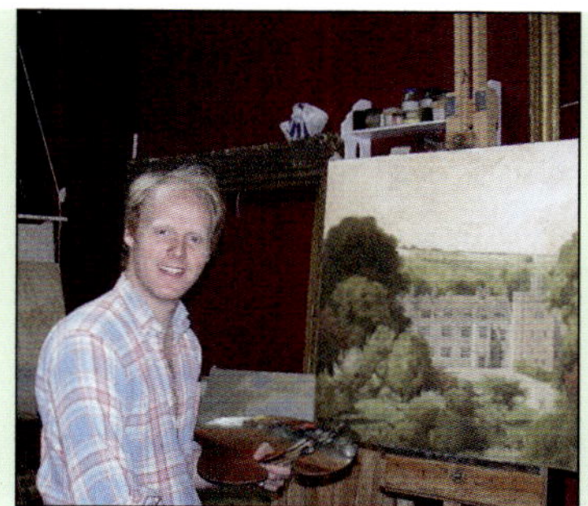

Artist painting. PHOTO: HETTIE SMYLY

Looking at Dick's work you can see that the artists who influenced him belong to the classical eras, 'Van Dyck being the ultimate, but then Rubens' landscapes are exquisite and I love Lawrence for the oiliness of his paint. He was technically superb. There are also Sargent and Romney for their firmness of stroke. I admire Canaletto for his draughtsmanship and crisp architecture and Fragonard for being able to create atmosphere. Otherwise there are Wilson and various other eighteenth-century painters with their fine detail of leaves and their capacity to create that little bit of magic. Galleries are a constant inspiration.' Recently, when Dick revisited the Scottish National Gallery for two hours he was astounded to find so much fresh inspiration, despite having been there many times before.

Dick's talent was evident early on as he won the Senior Art Prize at his prep school and then at Eton. He intended to study for a degree at Edinburgh University reading German, Italian and History of Art but, in his gap year (1991–92), he went to study in Florence at Charles Cecil's studio, which was set up about twenty years ago. This school follows in the tradition of the Ecole des Beaux Arts, Paris, of the 1920s, using its disciplines and techniques. The course was of three or four years' duration, but as Dick intended to go to university and was 'a young man in a hurry' he only did two terms before returning home. Nevertheless, he continued experimenting and using the school's techniques while at university. He ground colours, made varnishes 'which is such a performance' and practised the traditional methods of painting. At present he still tends to grind his own lead white, yellow ochre and occasionally other colours. Otherwise he uses Michael Harding oils.

Halfway through his first year at Edinburgh, he had a discussion with his parents about the feasibility of making a career as an artist. As they were very supportive, he finished his year and returned to Florence. He continued at his accelerated pace. He immediately started painting portraits and still life pictures whereas now the students generally draw for a year before painting. In order to build up some work he painted other students and friends until he'd acquired enough clients of his own. In all he studied in Florence for just over a year.

Based in London, he took portrait commissions. Since then, he has completed over 250 portraits in Britain and on the Continent, and has exhibited at the Royal Society of Portrait Painters. He then became interested in wildlife painting. Having been trained to work from life, he found that working from stuffed animals achieved a very realistic result. He acquired a collection including a 'pair of bonking foxes', and produced a sell-out exhibition.

Then in 2004 he painted a picture roughly based on a photograph of his parents' house and surroundings, inspired by eighteenth-century landscapes. 'After a second attempt I was really interested and excited, and thought maybe there is some scope in this.' With the help of a 'flyer' enough work was generated to start on an entirely new genre. 'Painting houses/gardens is often less stressful than painting portraits as you are

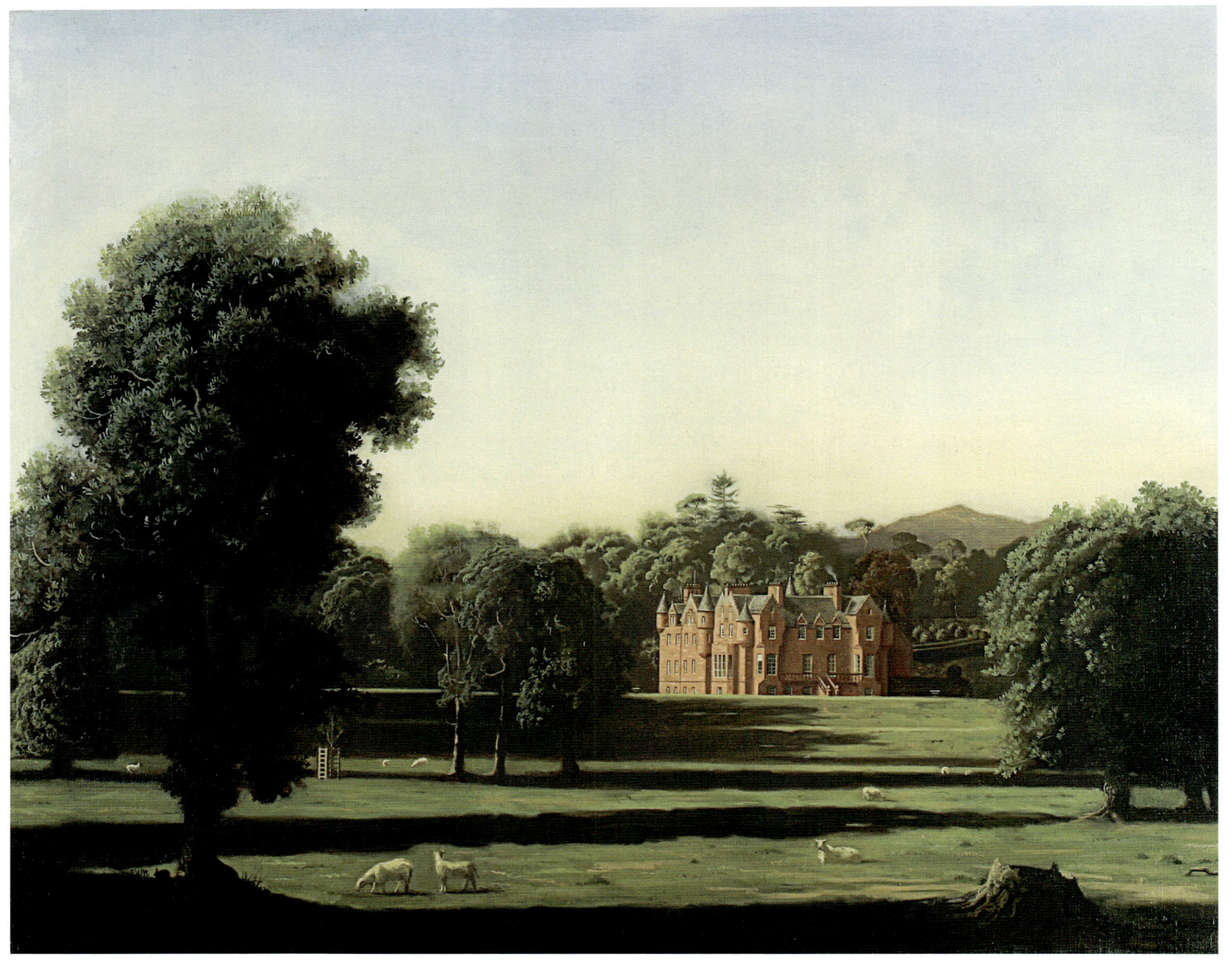

Dick Smyly, *A House in the Scottish Borders*, 2005, oil on canvas, 30 × 40in. PHOTO: NIALL MACDIARMID

FACING PAGE Dick Smyly, *A House and Garden in Ireland*, 2006, oil on canvas, 50 × 60in. PHOTO: NIALL MACDIARMID

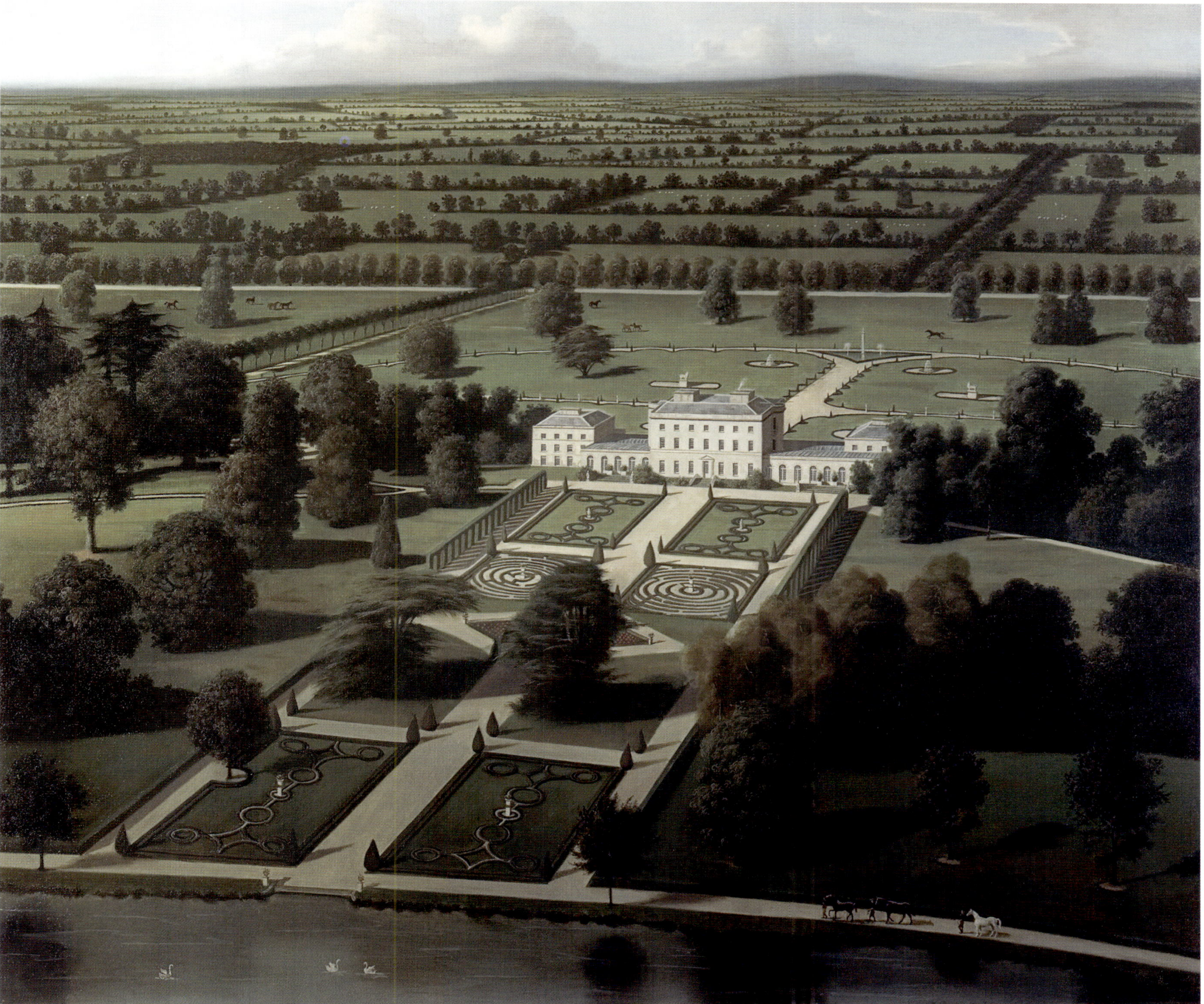

not pushing against time and there is more freedom to express yourself, to experiment with different light, skies and ways of silhouetting trees.'

Dick doesn't exhibit as he has enough work from word of mouth. There was a short article in *Country Life* which started the phone buzzing. Posted on one wall of his studio there is a map with pins showing where he has worked. In certain areas there are tight clusters indicating where the word of mouth has got about, but principally in and around London and South East England, and in Scotland.

To date he has done twenty to thirty pictures on the house/garden theme, but he has twelve to fifteen on his books and continues to take portrait commissions.

It is refreshing that Dick admits to being ambitious and to trying to hold his own financially with his contemporaries who have more conventional careers in, say, the City of London. This challenge entails becoming better paid and internationally known. To this end he concentrates on fewer, but better paintings that are breaking new ground. A good example being a recent work of an aerial view of a garden in Ireland. He cannot resist, however, doing smaller ones for friends on request.

Virtually all Dick's work is on commission. He begins a new work by wandering around and taking 'loads of photographs' for about a day. Occasionally he'll go back if he can't get the colour right or to check for details. The actual painting takes about a month if it's of average size, which is probably approximately 30 × 40 inches. 'The problem with working in the open is that the sun is always moving round and the dust gets on your palette and then there is the temperamental weather. After all, Canaletto used his camera obscura to get a rough outline and then returned to his studio to try to do as Guy de Maupassant

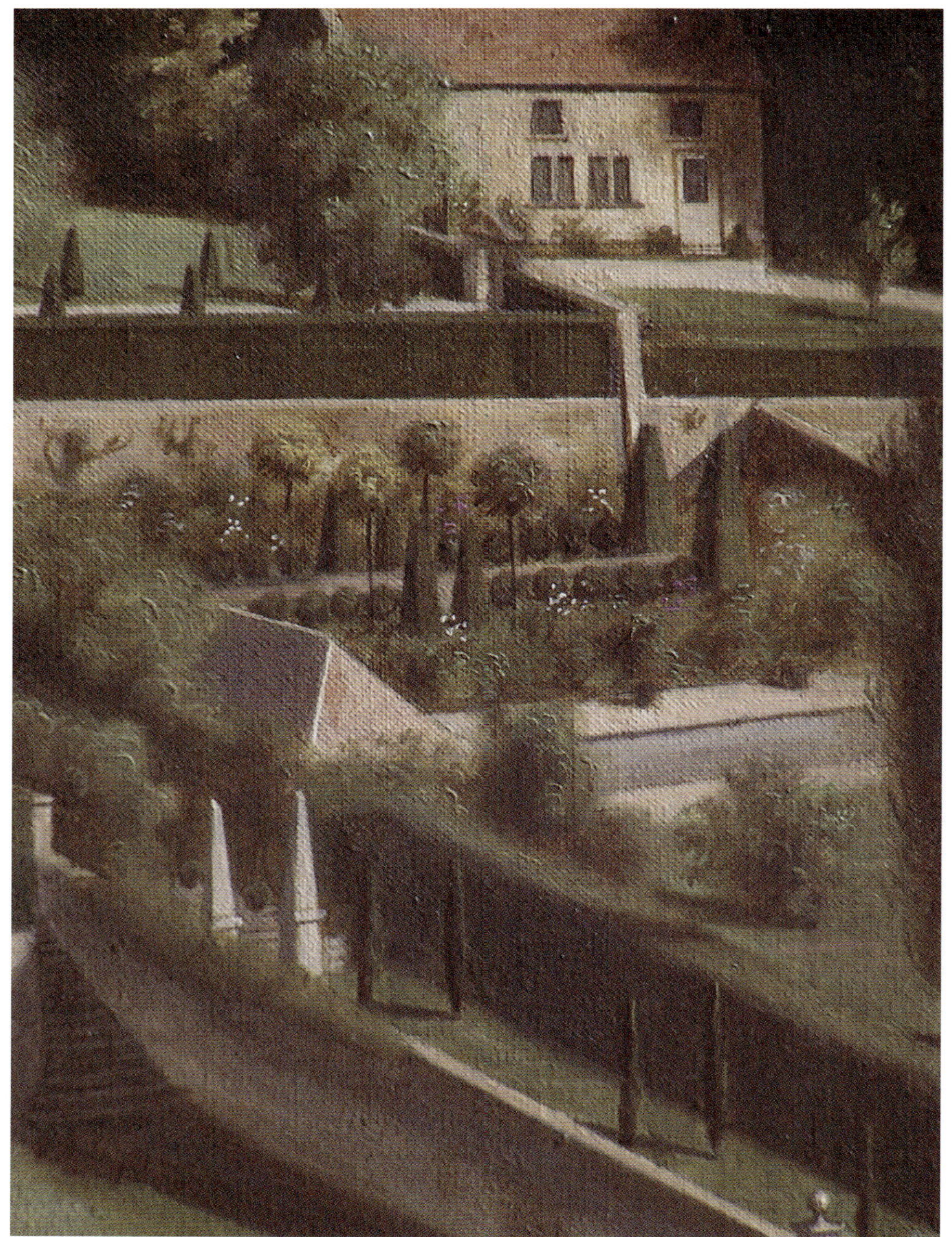

RIGHT Dick Smyly, detail from *Garden in Oxfordshire*, 2007, oil on canvas. PHOTO: NIALL MACDIARMID

FACING PAGE Dick Smyly, *Gaddesby*, 2006, oil on canvas, 30 × 40in. PHOTO: NIALL MACDIARMID

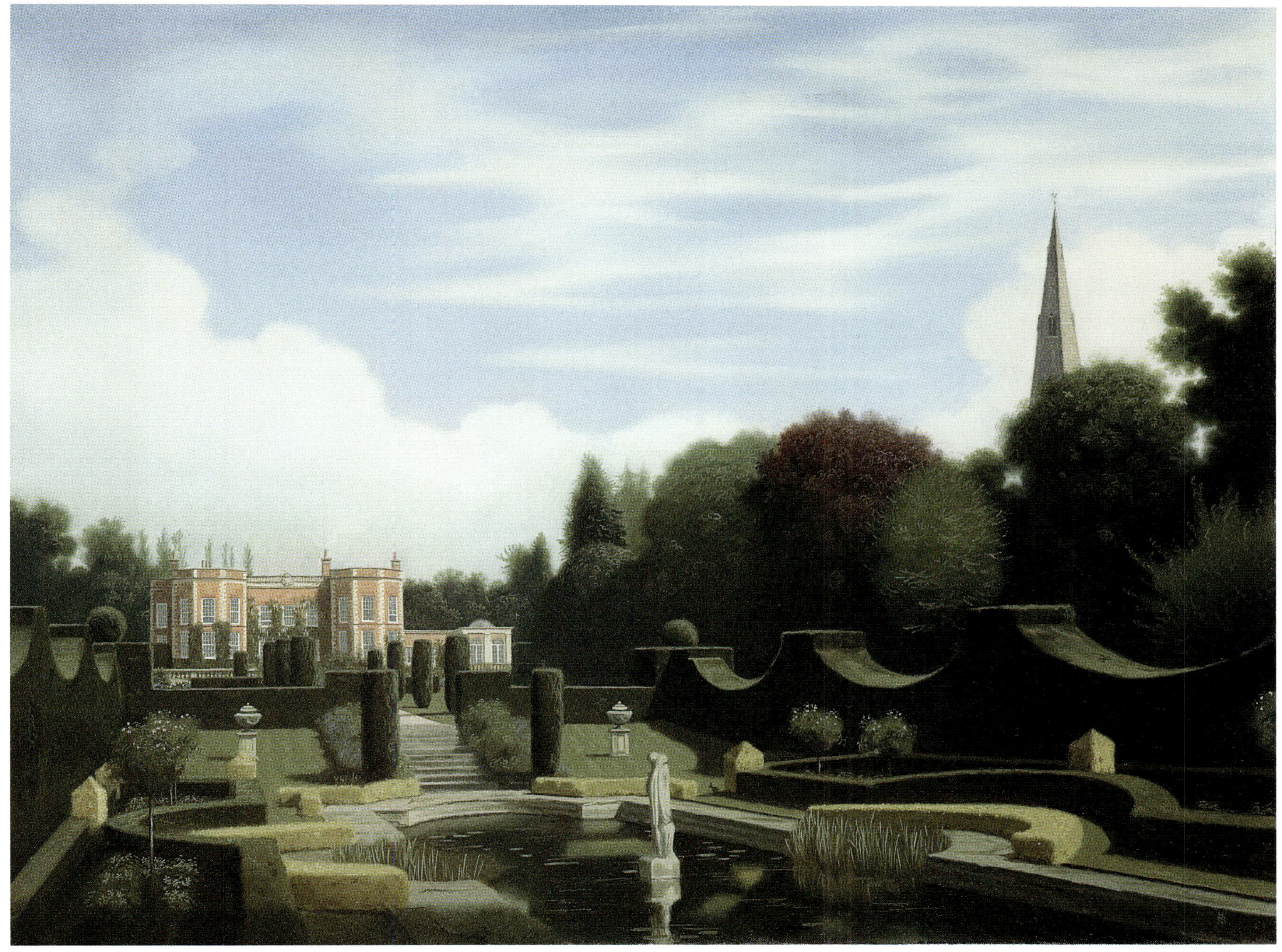

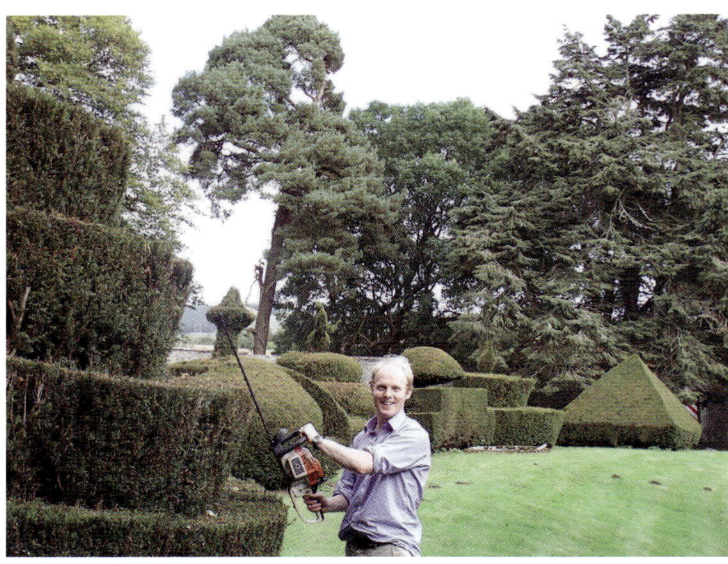

Dick Smyly, artist clipping hedges at home. PHOTO: HETTIE SMYLY

said, "attempt to create something more beautiful than reality".' Dick's canvases are Belgian linen, which he prepares with rabbit-skin glue and then two coats of primer. As for the materials, if he is in Florence, he stocks up with as much as possible, otherwise he goes to Cornelissens or Green & Stone. His working hours depend on the daylight as he doesn't feel able to work by artificial light, as 'you can't see the colours properly'. So that in summer he might paint from 7.00–7.00 pm or even 8.00 pm by which time 'I'm about to drop.' In winter the hours are more like 9.00–5.30 pm or 'say like yesterday, the light went around 3.30, ridiculously early, which is infuriating.' On receiving a new commission he expects his clients to trust his approach and therefore doesn't present preliminary drawings.

Most artists seem to depend on a critic: with Matisse it was his children, and in Dick's case it is his wife as she 'has an extraordinary eye, although she doesn't herself paint. I will often resist her suggestions to begin with but she has an uncanny instinct to see something wrong in a picture and is almost always right.'

It's intriguing to know if garden painters enjoy gardening themselves. Dick admits to being a 'very keen gardener and I probably let it take up too much of my time.' One of his passions is hedges (which is evident in several of his recent paintings that show detailed topiary). He is in charge of cutting and shaping a variety of unusually shaped yew hedges at his home in the Scottish Borders. Another project is an old Victorian woodland walk which goes down beside a river there. He has cleared the thick shrub by chainsaw and has been replanting it with acid-loving plants such as azaleas, rhododendrons, camellias and magnolias, and also specimen trees such as redwoods and pines.

The American artist James Mcneill Whistler used a symbol of a butterfly to put on all his work. Dick uses rabbits as his trademark. Often they are hardly discernible, gambolling about, rather amusingly, in some dark corner of his work.

These paintings are enchanting. It's possible to detect trees in the style of Felix Kelly and skies similar to those of Paul Sandby. Initially you are aware of rather a sombre quality gained by the use of greeny-grey, quite dark, long shadows, but then you realise that these are designed to contrast with areas of light and to create atmosphere. The tones depicting the trees, shrubs and hedges are fairly similar so the images are more about form and shape than about colour. There are vast, varied and dramatically depicted skies which vary considerably from one picture to another. Overall what colour there is in small areas is bright and clear and often reserved for the architecture that may be depicted. The general effect has a sense of drama and grandeur. It's early days for this artist, and it will be interesting to follow where his considerable talent takes him next.

Jonathan Warrender

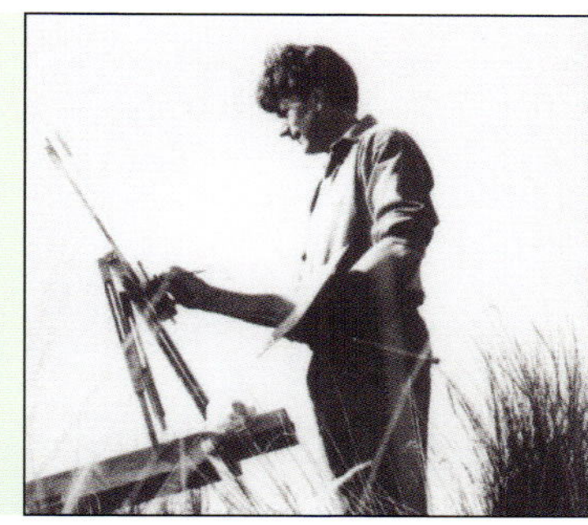

In 1998 I was commissioned to paint a most beautiful garden near Stow-on-the-Wold, Gloucestershire, owned by Ian and Caroline Bond. When I arrived, one of the first things I noticed was a bird's eye view picture of the same garden painted by Jonathan Warrender. The technique of this very accomplished painting intrigued me so much that I have never forgotten it.

Jonathan spent many hours in the art room at Downside School because of his dyslexia. He then furthered his education at the Camberwell School of Art in the 1970s. He didn't feel particularly at ease at the college as Abstract and Kinetic Art were all the rage. Being dyslexic he has found that he cannot draw from memory, because he cannot retain an image. He can draw whatever he is looking at, but finds it difficult to think images through in an abstract way. He was more comfortable with traditional schooling where he felt more secure and proved to be more skilful. He feels that he is not so much a painter of the sort where talent just flows, but a hard worker, a grafter.

Jonathan comes from a creative family who for generations have painted or written in various forms. His father's great-aunt Margaret was responsible for establishing the Hawthorn Prize. Coming from this background, Jonathan feels particular commitment to his vocation. He sees it as a chance to reintroduce people to familiar surroundings by depicting them in his own unique way.

In the late 1970s, Andrew Festing, who worked for Sotheby's, suggested to Jonathan that he should copy paintings for owners who were selling, say, a Gainsborough in the auction room, and wanted a record of the picture. He continued to do this for five or six years, making a reasonable living at it. Eventually one of the paintings that he was asked to copy was an early painting of the school of Jan Siebrechts, a sort of bird's eye view. 'I looked at the view and it reminded me of an escarpment in Somerset, near the Mendips, where I was brought up,

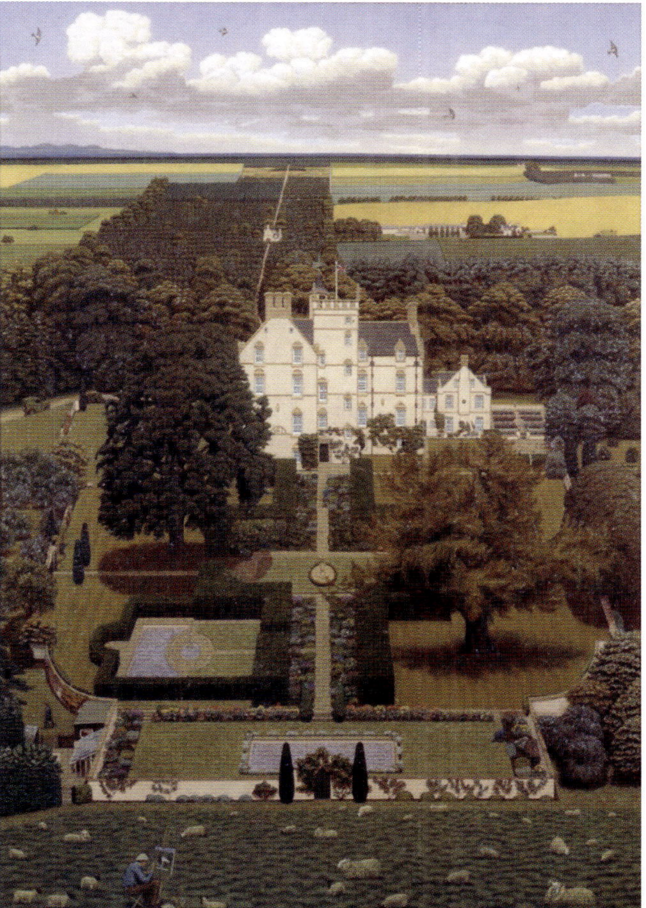

Jonathan Warrender, *Innes House*, 1980, oil on canvas, 3ft × 2ft 2in.
PHOTO: HESTER PHOTOGRAPHY

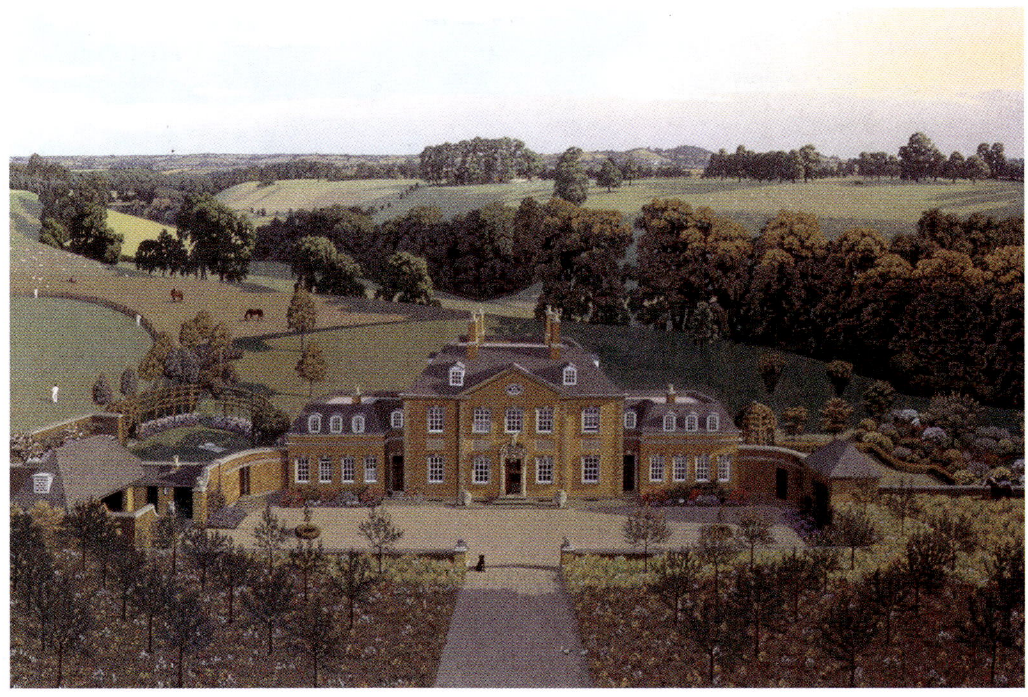

LEFT Jonathan Warrender, *House and Garden in Warwickshire*, 1993, oil on canvas, 3ft 4in × 5ft.
PHOTO: PRUDENCE CUMING

RIGHT Jonathan Warrender, *Stowell Park*, 1989, oil on canvas, 3ft 7in × 6ft.
PHOTO: MICHAEL J. BANNISTER

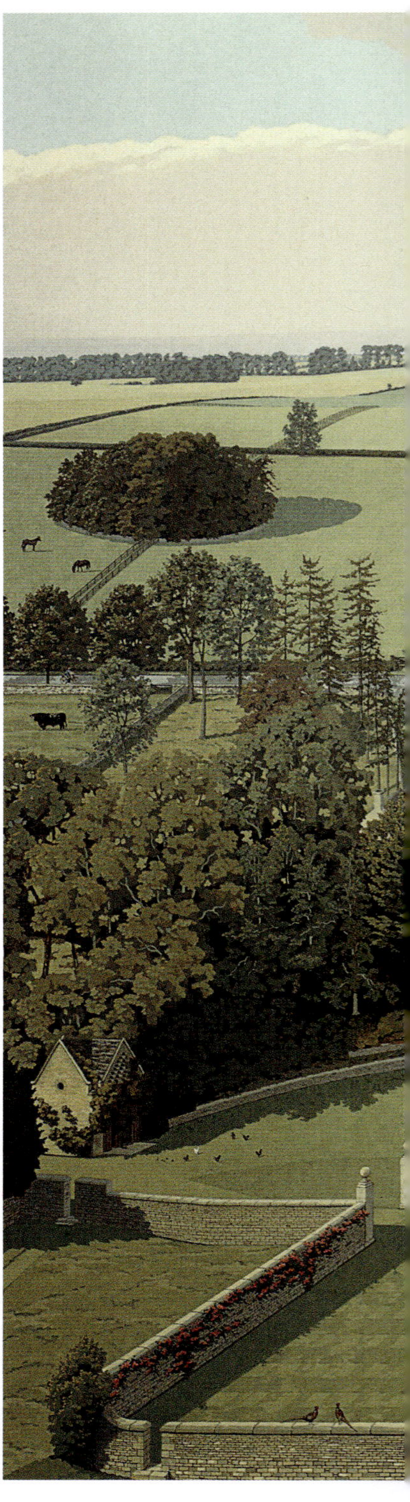

which had always seemed like a big map and plan and I thought I can do that – it seemed to make sense.'

Jonathan then waited for an opportunity to try to accomplish a similar picture by developing his own technique. The chance came in 1980–81 when he was asked to paint Innes House in Morayshire for Sir Iain Tennant. 'I did say, "Do you mind if I do it with a slightly unusual viewpoint?" but even so the painting did give him quite a surprise and he did think it was very odd, but eventually grew to love the picture enormously.'

Since that time Jonathan has always been in demand for such work, having completed nearly fifty and at times having commissions planned for three years in advance. These pictures can take up to six months to complete and he can, therefore, only take on two or three a year, often having to return the following year to finish a painting.

To create one of his images, Jonathan first walks round that part of the area that will be in the foreground – say, a quarter of a mile. He'll make a map and pace out the distances and the 'further you get back into the landscape the less precise and more "atmospheric" you have to be, and once I get the perspective right, I tip up the image – I feel my way round the canvas.' It is at this stage that he looks to see if the lawn seems the right size for the front of the house and that there is, say, the right proportion between the ha-ha and the herbaceous border. 'If I get the skeleton right I can then build on the bones of the painting with a certain amount of conviction. I do not set about a painting with the purpose of accurate recording but rather more to get the feel of the place, which begins to come when things are set one against another. There is an underlying proportion of scale in many houses and gardens that it is

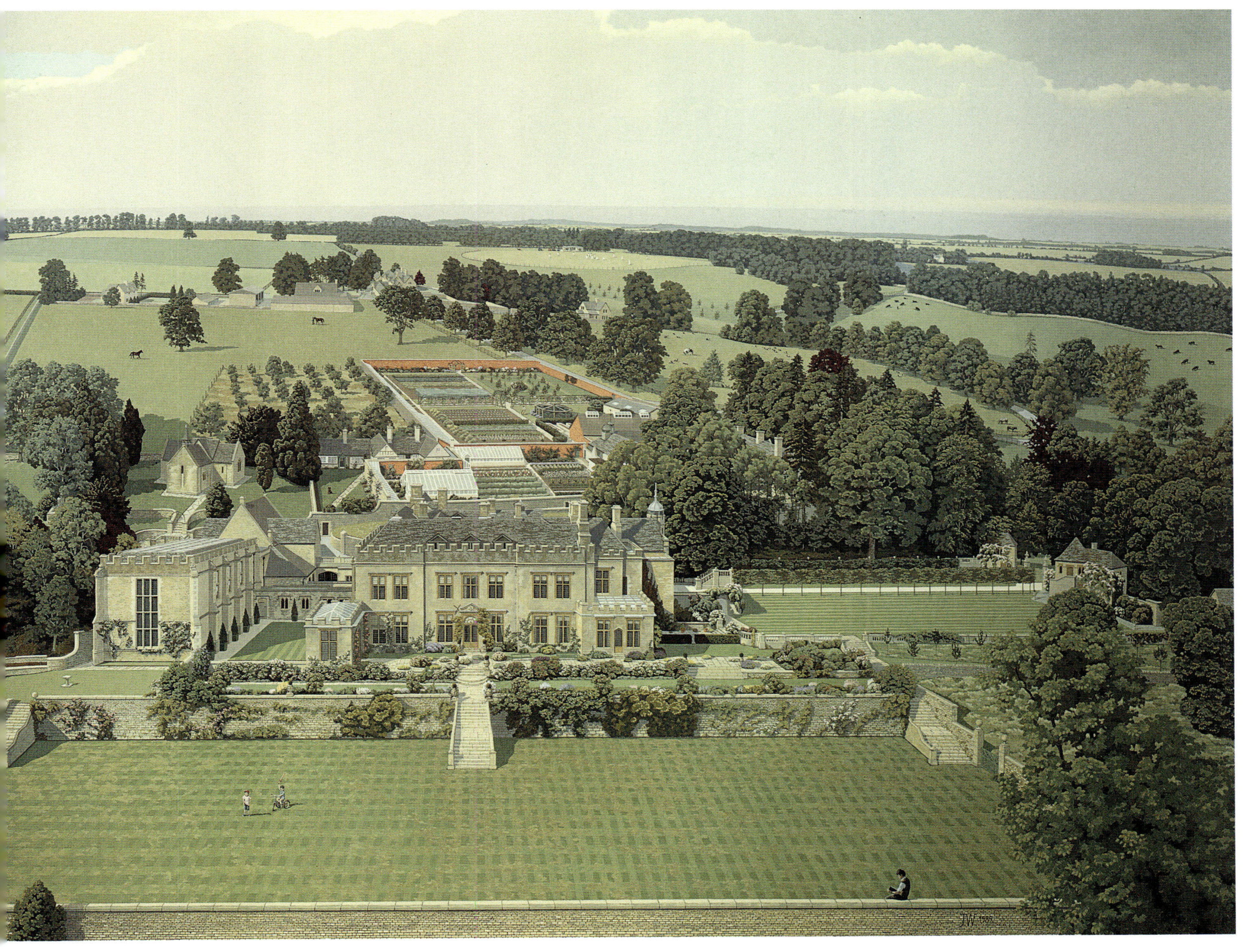

important to identify. When a "bird's eye" works well, it uses detail as a language of looking and the detail dictates the atmosphere that one wants to convey.'

The planning and execution of these pictures are very labour-intensive. Jonathan will make copious exquisite drawings of certain features – a prominent tree in the foreground or a front door with plants around it – that will appear in the painting. And he generally works from dawn to dusk, often standing for two to three hours at a time. Apart from the drawings he does some charming oil sketches of the same kind of features. He then uses these sketches to develop the painting itself, often returning with the canvas and moving round the garden to be sure that he has things to his satisfaction, before returning to his studio to complete the work.

Jonathan has found that as his work progresses he is able to convey more of the mood, drama and atmosphere of the image. 'The skies can have more life in them, but there is a danger that the naïvety that works so well in a bird's eye view can get lost, as narration and mood take over. There is more charm when images are rather stark and straightforward. It's possible to become too clever and then the paintings become an exercise in skill rather than in intuition and celebration of where you are.'

Jonathan has painted commissions both in this country and abroad but says that he would prefer to have found more work abroad where the light is better and there aren't so many rainy days, 'which you have to put up with.' He doesn't enjoy having to rely on photographs as he doesn't find this satisfactory, but if the weather is bad and he has allowed a certain amount of time then it becomes a necessity. At present he is working on a project in Provence which he is enjoying.

Light is obviously something to which Jonathan is very sensitive. He prefers to paint into the light because there is more definition within the scene and more contrast between light and shade – shadows play an important part in his work. In a recent picture, for an art collector, he has put the shadow of the man falling across the painting, as if looking at the scene, although 'he is standing offstage, he is in a sense being included in the image.'

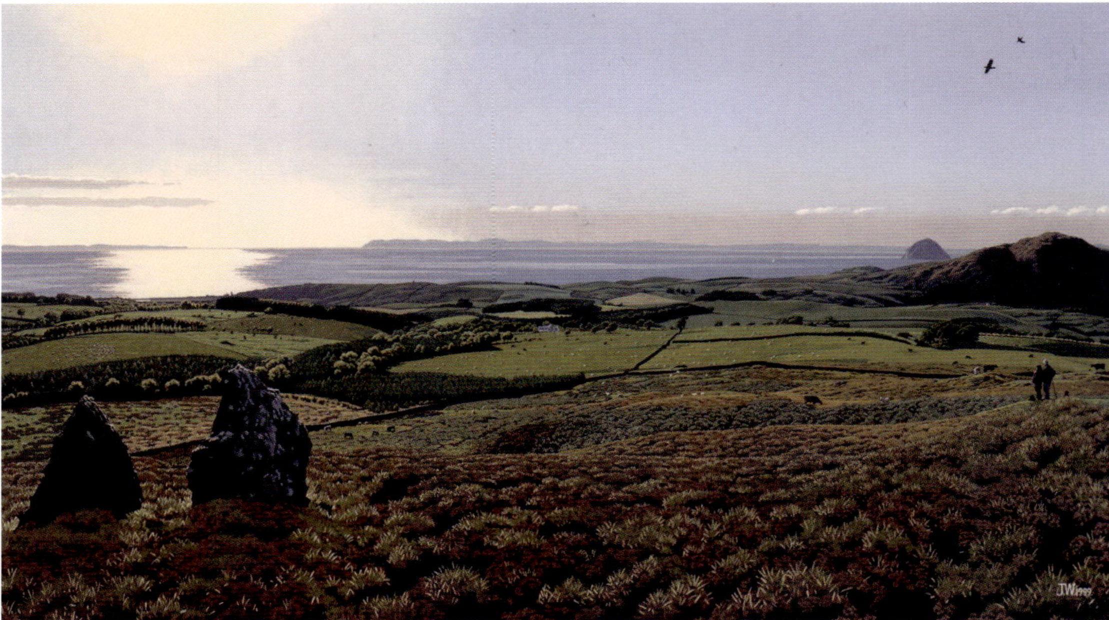

Jonathan Warrender, *Crailock, Ballantrae*, 1999, oil on canvas, 2ft 3in × 4ft 2in. PHOTO: GEOFFREY SHAKERLEY

Lately Jonathan has been diversifying into other directions as he likes the idea of depicting private as well as public places and also of facing new challenges which entail working and exhibiting in the USA. Nevertheless there are important commissions still in the pipeline and surely always will be, the mapping process and the depiction of a three-dimensional world being his speciality. It's obvious that he feels an intense affinity to nature when he describes some of his occupations in and around his home in Scotland – 'looking to see if a badger has cleared out its set, or where the otter cubs have been playing on the bank of the river where they were last year or whether I can find an oystercatcher's egg.' There is a clear link here with the preoccupation of his work.

FACING PAGE Jonathan Warrender, *Chilton Park*, 1995, oil on canvas, 4ft 6in × 3ft 3in. PHOTO: GEOFFREY SHAKERLEY

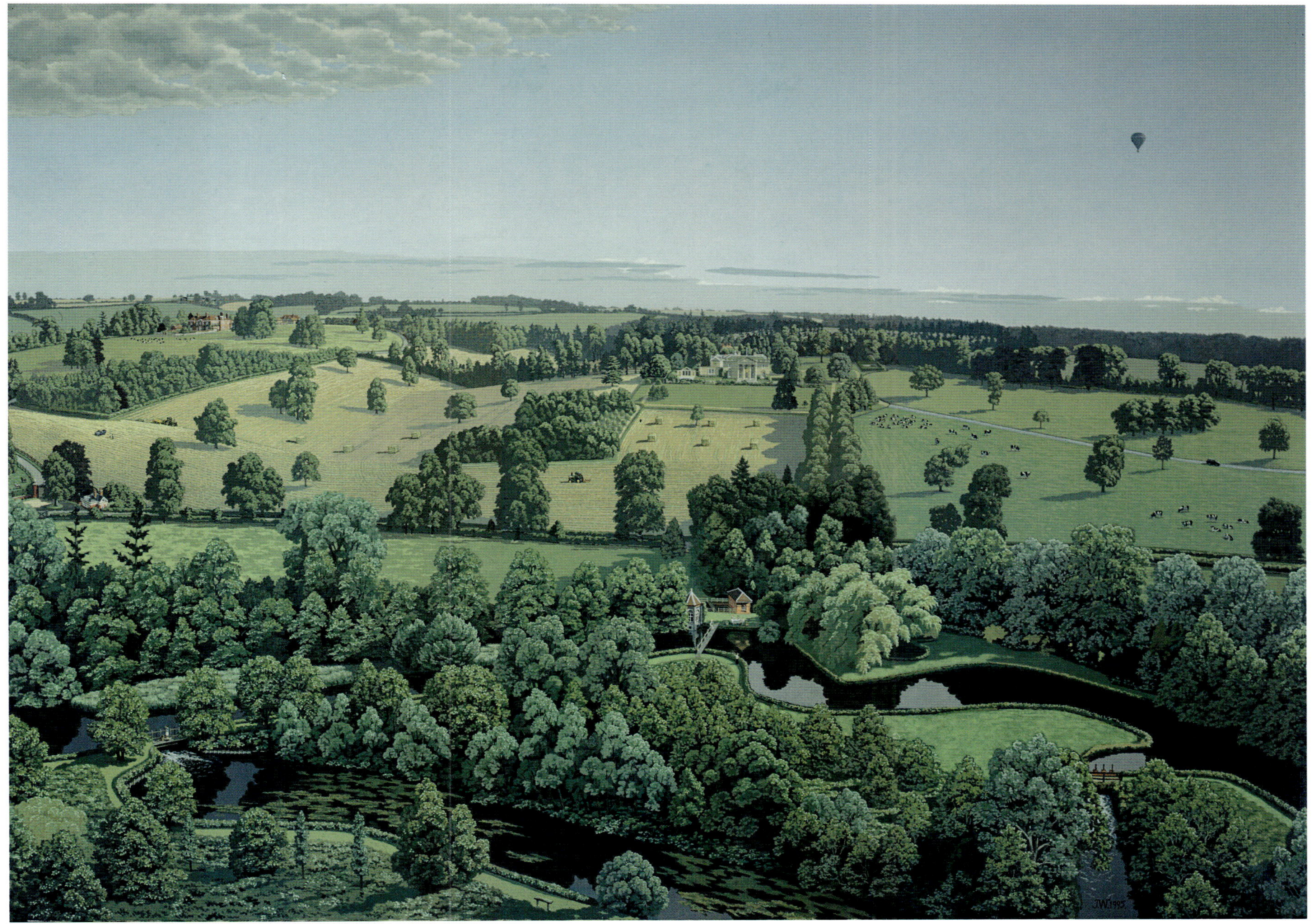

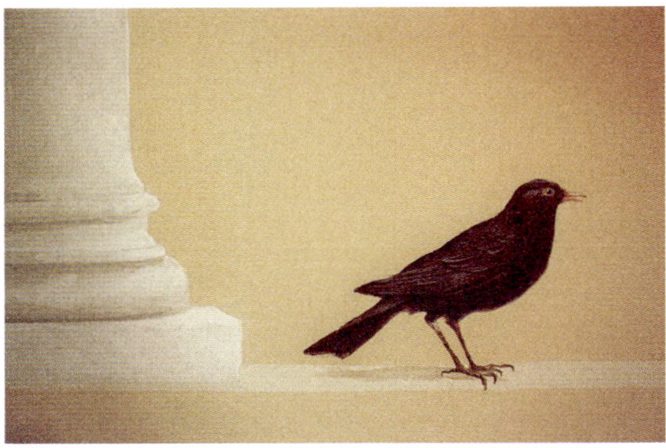

Michael Dillon, detail from a mural.